D0464261

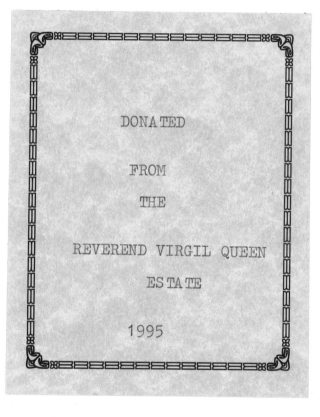

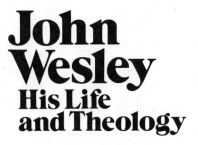

John Wesley
His Life and Theology

JOHN WESLEY, FOUNDER OF METHODISM

In those clear, piercing eyes behold
The very soul that over England
flamed!

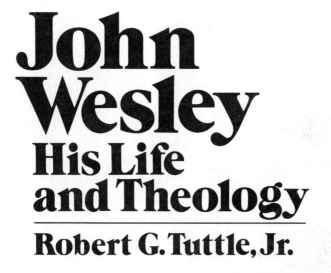

John Wesley

His Life and Theology

Robert G. Tuttle, Jr.

ZONDERVAN
PUBLISHING HOUSE   OF THE ZONDERVAN CORPORATION
GRAND RAPIDS, MICHIGAN 49506

JOHN WESLEY: HIS LIFE AND THEOLOGY
Copyright © 1978 by The Zondervan Corporation
Grand Rapids, Michigan

Library of Congress Cataloging in Publication Data

Tuttle, Robert G., 1941-
    John Wesley: his life and theology.
    Bibliography:
    1. Wesley, John, 1703-1791. 2. Methodists—England—Biography.
3. Evangelists—England—Biography.
BX8495.W5T73   287'.092'4 [B]   77-27583
ISBN 0-310-36660-7

287.092
W513t
1978

Printed in the United States of America

to my mother and father
LILLIAN ALLEN and ROBERT G. TUTTLE, SR.
who more than John Wesley would
understand their influence upon my life

Contents

Preface

This biography is intended to bring people into the fullness of faith in Jesus Christ by telling the story of a man whose life was totally committed: not to a cause—not to a religion—not even to a revival— *but to God.* Some years ago I entered the Wheaton Graduate School of Theology. During one of my first interviews with my adviser, Dean Merrill C. Tenney, he told me the story of an evangelist standing before a portrait of John Wesley in a well-known museum. After asking the attendant if it was all right to pray, the evangelist bowed his head and said: "Lord, do it again!" At the World Congress on Evangelization in Lausanne, Switzerland, there was not a single day that John Wesley was not quoted at some length in one of the plenary sessions. Obviously, many feel that John Wesley has a relevant word for these troubled times. Yet, no one has written so much that is read so little. Out of eight volumes of Journals, two volumes of Sermons, eight volumes of Letters, not to mention books (including those pertaining to matters from medical cures to language grammars), tracts, treatises, hymns, and a series of extracts composing a fifty-volume collection of works on practical divinity entitled *The Christian Library,* few have read more than Volume I of the Journals or the standard forty-four sermons.[1]

This book, therefore, has several primary objectives. First, I want to portray an interesting and readable biography which struggles with a man of history and emotion, while at the same time demonstrate an appreciation for the incredible detail available to us through his *Diaries, Journals,* and *Letters.* Second, I want to present a fairly

[1]Many of the tracts, treatises and extracts are included in the complete works edited by Thomas Jackson, an earlier Joseph Benson edition, and the first edition edited by William Pine. Although the Jackson edition is by far the most reliable, both Jackson and Benson omit several thousand pages of extracts (without so much as a footnote) included in the first Pine edition. It should also be mentioned that there is a new edition of Wesley's complete works being published over the next several years which should be extremely inclusive and reliable.

comprehensive theological analysis which takes into account a practical theologian whose theological thrust,
being geared to his own needs and to the needs of his
people, seems to shift as needs shift. Like most theologians, Wesley was remarkably consistent, yet appears con-
tradictory if proper perspective is not given to the man
whose life stretched across the entire eighteenth century.[2]
Wesley's thoughts, like Fénelon's "soul," seem to say: *moi
progressus ad infinitum* (my progress is without end).[3]

Furthermore, I wrote this biography in the hopes of
sparking the kind of interest that would cause you to go out
and read Wesley yourself. In other words, to read this book
alone is not to know Wesley. To know Wesley you must
also read Wesley. That is not to say that this is not a
scholarly work. I have read and reread all of Wesley's
works and have made an honest attempt to represent him
fairly, as well as with a tremendous amount of love and
affection. It is just that I am personally convinced that there
is absolutely no substitute for primary sources. I remember
as a seminary student that I did not like John Calvin until I
read John Calvin. Mr. Wesley not only has been used but
also greatly abused by many who have had neither the
time nor the patience to study the man (an evangelist, a
priest, a theologian), as well as the movement (the Revival,
the organized societies, the "people called Methodists").

Finally, I wrote this biography to inspire. Ultimately the
source for revival must be found *in God*. Today many
scholars would have us believe that the eighteenth-century
Evangelical Revival in England was inevitable. If John
Wesley had not provided the necessary catalyst, it would
have been provided by someone else. There is, of course,

[2]Nehemiah Curnock, editor of the *Standard Journals*, somewhat play-
fully writes that Wesley was "no martyr to the bugbear of consistency"
(*Journal*, Vol. I, p. 33). The truth of the matter is that Wesley could
apparently contradict himself without the slightest suspicion of inconsistency. Consequently, any serious study of John Wesley must span the
thoughts of a lifetime, judging only the continuous threads and never
the isolated statements apart from their context. Little wonder that Dr.
Bett in his *The Spirit of Methodism*, exhorts his readers not to misjudge
Wesley by an uninformed interpretation of his own words.
[3]Françoise de Salignac de La Mothe Fénelon (1651-1715), was a French
mystic and religious writer.

some logic in this. The times were ripe for a moral and spiritual change in direction. But personally, I believe that ultimately the *primary* reason for the revival must be found elsewhere. Let me explain.

Many who are more in sympathy with Wesley and his movement insist that the reason for the revival must be found in the man himself. Some point to the evangelical tactics of John Wesley as the primary reason for his success. This is somewhat misleading however. Wesley obviously adapted his methods to suit the times. But it should be remembered that Wesley's father (among others) was not entirely unsympathetic toward these tactics—but to little avail—and that Wesley himself was evangelical-minded long before the outbreak of any revival. Others emphasize Wesley's strong devotional piety or his concern for social reform as the reason for his success. But, here again, even a casual examination of Wesley's Oxford diaries reveal these characteristics in him more than ten years before the beginning of the Revival. Many of Wesley's contemporaries claimed that the reason for his success lay in his "natural knack of persuasion." One author finds their innocence amusing as he reminds his readers that one does not usually persuade the Englishman to give up the world and embrace God; but, with similar naivete, attributes Wesley's success, first to his extempore preaching and then to his penetrating logic.[4] Although Wesley's preaching ability probably could not match that of George Whitefield or Jonathan Edwards, few would deny that he had a unique ability to evoke response. As the years progressed, he obviously mastered his technique. However, the fact remains that this is still not the key. Early in the Revival, for example, Wesley could even read his sermons with remarkable results. On one occasion, he is described as preaching a sermon standing like a statue (the only thing that moved was his mouth), and reading so rapidly that one could hardly follow his logic. Yet, people were struck to the heart with overwhelming conviction.

It is the assumption here, therefore, that the primary

---

[4]Ronald Knox, *Enthusiasm*, pp. 513f.

reason for Wesley's impact on eighteenth-century English society lies not only in the moral and social environment, nor even in Wesley's own ability as an evangelist extraordinare, but in the *power of God*. This power manifested itself in an imperfect instrument of obedience to bring about change in the religious fiber of a nation. Man alone could not effect this change. Wesley himself claimed that it took no less of a miracle to resurrect a dead soul than to resurrect a dead body.[5] Alexander Knox, a personal friend of Wesley's, asked the appropriate question: "How was he so competent to form a religious polity so compact, effective, and permanent?" Knox answers: *"Only by the Grace of God. . . .* I can only express my firm conviction that he (like most reformers) was totally incapable of perceiving such a scheme. This would have implied an exercise of forethought and politic contrivance, than which nothing could be more opposite to his whole mental constitution."[6]

John Wesley, at the right time, with remarkable determination and considerable ability, tapped the even greater power of God, the power to create and recreate, the power of birth and rebirth. This biography, therefore, seeks to answer the obvious question. How? How did John Wesley link himself, the instrument of potential revival, to the enabling power of God?

The outline of the book is straightforward. There are four parts. Each part, however, has three phases. The first phase of each part is a chapter written in the first person entitled, "Setting the Stage." Since it is impossible to cover Wesley's entire life in the kind of detail available through the Diaries, Journals, and Letters (at least in one volume), these four chapters together provide us with the opportunity to look at John Wesley, "up close and personal." As I searched Mr. Wesley's life for a vehicle to give the variety of our objectives flow and continuity, I noticed a period of a month, late in his life. This month included several "quiet days" for reflection (a rare thing in Wesley's life),

---

[5]*Journal*, Vol. V, p. 314.

[6]Robert Southey, *The Life of Wesley*, Vol. 2, pp. 293ff. Italics mine.

and part of a journey, so typical to the eighteenth-century Revival as a whole. Focusing upon nineteen days of this journey as the "stage," I demonstrate the kind of detail accessible through a study of Wesley's complete works. On March 3, 1788, he traveled to Bristol where he remained until March 17. He then headed north, preaching at least twice a day and visiting the societies. Each of the four parts begins by picking him up at some point along the way where I, playing the part of Mr. Wesley at eighty-four years of age, will describe the journey itself and then share with you, the reader, "my" biographical notes recently penned at Bristol.

The second phase of each part consists of four chapters of biographical material, also in the first person. These sixteen chapters together describe Wesley's "biographical notes" and provide the general overview. They supply the information available in most such studies except for the fact that they are told *as Wesley himself would probably have perceived them.*

The third phase of each part is a chapter entitled, "The Analysis." These four analysis chapters together serve two purposes. First, they enable me to develop my own interpretation. This allows me to make my own observations. Second, they reduce the temptation of putting words into Mr. Wesley's mouth during the biographical chapters, as I seek to explain his personal development.

A further word about the use of the first person might be appropriate. The study of John Wesley represents more than three full years of my life. While completing an advanced degree on Wesley in Bristol, England, I took the first six months, reading ten to twelve hours a day, six to seven days a week, just to work through the primary sources alone. There were times when I felt that I was "becoming" John Wesley—rising early, fasting one day a week, and practicing regular prayers. As I was reading, I felt that I could anticipate the mind of Wesley. So, why not give pen to my "little neurosis"? Thus, the first person, by which I intend simply to set the mood for a man struggling with *his* own time. This is not an attempt to make Mr.

Wesley a twentieth-century man. I try to use the kinds of words and phrases that I believe he would have used without directly quoting where he has conversation with you, the reader, except where quotations have been indicated. I have made an effort to document most of what I have Mr. Wesley saying with footnotes, corresponding with his *Works*, which include an occasional comment of my own and from the study of others. This is not so much to prove my legitimacy as to underscore again the importance of working with primary sources and to provide a basis for those who would like to engage in a more detailed study of their own.[7]

This book, therefore, is not an attempt to master any particular kind of literary style. I want to portray a man, a very real man, in such a way that you might know that he faced problems in a very real world, in many ways much like our own. I want you to be inspired by his greatness, yet feel his humanness, as if to say, "by God's grace, it can happen again."

---

[7] All subsequent references to the *Works* are to the Jackson edition; to the *Letters*, the Telford edition; to the *Journals*, the Curnock edition; to the *Sermons*, the Sugden edition. The *Diary* is incomplete with parts either missing or not yet translated from the cipher that Wesley used to ensure confidentiality. Portions of the *Diary* are included in the Curnock edition of the *Journals*. It should also be mentioned that the key to the cipher used in the portions not yet translated has recently been found. When these portions are made available they should provide the student of Wesley with additional source for study and evaluation. A facsimile of the page from Curnock showing the *Journal* and *Dairy* is on the following page.

Sample of Wesley's Journal and Diary

[*Sat.* 18.—I baptized at his desire Ambrosius Tackner, aged thirty; he had received only lay baptism before. We dined on shore with Mr. Delamotte's father, who was come down on purpose to see him, and was now fully reconciled (which is of the power of God) to what he at first vigorously opposed.]

Sun. 19.—The weather being fair and calm, we had the morning service on quarter-deck.[1] I now first preached extempore [to a numerous and as it then seemed serious congregation.] We then celebrated the Holy Eucharist, [Ambrosius Tackner] and two more communicating with us—a little flock, which we did not doubt God would increase in due time.

Mon. 20.—Believing the denying ourselves, even in the smallest instances, might, by the blessing of God, be helpful to us, we [my brother and I] wholly left off the use of flesh and wine, and confined ourselves to vegetable food, chiefly rice and biscuit, [a diet which has agreed with us hitherto perfectly well.] In the afternoon Mr. David Nitschmann, Bishop of the Moravians,[2]

Saturday 18.

4½ Dressed; prayed; began Genesis 6; Deacon ¾; writ to Varanese,

7 Miss Sally Andrews, Sister Emilia 8; talked; writ to Salmon and

9 Clayton; 10. Falcon with Tackner; baptized him!

11 Delamotte Senior; read Whiston's Catechism.

1 ½ dinner, 2½ on board. Conversed 3½. German. 4. Cabin.

4 Writ to Sister Kezia, Mr. Vernon, Mr. Hutcheson, my mother,

5 Rivington. 5½ talked. 6¼ devotion ½ sung 7. German with Tackner.

7 Conversed, prayer, 9¼.

Sunday 19.

4 Dressed; prayed, Scripture. 6. Deacon, 7. Kempis.

8 Xavier; talked 10. Read prayers, preached extempore, Eucharist three

11 communicants. 12. Xavier. 1. dined, devotion. prayer. 2. Read with Tackner.

3. Read prayers, expounded. 4. Sat in with Hermsdorf. 5. talked; conversed with

6 Mrs. Tackner. ½ prayed, conversed. 6½ sung. 7¼ conversed with Oglethorpe.

8 Sung with Germans, ¾, with Oglethorpe [lit. 'sat in,' i.e. conversed with him in private; not talked casually, but seriously and with a purpose]; Prayer 9.40.

THE STAGE

Newcastle-upon-Tyne

Macclesfield

Epworth

Birmingham

Oxford

London

Bristol

Acknowledgments

Perhaps the one most responsible for this volume (though he does not know it) is a young friend I first met nearly ten years ago in an Anglican Theological College in Bristol, England. For a time the enrollment at this particular college was so low that students not attending the college classes were allowed to rent rooms. I was studying theology at a nearby university and my friend was teaching French in one of the local schools. As we were introduced he quickly informed me that he was an atheist and that I was not to discuss the Scriptures in his presence since he knew them as well as I did and their demands were foolishness to him. Somewhat to my surprise I readily complied. As our rooms were adjoining however, we had opportunity to spend a great deal of time together. I shall never forget the statement he made to me some three months later: "Tuttle, you trouble me. You are having more fun doing God's thing than I am doing my own thing." He then asked if he could read the first draft of a dissertation that I was then completing in order to make any necessary corrections in diction and punctuation. Since he had been an English major at Oxford a few years earlier I gratefully handed him the manuscript. Then, much to my surprise, a few weeks later a quotation from John Wesley in a footnote of that manuscript led him to faith in Christ. My conclusion: If the words of Wesley could do that for him then perhaps they could do the same for someone else. Thus the seeds for this book had been planted.

Since that time I have managed to keep in touch with both Wesley and my friend. The book, however, has been a long time in the making. It was not until I found someone (no doubt "an angel unawares") who would painstakingly transcribe notes and tapes that I dared to set aside enough time to do the work necessary for such an assignment. My "angel" is Miss Dorothy Tucker of Colorado Springs, Colorado. Without her patience and encouragement this book would still be a dream yet unfulfilled.

I must also express appreciation to the editors at the Zondervan Corporation who were bold enough to extend to me a contract on an uncompleted manuscript. In addition I must also mention my colleagues and students at Fuller Seminary, especially Mr. Tom Albin, Miss Janet Gathright, and Mr. Michael Weekes who carefully read the manuscript making suggestions and comments both for clarity and understanding.

Finally, though mention here hardly seems adequate, I want to express appreciation to my wife, Pati, and son, Eric. In a family one sacrifice, sacrifices all. I say to them as well as to all of the above mentioned, thank you.

ROBERT G. TUTTLE, JR.

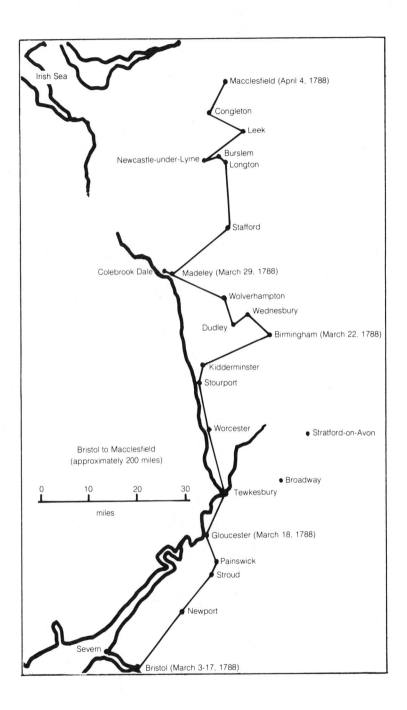

Irish Sea

Macclesfield (April 4, 1788)

Congleton

Leek

Newcastle-under-Lyme

Burslem
Longton

Stafford

Colebrook Dale

Madeley (March 29, 1788)

Wolverhampton

Wednesbury

Dudley

Birmingham (March 22, 1788)

Kidderminster

Stourport

Worcester

Stratford-on-Avon

Bristol to Macclesfield
(approximately 200 miles)

Broadway

0   10   20   30

Tewkesbury

miles

Gloucester (March 18, 1788)

Painswick

Stroud

Newport

Severn

Bristol (March 3-17, 1788)

Part I
The Early Years

1

Setting the Stage

Only let your whole family stir themselves up and be instant in prayer; then I have only to say to each, "If thou canst believe, thou shall see the glory of God!" John Wesley

Monday, March 17, 1788 (5:00 A.M.), Bristol, England. Mr. Wesley is alone, but speaks to you, the reader, as though you were there in the room with him.

Today I begin my journey north, a custom I have practiced in the early spring for many years now. This evening I expect to preach at Stroud. I am now in my sitting room just off the Common Room above the Methodist chapel called the New Room in the Horsefair, Bristol. My bedroom is to my left. It is small, just six by ten. I had a desk built into the window to conserve space and to catch the light so I can save on candles. The sitting room is larger, approximately ten by ten. These two rooms have been my home in Bristol since the beginning of the Revival in Kingswood, just a few miles away, in 1739, nearly fifty years ago. On May 12, 1739, the cornerstone for this, the first of our Methodist chapels, was laid. Behind me a door leads into the Common Room. There those of us in residence take our meals together. Off the Common Room there are other rooms, sleeping quarters for our Methodist preachers who come to work with the local societies, classes, and bands. At one end of the Common Room there are windows looking out on the courtyard. At the other end, there is a window which looks down into the chapel below. From that window I can watch our young preachers deliver their sermons without their being aware of my presence. I marvel at how some of them have so quickly grown in grace. Even now I

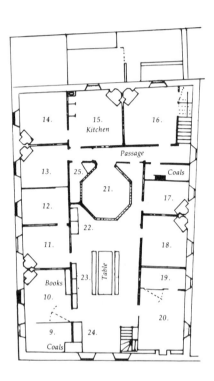

THE FIRST FLOOR PLAN

REFERENCE

9. J. Wesley's Bedroom
10. do. Sitting Room.
11.-20. Students' Rooms
21. Lantern light.
22.-24. Cupboards.
25. Pantry.
26. Porch (former).

can hear some of our society shuffling across the floor as they prepare for early communion. We frequently serve communion as early as 4:00 A.M., especially on Holy Days so as not to conflict with any of the services held by the Church of England. God forbid that our Methodists should not also be faithful members of the Established Church. What good is the leaven without the loaf?

Yesterday was Palm Sunday. I preached here at 4:00 and 8:00 in the morning before preaching at the Mayor's Chapel at 11:00. I still contend that early morning preaching not only prevents our being in competition with the Church of England, but it also develops discipline as well. "Give up this, and Methodism too will degenerate into a mere sect, only distinguished by some opinions and modes of worship."[1] Some months ago I was in London and "went down at half-hour past five, but found no Preacher in the chapel, though we had three or four in the house: So I preached myself. Afterwards, inquiring why none of my family attended the morning preaching, they said, it was because they sat up too late. I resolved to put a stop to this; and therefore ordered, that, 1. Every one under my roof should go to bed at nine; that, 2. Every one might attend the morning preaching: And so they have done ever since."[2]

The same sermon that I preached yesterday at the Mayor's Chapel to most of the aldermen of the city, and to a multitude of high and low, I preached in our own chapel at 5:00 in the evening. My text was Luke 16:31: "If they hear not Moses and the prophets, neither will they be persuaded, though one rose from the dead." To both congregations I sought to explain, and apply, that awesome passage of Scripture—the rich man and Lazarus. Surely, there is still work to be done, even in our strongest societies. Just last year I noted in my *Journal* how the Bristol Society has increased in grace and number.[3] If we do not press on toward the mark of our high calling, however, it will all soon wear off.

[1]*Works*, Vol. IV, p. 267.
[2]Ibid., p. 406.
[3]Ibid., p. 362.

Perhaps it is appropriate that we should be introduced to one another during Holy Week. This is a time to consider our common ground as followers of Christ. "The true members of the Church of Christ 'endeavour,' with all possible diligence, with all care and pains, with unwearied patience, (and all will be little enough), to 'keep the unity of the Spirit in the bond of peace;' to preserve inviolate the same spirit of lowliness and meekness, of longsuffering, mutual forbearance, and love; and all these cemented and knit together by that sacred tie,—the peace of God filling the heart. Thus only can we be and continue living members of that Church which is the body of Christ."[4]

The morning here in Bristol is lovely and mild, for which I am grateful. Although, "the rush of numerous years" have occasioned me little suffering, it is true that I am not as agile as I was in times past.[5] "I do not run or walk so fast as I did; my sight is a little decayed; my left eye is grown dim, and hardly serves me to read; I have daily some pain in the ball of my right eye, as also in my right temple, (occasioned by a blow received some months since,) and in my right shoulder and arm, which I impute partly to a sprain, and partly to the rheumatism. I find likewise some decay in my memory, with regard to names and things lately passed, but not at all with regard to what I have read or heard twenty, forty, or sixty years ago; neither do I find any decay in my hearing, smell, taste, or appetite; (though I want but a third part of the food I did once;) nor do I feel any such things as weariness, either in travelling or preaching; And I am not conscious of any decay in writing sermons; which I do as readily, and, I believe, as correctly, as ever.

"To what cause can I impute this, that I am as I am? First, doubtless, to the power of God, fitting me for the work to which I am called, as long as He pleases to continue me therein; and, next, subordinately to this, to the prayers of his children.

---

[4]*Works*, Vol. VI, p. 399.
[5]On June 28, 1788, Wesley would be eighty-five.

"May we not impute it, as inferior means, 1. To my constant exercise and change of air? 2. To my never having lost a night's sleep, sick or well, at land or at sea, since I was born? 3. To my having sleep at command, so that whenever I feel myself almost worn out, I call it, and it comes, day or night? 4. To my having constantly, for above sixty years, risen at four in the morning? 5. To my constant preaching at five in the morning for above fifty years? 6. To my having had so little pain in my life, and so little sorrow or anxious care?

"Even now, though I find pain daily in my eye, or temple, or arm; yet it is never violent, and seldom lasts many minutes at a time.

"Whether or not this is sent to give me warning that I am shortly to quit this tabernacle, I do not know; but, be it one way or the other, I have only to say:

> My remnant of days
> I spend to his praise
> Who died the whole world to redeem:
> Be they many or few,
> My days are his due,
> And they all are devoted to Him!"[6]

For two weeks now I have been in Bristol, primarily resting, yet also managing to transact some business, visit our school at Kingswood, attend the Select Society, classes, and bands, write letters, converse with numerous friends, prepare sermons, and preach at least once a day (with but one exception).[7] So, these days have not been idle nor without some excitement. In fact, as a result of a sermon preached against slavery on the Thursday after my arrival the crowd was exceedingly large, including high and low,

[6]*Works,* Vol. IV, pp. 427f. The lines at the end are from Charles Wesley's birthday hymn CXC, v. 14, *Hymns and Sacred Poems,* 1749; Osborn's edition, Vol. V, p. 403.

[7]A word of explanation might be helpful here. As for the school at Kingswood, Wesley took it over from George Whitefield. It was built originally for the sons of colliers or miners. Wesley soon included their daughters as well. The same building was then also used as a boarding school for orphan girls and as an adult school. Then in 1748 Wesley erected another boarding school beside the old school for the sons of Methodists. As for the explanation of the Methodist Societies, classes, and bands, see pp. 277-282.

rich and poor. The text was that ancient prophecy, Genesis 9:27: "'God shall enlarge Japhet. And he shall dwell in the tents of Shem; and Canaan shall be his servant.' About the middle of the discourse, while there was on every side attention still as night, a vehement noise arose, none could tell why, a shot like lightning through the whole congregation. The terror and confusion were inexpressible. You might have imagined it was a city taken by storm. The people rushed upon each other with the utmost violence; the benches were broke in pieces; and nine-tenths of the congregation appeared to be struck with the same panic. In about six minutes the storm ceased, almost as suddenly as it arose; and, all being calm, I went on without the least interruption.

"It was the strangest incident of that kind I ever remember; and I believe none can account for it, without supposing some preternatural influence. Satan fought, lest his kingdom should be delivered up. We set *Friday* apart as a day of fasting and prayer, that God would remember those poor outcasts of men; and (what seems impossible with men, considering the wealth and power of their oppressors) make a way for them to escape, and break their chains in sunder."[8]

In spite of all, however, I still have had some time for reminiscing, including a review of my *Journal* and *Diary* notes in order to bring them up to date. This is especially significant since my brother, Charles, lies ill in London with a disease that most say will kill him. Just this morning I have been praying and writing for over an hour. It occurs

---

[8]*Works,* Vol. IV, p. 408. Bristol at this time was the third largest city in England and was the center of the slave market, being one corner of the "Triangle Trade." English goods were exchanged for slaves in West Africa who were then sold in Bristol to be exchanged for sugar, rum, and tobacco in the West Indies and America. Wesley for some years had been one of the first to speak out strongly against slavery. His tract "Thoughts Upon Slavery," published in 1774, had been circulating for some years. It should be remembered that he made this point not without persecution. There would be times when only the pulpit rail (which provided time for his escape) prevented Wesley himself from falling victim to just such violence.

to me that you might like to see a letter written to Charles just a few moments ago.

> Bristol, March 17, 1788
> between four and five.
>
> Dear brother—I am just setting out on my northern journey. But I must snatch time to write two or three lines. I stand and admire the wise and gracious dispensation of divine providence! Never was there before so loud a call to all that are under your roof. If they have not hitherto sufficiently regarded either you or the Lord God of their fathers, what was more calculated to convince them than to see you hovering so long above the borders of the grave? And I verily believe, if they receive the admonition, God will raise you up again. I know you have the sentence of death in yourself; so had I more than twelve years ago. I know nature is utterly exhausted; but is not nature subject to *His* word? I do not depend upon physicians, but upon Him that raiseth the dead. Only let your whole family stir themselves up and be instant in prayer; then I have only to say to each, 'If thou canst believe, thou shall see the glory of God!' Be strong in the Lord and in the power of his might. Adieu!
>
> John Wesley[9]

Enough of this. If I linger too long with my thoughts upon my brother, I might, as he was so prone to do, become melancholy. At any rate, I must take to my chaise in half an hour and I want time enough (since you have been kind enough to show interest in my autobiographical notes) to tell you my story.[10]

The purpose for this "meeting" with you, my reader (which we will resume periodically during my journey north), is to share the labors of my reminiscing these past few weeks. As I have anticipated Charles' death, my entire life has passed before me. This I have written down thinking that you, perhaps prompted by the verdict of history some years hence, might come to these pages looking for hope, inspiration, and faith from the life of a man (if I may pass judgment upon myself) who has weighed the cost of greatness. In so doing I have found that one road often leads to compromise, comfort, and mediocrity, while

---

[9]*Letters*, Vol. VIII, pp. 45-46. This was to be John's last letter to his brother Charles.

[10]A "chaise" is an open, horse-drawn carriage.

another leads to self-discipline, self-sacrifice, and great-ness. If you, dear friend, should by some act of grace, attribute the latter judgment to me and are constrained to bless the instrument, stop! *Give God the glory!*

Let us begin.

2

The Eighteenth Century

No age since the founding and forming of the Christian Church, was ever like, in open avowed atheism, blasphemies, and heresies, to the age we now live in.   Daniel Defoe

Allow me to say a few words about the age into which I was born. England, at the turn of the century, was mostly farm land pocked with small towns and scattered population. Fortunately Epworth (where I was born in 1703) was just a village, because the first thing you noticed about anything larger than a small village was the stench of human waste and rotting garbage. I will never forget the shock of my first journey to London. Every nook and cranny was made a public convenience. Many of the unpaved streets were narrow, often only six feet wide. Here in Bristol the streets were too narrow for carts, and sledges had to be used for moving goods, even though vast improvements have been made over the past few decades.[1] Most houses were one- or two-room hovels, frequently made only of weatherboard and a pitched roof and placed back to back. There were some larger houses (previously deserted by the rich) that were quickly inhabited not only by people but by their livestock as well. All refuse, including that of the butcher, was thrown into the streets to mold and decay, filling the city with filth and disease.

Some, understandably, refer to this period as the "cess-

---

[1]Rupert E. Davies, *The Church in Bristol*, p. 53. Davies writes: "As the century went on and Bristol became richer and richer, many of the meaner areas vanished, the centre of the city was rebuilt, and handsome squares and streets appeared, lined with dignified houses for the prosperous merchants."

pool" of the last two millenniums, if not for its filth then certainly for its morals. Debauchery was epidemic, affecting the nobility, the middle classes, the lower classes, the members of court, and even the members of Parliament. I am told that our late prime minister, the first Earl of Orford, Sir Robert Walpole, lived in an open state of adultery until God was gracious enough to take him from us in 1745. His often-quoted statement: "I am no saint, no spartan, no reformer," was perhaps the understatement of the century.

The farming techniques were improving but the industrial methods were extremely primitive. Life was cheap. I've watched them hang ten and twelve a day from the gallows at Tyburn near Marylebone in London where Charles now lies dying. They hung a ten-year-old boy one day for stealing a loaf of bread. I became so sick of reading the accounts of scores of murders and public executions where, I'm afraid that had I read farther, I would have found them described in vivid detail.

In spite of such decadence, this was also a period of increasing prosperity among the powerful few. Whereas the vast majority of the people were hungry and diseased (especially in the larger towns and cities), there was a fine veneer of sophistication above them. Though I rarely passed up an opportunity to give fair warning to the rich: "It is easier for a camel to go through the eye of a needle than for a rich man to enter into the kingdom of heaven," is it any wonder that God would call me to minister among the poor?[2] After all, did not our Lord Himself set a pretty good precedent? I remember writing to one in our Society: "I want you to converse more, abundantly more, with the poorest of the people, who, if they have not taste, have souls, which you may forward in their way to heaven. And they have (many of them) faith, and the love of God, in a larger measure than any persons I know. Creep in among these, in spite of dirt, and a hundred disgusting circumstances; . . . Do not confine your conversation to genteel

---

[2]See *Works*, Vol. VII, for Wesley's sermons on "The Danger of Riches" (pp. 1-15), and "On Riches" (pp. 214-222).

and elegant people. I should like this as well as you do: But I cannot discover a precedent for it in the life of our Lord, or any of his Apostles. My friend, let us walk as he walked."[3]

Philosophically, we Englishmen (to speak generally), since the close of the Thirty-Years' War (1618-1648), had meandered between arid intellectualism and spiritualism. During the Commonwealth, for example, the mystic "inner light" shown bright, but by the turn of the century we English (now obsessed with the correct method of imparting knowledge) had tired, even of our Puritan strain, and, although still emotionally aggressive and extremely passionate, deplored anything that smacked of personal religion, now labeled *enthusiasm*.[4]

Although our seventeenth-century legacy had to do more with *experience* than knowledge, the issue was whether to judge experience by reason (natural revelation) or by faith (divine revelation).[5] Some seventeenth-century theologians were actually optimistic about the remarriage of faith and reason, but this was not to be. It is so much easier to run from east to west than to stop at the middle point! By the beginning of the eighteenth century the appeal to faith was nearly abandoned altogether and reason prevailed. Deism, for example, exalted reason to the point of totally obscuring the supernatural. "Accordingly, (we were and still are) surrounded with those (we find them on every side) who lay it down as an undoubted principle, that reason is the highest gift of God. They paint it in the fairest colours; they extol it to the skies. They are fond of expatiating in its praise; they make it little less than divine. They are wont to describe it as very near, if not quite, infallible. They look upon it as the all-sufficient director of all the children of men; able, by its native light, to guide them into all truth, and lead them into all virtue."[6] Let me illustrate still further.

---

[3] *Works*, Vol. XII, p. 301.

[4] It should perhaps be noted that the term "enthusiasm" as a label was little better than calling one a "mad dog."

[5] The ontological approach of philosophers like Descartes played a significant role in the emphasis on experience.

[6] *Works*, Vol. VI, p. 351.

Mr. Toland's *Christianity Not Mysterious* and Mr. Tindal's *Christianity As Old As Creation*, two masterpieces of infidelity, in an attempt to reduce religion to its bare essentials, believe God but not his word. They say: "I think the Bible is the finest book I ever read in my life; yet I have an unsuperable objection to it: It is *too good*. It lays down such a plan of life, such a scheme of doctrine and practice, as is far too excellent for weak, silly men to aim at, or attempt to copy after."[7] My answer? If "all things are possible with God, then all things are possible to him that believeth"; but alas, England had few who would proclaim such a word. It would take a true revival to reunite "the two so long divided, knowledge and vital piety."

So, evangelical faith was locked in by a frozen determinism which separated creation from its creator. Man, according to Dr. Clarke, left to himself and if given enough time would reason his way to God.[8] I, on the other hand (by no means disparaging of reason altogether), would eventually discover that reason alone cannot produce faith, but utter despair. I found the truth of this by sad experience more than sixty years ago. "After carefully heaping up the strongest arguments which I could find, either in ancient or modern authors, for the very being of a God, and (which is nearly connected with it) the existence of an invisible world," I was still not convinced.[9] Nonetheless, being ignorant to the way of faith, I pursued the thought by reason alone, "til there was no spirit in me, and I was ready to choose strangling rather than life."[10]

I remember dining with a deist some forty-five years ago who, in answer to my question: "Do you believe there is a God?" replied simply, "I know there is a God; and I believe Him to be the soul of all, . . . But farther than this, I know not: All is dark; my thought is lost. Whence I come, I know not; nor what or why I am; nor whither I am going: But this I know, I am unhappy; I am weary of life; I wish it were at

---

[7]*Works*, Vol. VII, p. 298.
[8]Dr. Clarke is a reference to Samuel Clarke, a prominent deist.
[9]*Works*, Vol. VI, p.356.
[10]Ibid.

an end."[11] Are you then surprised that I would shortly thereafter accept the rather disagreeable chore of writing a large treatise entitled: "An Earnest Appeal to Men of Reason and Religion," soon to be followed by "A Farther Appeal," which, I am led to believe, have brought many to a better mind.[12]

The ecclesiastical scene was affected by the philosophical scene. Although the Church for some years had had little effect on the working classes, indifference and irreligion was now equally prevalent among the middle- and upper-class society as well. I remember words written by Mr. Defoe while I was still at Oxford: "No age since the founding and forming of the Christian Church, was ever like, in open avowed atheism, blasphemies, and heresies, to the age we now live in."[13] The simple fact is that hardly anyone appeared to act by any principle of religion. Everywhere those who should have known better, entirely discarded it and were ready to admit to their disbelief in ordinary discourse.

By and large an "impoverished" church was impotent against the onslaught of secular philosophy. "Few clergymen cared to discourse on the subject; and if they did, they generally expected that a few weak reasons should eradicate at once strong and deep-rooted prejudices."[14] Furthermore, while thinking people were casting great doubt on the truth of the Christian faith, the local parishes were all too often held "in plurality." That is, one rector drew an income from several livings, while the actual work among the people was done by an ill-educated, underpaid, and half-starved curate. The rector kept in good relationship with the wealthy merchants who enabled him to enjoy relative domestic ease.

The Established Church was also highly political. Queen

---

[11]*Works* Vol. I, p. 290.
[12]The "Earnest Appeal" can be found in the *Works*, Vol. VIII, pp. 3-134 and the "Farther Appeal" can be found in the same volume pp. 136-247. Also, *Works*, Vol. I, p. 532 gives an example of a deist (a Mr. Lampe) who was converted by the "Earnest Appeal."
[13]V. H. H. Green, *The Young Mr. Wesley*, p. 8.
[14]*Works* Vol. II, p. 349.

Anne (1702-1714), the younger daughter of James II, once again took a High Church line which stressed the importance of the connection between church and State more and more. Dissenters were persecuted. The stage, therefore, was set for revival within the Church of England. That is the way it was. I will say no more. I dare not carry this too far. Some future generation might conclude that our Revival was more ecclesiastical, sociological, or even political, than a movement of God's Spirit. The church does not have to be decadent to the point of collapse (as some weak-minded historians would have us believe) to be ripe for revival. Although most of the clergymen with real integrity were "non-jurors" (those who refused to take the oath to William III because he was not considered to have succeeded legally to his office) there were a few exceptions to the general rule of degeneracy within the Established Church. One such exception was my father, Samuel Wesley, who moved to Epworth with my mother, Susanna, in 1697, following the resignation of his naval chaplaincy after only a few months duty on a man-of-war.[15] Allow me to describe for you now the scene at Epworth. The influences there were significant indeed.

---

[15]Some accounts place the dates of the Wesley's arrival at Epworth two years earlier, or 1695.

3

The Home Environment

There are few, if any, that would entirely devote above twenty years of the prime of life in hopes to save the souls of their children, which they think may be saved without so much ado; for that was my principal intention, however unskillfully and unsuccessfully managed.   Susanna Wesley

I was past thirty years of age before I found out the particular circumstances surrounding my birth. My father and I were visiting together in London. It was November 30, 1733. I remember the occasion with remarkable clarity. Father was most anxious for me to return with him to Epworth so that I might assume full responsibility for the parish following his death.[1] He was unusually melancholy and recalled with some emotion and great candor (perhaps more than he was aware, since most of what he was to say to me I was hearing for the first time) the early years at Epworth.

On November 12, 1688, three months after his ordination as deacon in the Church of England, my father married Susanna Annesley.[2] Although both my father and mother had rich heritages among the Dissenting Churches, the would-be dissenting minister and his wife both blossomed into loyal Anglicans. It seems that my father was given the task of refuting an Anglican polemic against the Dissenters, but in the course of working this out came to

---

[1]John was in residence at Oxford during this time. The events surrounding his father Samuel's attempt to persuade him to return to Epworth appear in chapter 9.

[2]Samuel (born in 1662, he was 26) and Susanna (born in 1669, she was 19) were married in the old parish church at Marylebone, London.

the conclusion that the Anglican attacks were valid. Henceforth, he was a stern opponent of Dissent. My mother had a similar experience, but quite independently of my father. Although she had watched the personal sacrifices that her father (Dr. Samuel Annesley) had made in his struggles against the Established Church, she also returned to the Church of England.

Even though my father was ordained priest on February 24, 1689, he was at first unable to secure a living and had to struggle by on what little he could earn by writing.[3] He was also a political activist of sorts. Although his activism would eventually place his ministry in some jeopardy with his people, his faithfulness to the Established Church, coupled with the good will of a nobleman for whom he was serving as domestic chaplain, the Marquis of Normanby, enabled him to obtain the small living of South Ormsby, in Lincolnshire, in 1690. This was the same year my older brother, Samuel, Jr., was born, the first of nineteen children, of which only ten survived infancy.[4]

While at South Ormsby, my father missed his one opportunity for some notoriety. In 1694 the same Marquis who had secured the living for him in Lincolnshire, suggested to the Archbishop of Canterbury that my father might be a suitable candidate for an Irish bishopric. This, however, was not to be. So, my father settled into the work of the parish with integrity and devotion. He showed no

---

[3]Just how little can be judged by Samuel's first book, rather oddly entitled, *Maggots: Or Poems on Several Subjects Never Before Handled,* published in 1685, and dedicated to his former headmaster at Dorchester Grammar School, Henry Dolling. There is also a suggestion that he might have had some income from a domestic chaplaincy held during this same period in the home of the Marquis of Normanby. See Luke Tyerman, *The Life and Times of the Rev. Samuel Wesley, MA,* pp. 194-202.

[4]The ten children are Samuel, Jr. (born 1690 and nicknamed Sammy); Emilia (born 1691); Susanna (born 1695 and nicknamed Sukey); Mary (born 1696 and nicknamed Molly); Mehetebel (born 1697 and nicknamed Hetty); Ann (born 1702 and nicknamed Nancy); John (born 1703 and nicknamed Jacky); Martha (born 1707 and nicknamed Patty); Charles (born 1708); and Kezziah (born 1710 and nicknamed Kezzy). There are some rather strange stories associated with the deaths of some of the infants including a child born in 1705 that was accidentally smothered by its nurse, and thrown dead into its mother's arms. Samuel Wesley writes on the occasion concerning Susanna: "She composed herself as well as she could, and that day got it buried."

favoritism whatsoever. Even the Marquis himself was not exempt from his strong sense of duty. As a matter of fact, his rebuke of the Marquis' mistress caused the loss of his living in South Ormsby, though he remained the Marquis' chaplain for some years and under such friendly circumstances that he dedicated his *History of the Old and New Testament* to the Marchioness of Normanby in 1701.

In 1697 (after resigning his naval commission which he held only for a few months), the Crown appointed my father to Epworth, also in Lincolnshire. Epworth was one of the principal villages on the "Isle of Axholme," the watery flats formed by the rivers Trent, Don, and Idle. Since the villagers lived by agriculture, fishing, and the hunting of waterfowl, they depended upon the water. The river flooding made their land fertile and provided suitable cover for ducks and geese. On the other hand, the same water that provided their livelihood also threatened their crops and homes, frequently forcing them to seek refuge on the nearby hills. Though Charles I commissioned a Cornelius Vermuyden to drain the whole countryside in 1626, there was still the problem. Added to that, a third of the land that was then reclaimed was taken over by the Crown, a third given to Vermuyden himself, and a third left to the villagers, without so much as a notice to the people involved. The farmers, therefore, were bitter. Riot was always just below the surface. There was a long, enduring resentment against the government. These farmers frequently defied authority, even rough handling the tax collectors. It is said that not even Oliver Cromwell could subdue the people of Epworth.

Strangers were generally unwelcome. You can imagine the reception granted my parents when they assumed their duties under the sign of Royal favor. My father was disliked even more when he insisted on befriending the tax collectors recently turned out. Nevertheless, this was the place that my father described so affectionately that November morning in 1733. This was the place where he spent the last thirty-eight years of his life without much hope for improvement except that the smaller living of

Wroot was added to the Epworth living in 1725. It is significant to me that in spite of hardships and even imprisonment, as well as tremendous persecution and abuse, my father remained undaunted.[5] To be sure, there were times when he would have cherished the idea (to use his own words) "of becoming a missionary in India, China, or Abyssinia," but Epworth was to be his calling. I remember a letter he wrote to the Archbishop of York after a particularly bad period in 1705: "Most of my friends advise me to leave Epworth if e'er I should get from hence. I confess I am not of that mind, because I may yet do good there; and 'tis like a coward to desert my post because the enemy fire thick upon me. They have only wounded me yet, and I believe can't kill me."

I vaguely remember our first home at Epworth, a comfortable, old, seven-room thatched building that was able to accommodate our rapidly growing family. There was even sufficient land for breeding cattle, which could have made life almost enjoyable except for the resentment of our "good" neighbors who made life, at times, almost intolerable. For most of the villagers, religion was little more than a bad joke. Before my parents arrived, the people of Epworth were somewhat amused by the paunchy little priests who dared not ruffle anything more than the goosedown pillows under their sleepy heads. The taverns were filled with those who told bawdy tales and spoke of political intrigue. They hated anything that smacked of true religion. My parents not only practiced true religion, however, but held strong loyalist views as well. They were therefore hated for the reasons they received their living to begin with, their high churchmanship and their Toryism. Again, you can imagine the difficult time anticipated by a parish priest who not only called his irreligious parishioners to genuine piety, but was liturgically high

---

[5]In 1705, Samuel Wesley was arrested in the churchyard immediately after a baptism and put in the Lincoln Castle prison in accordance with the harsh laws of the time concerning the payment of debts. The collection of the debt was politically motivated and was initiated after his enemies had burned his flax, and perhaps caused him to lose his military chaplainship. He remained in prison for four months.

church and politically loyal to a system that had apparently been robbing them blind.

If my father had trouble with the good people of Epworth, there was trouble at home as well. My mother, the last of twenty-five children, was quite resolute and strongly independent. This fact worked both to advantage and disadvantage. On the one hand it is fortunate that my father had a wife of such sterling quality. Where he was weak, she was invariably strong, business-like, practical, efficient, and determined. She was a woman of remarkable gifts, but her independent spirit sometimes led to trouble. It was during that same November visit that my father told me the following story which I then heard for the first time. Although my parents had much in common, they did have certain differences. It seems that my father noticed on one occasion that my mother failed to repeat the "Amen" to the prayer for King William III. He then called my mother to his study and asked her why. I have since found the following comments in my mother's own hand concerning the same event: "I was a little surprised at the question, and don't well know what I answered, but too well I remember what followed. He immediately kneeled down and imprecated the divine vengeance upon himself and all his posterity if ever he touched me more or came into a bed with me before I had begged God's pardon and his, for not saying Amen to the prayer for the King."[6] Although they slept separately that night, they did go to Communion together the next morning. My father, however, remained completely firm and impenitent even when the King's death on March 8 led to the accession of Queen Anne (for whom my mother, as a loyal supporter of the Stuarts, would certainly have been ready to say the "Amen"). Subsequently, he left Epworth for London claiming to seek another service chaplaincy. My mother, understandably, was worried and upset at my father's departure from her bed and his parish. Again, I have since found these words in my mother's own hand, this time written in confidence

---

[6]See *Proceedings of the Wesley Historical Society*, XXIX, pp. 50-57.

to Lady Yarborough at Snaith Hall: "I am more easy in the thoughts of parting because I think we are not likely to live happily together, but I have six very little children, who though he tells me he will take good care of, yet if anything should befall him at sea, we should be in no very good condition. I have unsuccessfully represented to him the unlawfulness and unreasonableness of his Oath; that the Man in that case has no more power over his own body than the Woman over hers; that since I am willing to let him quietly enjoy his opinions, he ought not to deprive me of my little liberty of conscience."[7]

Toward the end of the summer, my father returned home. He had intended to stay only a few days before leaving again, but stayed on, and a fire, set by one of our servants which destroyed part of the rectory, served to bring the disastrous episode to a close. Indeed, the pregnancy which resulted from the reconciliation was terminated by the birth of John Benjamin Wesley on June 17, 1703.[8]

One of my earliest memories is of another fire in that same rectory (although I remember the damp smell of the smoke more than the actual event). This was a Thursday night, February 9, 1709, I believe between 11:00 and midnight, which completely destroyed the building. All were quickly evacuated except for me. As my rescue came none too soon, I have frequently thought of myself (to use those words of the prophets) as a "brand plucked from the burning."[9] From that moment on, my mother seemed to take special pains to see that I was wholly committed to God. After my older brother, Samuel, entered Westminster in 1704, the household was dominated by women. My younger brother, Charles, joined me and my six sisters in 1708, only to be followed by yet another sister just two years later. It occurs to me now that some of you might be interested in learning about our routine as inspired by the leadership of our rather unusual mother.

---

[7]Ibid.

[8]A later calendar change would move Wesley's birthdate to June 28.

[9]Amos 4:11; Zechariah 3:2. It is interesting that John was the only child given a middle name. Benjamin was also the name of a child that had previously died in infancy.

Mother claimed no special insight. As a matter of fact, it was only with great difficulty that I persuaded her to put into writing her method of educating and training children. I have a letter dated February 21, 1732, where she writes following a request made by me: "The writing anything about my way of education I am much averse to. It cannot, I think, be of service to anyone to know how I, who have lived such a retired life for so many years, used to employ my time and care in bringing up my children. No one can, without renouncing the world, in the most literal sense, observe my method; and there are few, if any, that would entirely devote above twenty years of the prime of life in hopes to save the souls of their children, which they think may be saved without so much ado; for that was my principle intention, however unskillfully and unsuccessfully managed."[10]

Then on July 24, 1732, she wrote: "According to your desire, I have collected the principal rules I observed in educating my family." She then described at some length our regular method of living. "When we turned a year old (and some before), we were taught to fear the rod and to cry softly, by which means we escaped abundance of correction which we might otherwise have had." We sat with our parents at mealtimes and were allowed "to eat and drink (small beer) as much as we would, but not to call for anything." If we wanted anything, we were allowed to whisper our requirements to one of the servants. We were not permitted either to be finicky or greedy over our food. We were absolutely forbidden to eat anything between meals and if one of us dared "to go into the kitchen to ask anything of the servants . . . we were certainly beat."[11]

For mother the root of all sin and misery was self-will. She felt that whatever encouraged this within us simply insured our wretchedness and irreligion. She wrote further that whatever checked and mortified this, promoted our future happiness and piety. She believed that

---

[10]See Rebecca Harmon, *Susanna, Mother of the Wesleys*, pp. 57-62, who gives this and the following letters in full and describes their impact in detail.
[11]Ibid.

religion was nothing else than doing the will of God and not our own: That the one grand impediment to our temporal and eternal happiness was this self-will. No indulgence of it could be trivial and no denial unprofitable. Heaven or hell depended on this alone, so that any parent who sought to subdue this worked together with God in the renewing and saving of a soul. She felt that the parent who indulged it did the devil's work; made religion impracticable, salvation unattainable, and did all that lies in the parent to damn the child's body and soul forever.[12]

Added to this were several rules observed among us: 1) If we would confess our faults, we were not beaten. 2) No sinful action, as lying, playing at church or playing on the Lord's day, disobedience, quarreling, or any form of disrespectfulness should ever pass unpunished. 3) No child was ever beaten twice for the same fault, and if we amended we were never upbraided with it afterward. 4) Every single act of obedience, especially when it crossed upon our own inclinations, was always commended, and frequently rewarded according to the merits of the case. 5) If ever we performed an act of obedience, or did anything with an intention to please, though the performance was not well, yet the obedience and intention was kindly accepted, and the child was directed, with sweetness, how to do better for the future. 6) We were expected to respect the property of others, even in the smallest matter. 7) Promises were to be strictly observed; once a gift was given, for example, it was not to be taken back. 8) My sisters were taught not only to work but also to read. Mother, quite frankly, was offended by women who could sew but could not read fit to be heard.[13]

So, my mother managed a discipline, which although austere, was never cruel. It is important to remember that her instructions related not only to the development of the child through discipline and education, but was profoundly religious as well. And, lest you think that she related well only to her children, let me describe briefly one

---

[12]Ibid.
[13]Ibid.

curious result of all this. Our family devotions were held not only for us but for the servants as well. Devotional meetings were frequently held in the rectory kitchen on Sunday evening. When my father was away my mother took charge. Once when my father was spending most of his time in London as a member of Convocation (November 1710 until February 1712) some members of the congregation joined our little meetings. At first there were only thirty or forty but by the time my father returned the attendance had reached more than 200. Although mother was criticized by many of the other villagers, she simply laid this aside saying "that she had long taken leave of the world, and that everything which conduces to the salvation of souls appears odd to others."[14]

Thus, we were all taught to admire a sense of vital piety leading to a wholehearted devotion to God. Contributing to this no doubt was the fact that both my parents knew no halfway measures. This can be seen most clearly in their views of religion, both High Church and Puritan.

My father, for example (as I have already mentioned), was not only a High Churchman, but a strong Loyalist as well.[15] My mother was also High Church but had strong Jacobite sympathies, accepting the ascension of William and Mary de facto but not de jure.[16] Again, as we have already noted, this would inevitably put her at cross purposes at some point with my father. Yet, it is not surprising that I too should develop an appreciation for the High Church tradition.

Both my parents also had strong Puritan roots. The Puritans sought to purify the church from all unscriptural forms of public worship. In their fundamental appeal to the Scriptures, they also looked to reason and experience embodying a "conception of the Christian life in terms of

---

[14]*Journal*, Vol. III, p. 33.

[15]All three of his principal works were dedicated to Royalty. For example, Samuel's book, *Studies in the Book of Job*, was presented in person by John to Queen Caroline on October 12, 1735; see chapter 10.

[16]Jacobite is the name given to the Stuart partians. The Stuart King James II, had been expelled in the Glorious Revolution (1688) as a Roman Catholic and his supporters kept alive the hope of his return to power.

disciplined living, moral rigorism, and Christianity in earnest."[17] Is it not natural, therefore, that my parents should stress moral virtue and the place of reason in religion in our devotional training? Early in life I found myself becoming by nature a rigorist, a moralist, and a lover of reason. My father sometimes complained that reason, for example, was so prevalent in me (remember that this would have been underscored by the prevailing philosophy of the day) that I was unwilling to attend to even the barest necessities of life if I could not find a good reason for them.

I think that if this had been the extent of the influence of my earliest home environment, life for me would have been much easier. There was, however, still another influence that would put me at odds with myself forcing an impasse that would take years to resolve. This had to do with mysticism.

Devotional reading was an important part of my parents' discipline. Many of the devotional books being read by serious-minded Christians during the first part of this century were written by the Roman Catholic mystics. We were no exception. So, we read these as well. This would not have presented a problem had I not already been somewhat of a rigorist (relating to my High Church background), a moralist (relating to my Puritan background), and a legalist (since we have already established that I was, by nature, a lover of reason). The result of this was that the influence of much of my earliest devotional reading, which accelerated my appreciation of asceticism (held in common by both Puritan and mystic alike), quickly tapered off into a mystical contemplation that was so subjective that I no longer had sufficient roots to ground me in the evangelical faith.[18] Those who understand basic philosophy know that

---

[17]John Newton, *Susanna Wesley and the Puritan Tradition in Methodism*, p. 43.

[18]Part of the issue here had to do with a Puritan Christo-centric mediated *com*-union with God focusing upon justification on the one hand, over and against a mystic theo-centric *un*mediated *union* with God focusing upon sanctification on the other. The details outlining the nature of this impasse are given in "The Analysis, Part I."

it is impossible to be both an Aristotelian and a Platonist at the same time. Does reason lead to faith, or does faith lead to reason (or understanding)? This was my dilemma. The battleground proved to be the first thirteen years of my ministry.[19] Fortunately, the Scriptures finally won out, taking the strength of the one and counteracting the weaknesses of the other. Although the resolution of this impasse would eventually prove to be the particular genius of our so-called Methodist Revival, this was a long time coming.

Let me describe briefly a few of the devotional books that had such an influence on me and my parents during those early formative years. The few sparks of piety in the pre-Reformation church were mostly among the mystics. It is predictable, therefore, that there would have been, among the Puritans, an admiration for the mystical piety which (like Puritanism) began with a high regard for mortification and self-denial. Even though mysticism failed to acknowledge the essentials of the evangelical faith, *carefully* used, these mystics could strengthen the Puritan resolve to a pure and holy life. One should not be surprised, therefore, to find that my mother's father, Samuel Annesley, had an acquaintance with these mystics. He knew Gregory of Nyssa and referred to him when writing on "What it is to Love God with the Whole Heart."[20] He knew Francois de Sales and appealed to him when arguing "the love of God as a gift of the Spirit."[21] He also knew St. Teresa and referred to her well-known maxim, "All that is not God is nothing," in one of his sermons.[22] Consequently, it is easy to see how my mother's emphasis on the will, on humility, and on the outworkings of prayer in love toward one's neighbor, could be strongly reminiscent of the mysticism of St. Teresa and *The Interior Castle*.[23]

In addition, mother read the quasi-mystic Blaise Pascal,

---

[19]This is the story of Part II, "His Early Ministry."

[20]See *A Supplement to the Morning Exercise at Cripplegate*, ed. by Samuel Annesley, second edition (1676), pp. 4-5.

[21]Ibid., p. 12.

[22]Ibid., p. 26.

[23]Newton, *Susanna Wesley*, p. 136.

and told me that he was the one who helped rescue her from skepticism.[24] Pascal recommended a rigorous mortification to enable one to endure pain and suffering with joy and satisfaction. Although my mother disliked his glorification of spiritual trials to the extent of welcoming temptation, she did admire his exceptional piety and she quotes him both in her theological writings and in her private correspondence.[25]

Furthermore, the mystic Lorenzo Scupoli and his *Pugna Spiritualis* or *Spiritual Combat* (known through Castaniza's translation) held a central place in my mother's devotional reading. Undoubtedly she was predisposed toward the *Spiritual Combat* by her father's typically Puritan understanding of the Christian life as a Holy War. Scupoli, addressing the *understanding* and the *will*, argues that a man must "hate himself, renounce his own ego, and turn with wholehearted love to God." Although feeling and emotion may follow, Scupoli (like Pascal in many ways), found *Virtus Patientiae* the essential factor in Christian obedience, that is, the readiness to accept suffering and temptation as "grist for the mill of perfection." My mother heard in this particular type of mysticism the summons to continue the struggle for Christian perfection and to withdraw from the things of the world, for "the love of God alone is efficacious and all-powerful." This was to have a most profound influence upon me.

My mother also knew and recommended à Kempis, the Cambridge Platonists More and Norris, and the Scottish mystic, Henry Scougal, author of the influential *The Life of God in the Soul of Man*.[26] According to Scougal, love has an irresistible power. It is the force which transforms every-

---

[24]It is interesting to note that in philosophy mysticism is frequently pitted against skepticism and that Susanna (like John), though never disparaging of reason, reacts against the extreme rationalism of her day. See her letter to John dated August 18, 1725.

[25]Susanna would also object to Scupoli on the issue of "welcoming temptation." She frequently quotes the words from the Lord's prayer: "Lead us not into temptation." Cf. Newton, *Susanna Wesley*, p. 138.

[26]According to George Whitefield, this book led him to faith.

thing. It bestows its own quality upon every attribute of the soul and gives direction to them. The object of a man's love determines his worth. The one who loves vulgar things is himself vulgar. He who loves God participates *gradually* in the nobility of the divine world. Both my mother and I were much affected by Scougal.

Now, a brief word about my father is needed. Although he had the dull obstinacy of a rigid formalist, being more prone to political and ecclesiastical quarrels than to internal religion, he too was influenced by the mystics. As we have already mentioned, my father's life at Epworth was not an easy one and hardly conducive to spiritual indulgence, but the fact remains that he too knew a Kempis (according to many the springboard to mysticism), who was his "old friend and companion." He also frequently referred to Pascal and the French mystic de Renty. I remember a letter to me dated July 14, 1725, where he cautioned me against the "peril of levity" (paraphrasing Ecclesiastes 7:16-18, and quoting Ecclesiastes 11:9 and 12:14), stating that mortification is still an indispensable Christian duty.

Although there is much more to be said, allow me to summarize by simply saying that we were all living in those early days within an atmosphere that was at once High Church, Puritan, and mystical. I can now see that the several pilgrimages of faith for my parents and myself have interesting parallels along so many lines. This should become even more apparent as my story continues.

4

A Student: Charterhouse and Christ Church, Oxford

Being removed to the University for five years, I still said my prayers both in public and in private, and read, with the Scriptures, several other books of religion, especially comments on the New Testament. Yet I had not all this while so much as a notion of inward holiness. John Wesley

I remained at home until I was nearly eleven. Although I did not in my earlier years attend any public or private school, since my mother (as you might well imagine) had a poor opinion of the common methods of teaching and governing children, I did not seem to suffer. The influence of her pious instructions, softened by her tenderness, was so faithful and uniform that I found myself at no real disadvantage. In fact, I *appeared* so serious-minded about education as well as religion that my father allowed me to receive the sacrament at the age of eight.

I entered Charterhouse, a boarding school for boys in London, on January 28, 1714, in its centenary year.[1] I occupied one of the few free places for "poor scholars" having been nominated by the former Marquis of Normanby (my father's patron who some ten years earlier had been created Duke of Buckingham). The first two paragraphs in my *Journal* review for May 24, 1738, describe this period. Let me give them to you much as they stand, and then interpret them briefly.[2]

I believe until I was about ten years old I had not sinned

---

[1]Charterhouse had been founded on October 3, 1614. See Telford, *The Life of John Wesley*, p. 23 for greater detail.

[2]The following is a paraphrase. For the full account see *Works*, Vol. I, p. 98.

away that "washing of the Holy Ghost" which was given to me in baptism. I had been strictly educated and carefully taught that I could be saved only "by universal obedience," and "by keeping all the commandments of God." Those instructions, so far as they respected *outward* duties and sins, I glady received, and considered carefully. But all that was said to me of *inward* obedience, or holiness, I neither understood nor remembered. So much so that I was as ignorant of the true meaning of the law, as I was of the gospel of Christ.

The next six or seven years were spent at school. As outward restraints were now removed, I was much more negligent than before, even of outward duties. I was almost continually guilty of outward sins, which I committed knowingly, though they were not scandalous in the eyes of the world. I still read the Scriptures, however, and also said my prayers, morning and evening. What I then hoped to be saved by was: 1) not being so bad as other people, 2) having still a kindness for religion, and, 3) reading the Bible, going to church, and saying my prayers.[3]

Although I intended that these words should refer mostly to my inadequate view of saving faith, there is much here which has been misunderstood even by my closest friends. In spite of my "negligence," Charterhouse was a good experience. Even today, I rarely go to London without visiting there. It shall always be dear to me. I rarely miss an opportunity to renew acquaintance with my former Charterhouse schoolmates.[4]

The rigorous regulations and the modest style of living were reinforced by many letters from home. Each day was begun at 5:00. I washed, read prayers, wrote letters, and, true to a promise made to my father, ran three times around the garden before breakfast at 8:00. Breakfast consisted of bread, cheese, and beer (tea or coffee being much too expensive). These hard, frugal times were important to me. It was here, for example, that I first discovered

---

[3]*Works*, Vol. I, p. 98.
[4]*Works*, Vol. III, pp. 176, 335.

that one can manage quite well on a staple diet of bread alone.

Furthermore, Dr. Walker, my headmaster, seemed to favor me above all his other students. My mother had well prepared me to learn, and even though Dr. Walker was (according to those misguided people who would judge the effectiveness of the mind by the age of the body) past his prime, being sixty-seven years old, I seemed to excel almost from the start.

Equally important, during this time I drew closer to my older brother, Samuel, Jr. As an usher at Westminster he was becoming a reasonably responsible scholar and poet and challenged me greatly whenever our Sundays and holiday times brought us happily together. As my parents had advised me not to make the expensive trip home too frequently, many of my idle moments were spent with Samuel and his young wife in Dean's Yard where I was not only entertained but also carefully instructed by one who was as well equipped to teach as any one I have ever known. This was so much of an advantage that when I left for Christ Church, Oxford, I received a prize of twenty pounds in addition to an exhibition for the same amount. I will never forget an encounter with Dr. Sacheverell during my last week at school, when he greeted me with the words: "You are too young to go to the university; you cannot know Greek and Latin yet. Go back to school!"[5] Forgive me if I smile inwardly a bit when I say to you with some pride that Charterhouse prepared me admirably. It pleases me to know that my former school regards me as one of its "greatest" sons. Some years ago these few words of verse were written in my honor:

> *John Wesley was one of our company,*
> *Prophet untiring and fearless of tongue,*
> *Down the long years he went*
> *Spending yet never spent,*
> *Serving his God with a heart ever young.*[6]

I remember happily accepting the role of steward at the

---

[5]Dr. Henry Sacheverell, an opponent of the Dissenters, assisted Wesley's father in the controversy over "obedience to authority."

[6]*Letters*, Vol. I, p. 3.

Founders' Day dinner on December 12, 1727. I also remember spending an extended period at Charterhouse after my return from Germany in the late summer of 1738. In fact, Charterhouse was to become a kind of "place apart," where I could retire for months at a time without much interruption.[7]

Before going further I need to tell you about two aspects of my personality that seemed to take shape and form during these early years. One has to do with my inordinate fear of dying and the other with my interest in apparitions. Charterhouse, besides being a school for boys, was also an infirmary for old men. I became accustomed to seeing death. The less serious boys made jokes (which, I suppose, kept them from contemplating their own mortality), but I could not escape so easily. As the old men were carried out, I found myself plagued by haunting doubts. I would become depressed. During the worst of times I busied myself translating Latin to keep from thinking, but then, when I least expected it, the question: "What if I should die?" *Death* became the *enemy!* If I speak to you plainly I must admit that I became a man obsessed. I remember some years later discovering Dr. Cheyne's *Book of Health and Long Life,* whose advice I instantly put into practice.[8] I also developed an interest in medicine, eventually writing the *Primitive Physick: or, An Easy and Natural Method of Curing Most Diseases,* which was published in 1776. Then, as the years progressed the stirring testimonies of our dying Methodists (many of which appear in my *Journal*) brought me some relief; but even today, a now toothless enemy waits impatiently, though my victory over the fear itself is virtually won.

A second aspect of my personality (perhaps not entirely unrelated) concerns my interest in apparitions. While I

---

[7]It is likely that one of the first Methodist fellowship meetings met at Charterhouse and it was here that Wesley prepared either the first Methodist Hymnbook of 1739 or the edition of 1740. He also wrote to many of his friends from his Charterhouse rooms. See *Journal,* Vol. II, p. 77 and pp. 130-155, for example.

[8]Wesley read the fourth edition of this book which appeared in 1725 and commented upon it in a letter to his mother. See *Letters,* Vol. I, p. 11.

was away at Charterhouse some rather strange things began to happen at the Epworth rectory. My sisters, Sukey and Nancy, first heard the knockings of a "supernatural" visitant on December 1, 1716. Other sounds like groans and the crashing of bottles were soon to follow. Although my mother first suggested that the noises were made by rats and hired a villager, John Maw, to blow a horn throughout the house to scare them away, the disturbances continued. Eventually, even my father was convinced that the sounds (which included footsteps apparently made by someone wearing jack-boots, the banging of doors, the shattering of glass, the splintering of wood, the pouring of coins on the floor, and even the gobbling like that of a turkey cock, but all without any outward physical manifestation) were too regular and persistent for any natural causes. After some months, which included some sleepless nights, "Old Jeffrey" (so named by my sister, Emilia, after one who had died in the house), ceased to terrify and became more of a nuisance and a bore. My family came to accept the annoying "ghost" as a matter of fact. Even my younger sisters were no longer alarmed. Frequently when one or the other was doing her chores, like sweeping the floor, she often heard sweeping being done behind her, and only regretted that the visitant would not take the broom into his or its hands and do the work for her. Then, suddenly, the visitations ended as abruptly as they had begun.

When I went home following my years at Charterhouse, I made careful inquiry into everything that had happened. Again, following my years at Christ Church, Oxford, I discussed the affair with all whom I could, taking careful notes, which I used for a recent article in the *Arminian Magazine*. [9] You might well ask, what do I make of all this? Let me comment briefly.

It appears that Old Jeffrey was politically conscious. He was especially violent whenever my father prayed for King George I. It occurs to me that the visitations were perhaps intended to remind my father of the sinfulness of his deser-

---

[9] See *Arminian Magazine* (1784), pp. 548-550, 606-608, 654-656.

tion of my mother in 1702. "I fear his vow was not forgotten before God," nor apparently by this Jacobite "friend." Furthermore, some have questioned why I should include this, and many other such stories, in my *Works*. Admittedly it is hard to keep the middle way; "not to believe too little or too much!"[10] Yet, it is likewise true "that the English in general, and indeed most of the men of learning in Europe have given up all accounts of (demon possession) and apparitions, as mere old wives' fables. I am sorry for it; and I willingly take this opportunity of entering my solemn protest against this violent compliment which so many that believe the Bible pay to those who do not believe it. I owe them no such service. I take knowledge, these are at the bottom of the outcry which has been raised, and with such insolence spread throughout the nation, in direct opposition not only to the Bible, but to the suffrage of the wisest and best of men in all ages and nations. They well know, (whether Christians know it or not,) that the giving up (demon possession) is, in effect, giving up the Bible; and they know, on the other hand, that if but one account of the intercourse of men with separate spirits be admitted, their whole castle in the air (Deism, Atheism, Materialism) falls to the ground. I know no reason, therefore, why we should suffer even this weapon to be wrested out of our hands. Indeed there are numerous arguments besides, which abundantly confute their vain imaginations. But we need not be hooted out of one; Neither reason nor religion require this."[11]

It has always amused me that "one of the capital objections to all these accounts, which I have known urged over and over, is this, 'Did you ever see an apparition yourself?' No: Nor did I ever see a murder; yet I believe there is such a thing; yea, and that in one place or another murder is committed every day. Therefore I cannot, as a reasonable

---

[10]*Works*, Vol. III, p. 202. Here (Dec. 14, 1764) Wesley reads Baxter's book on "apparitions." Some of this he accepts; some he does not.

[11]*Works*, Vol. III, pp. 324f. These words were written as a preface to similar stories recorded in the *Journal*. The words in parentheses replace the words "witches" and "witchcraft." Demon possession is closer to Wesley's meaning as we now understand it.

man, deny the fact; although I never saw it, and perhaps never may. The testimony of unexceptionable witnesses fully convinces me both of the one and the other."[12] But enough of this. We must now return to the story of my days as a student.

I entered Christ Church, the most distinguished college in Oxford, on June 24, 1720. I was determined to learn as well as I could; but I was extremely poor. I remember seeing a friend have his cap and wig snatched as he was standing at a coffee-house door and thinking to myself: "I am pretty safe from such gentlemen, for unless they carry me away, carcass and all, they would have but a poor purchase." Had it not been for the generosity of my brother Samuel, my tutor, Dr. Sherman (who transmitted to me the rent of the rooms to which he was entitled but in which he did not reside), and a few friends who were kind enough to make small loans, I might well have starved. I remember a letter from my mother: "Dear Jacky, be not discouraged. Perhaps, not withstanding all, we shall pick up a few crumbs for you before the end of the year." She again advised me not to make the expensive journeys home but to use that money for a wiser and a better purpose, namely to pay debts, and make things easier for myself.

Again, let me share with you and then interpret briefly a paragraph from my *Journal* review for May 24, 1738, corresponding with these years as an undergraduate. "Being removed to the university for five years, I still said my prayers both in public and in private, and read, with the Scriptures, several other books of religion, especially comments on the New Testament. Yet I had not all this while so much as a notion of inward holiness; nay, went on habitually, and, for the most part, very contentedly in some or other known sin: Indeed, with some intermission and short struggles, especially before and after the Holy Communion, which I was obliged to receive thrice a year. I cannot well tell what I hoped to be saved by now, when I was continually sinning against that little light I had; un-

---

[12]Ibid.

less by those transient fits of what many Divines taught me to call repentance."[13]

Although I retained a kindliness toward religion, religion was not yet "the business of my life"; I was not yet *homo unius libri* (a man of one book). As an undergraduate I pursued my studies with great advantage under the direction of Dr. Wiggin, a gentleman eminent for his knowledge of classical literature. I then studied under his successor, Henry Sherman, a friend of my brother Samuel's. As a young student, I soon developed classical tastes as well. My writing, so I was told, gained polish and wit. I even tried my hand at poetry though most of this was either an imitation or translation of the Latin. I remember sending my father an imitation of the 65th Psalm. I shall never forget his reply: "I like your verses on the 65th Psalm and would not have you bury your talent."[14]

Much of what I was expected to learn, however, was "an idle, useless interruption of useful studies, horribly shockingly superficial, an insult upon common sense."[14] So, I pursued what I liked best. I became fascinated with logic. I regarded Aldrich's *Compendium Artis Logicae* with profound reverence and eventually published my own translation of this remarkable work. Consequently, it was during this period that I was first attracted to a method of debate (which I frequently employ even now) known as *argumentum ad hominem* or *reductio ad absurdum* where, by appealing to an opponent's own prejudice, I could use their own arguments against them, and then, if need be, reduce them to the absurd.[15]

---

[13]*Works,* Vol. I, p. 98.

[14]See Green, *The Young Mr. Wesley,* p. 62n.

[15]Later on, for example, we find Wesley using Thomas à Kempis (a Catholic) against the Catholic polemic in Ireland; he used Fénelon's *Simplicity* against mystical refinement in religion; Madame Bourignon (a mystic) is used against the mystical antinomian concept of grace; Gregory Lopez is used against Madame Guyon; Anna Maria Van Schurmann is used against William Law; and even the mystical divinity of Dionysius is used against the Moravian "Stillness" at Fetterlane. The latter backfired when some in the Society failed to see the error of the argument even when reduced to the absurd. It should also be added that this may have been an effective form of debate, but it has been confus-

Before concluding the story of this particular period of my life I should also add that while at Oxford I was still haunted by thoughts of death and I continued my interest in the supernatural. I remember being impressed by the story of a young man reputed to be seized by a demon. On another occasion I remember wanting to visit a house near Oxford that was said to be haunted.[16]

So, I found myself during these early Oxford years strengthening my analytical prowess. This accentuated my intellectual impetuosity. I grew impatient. Perhaps this is why my brother Charles always claimed that I could never keep a secret. Although I spent hours in reflection, this bore no proportion to my quickness of apprehension. It was extremely difficult for me to delay either in reasoning or in acting. I was young. I was happy (of sorts), but something was missing. Then, during the year following my undergraduate work, several things began to happen almost all at once.

---

ing for the historian. Wesley, if not carefully read, frequently gives the appearance of self-contradiction; but, when his arguments are examined closely, an interesting consistency is revealed.

[16]See *Letters*, Vol. I, pp. 6, 13-14, and cf. p. 168n.

5

A Religious Conversion

Dear Jacky—The alteration of your temper has occasioned me much speculation. I . . . hope it may proceed from the operation of God's Holy Spirit, that by taking away your relish of sensual enjoyments, he may prepare and dispose your mind for a more serious and close application to things of a more sublime and spiritual nature. . . . In good earnest, resolve to make religion the business of your life.   Susanna Wesley

For me, the fact that I should consider Holy Orders was as normal as breathing. My ancestors on both sides of the family had distinguished themselves by service to the church; but, a dilemma was presenting itself. I had received my B.A. degree toward the end of 1724, *but what to do?* Up to that point I had not practiced to any remarkable degree, the kind of piety so necessary for the Christian ministry. Although I had not been a blatant sinner, if I was to come to any kind of commitment in regard to ordination, some changes had to be made.

I remember reading the words of Montesquieu some years later: "In England there is no religion and the subject, if mentioned in society, evokes nothing but laughter." It pains me to admit that a Frenchman could make such a judgment upon our little kingdom, but he was right. It would take courage to follow Christian service in the tradition of my forefathers. The Oxford community was noted for its jibes aimed at those who studied theology. They were characterized as second-rate weaklings (and not altogether without reason) whose primary "calling" was to secure all the fat, comfortable benefices they could.

Such a calling for me, however, would have to find roots in integrity and a willingness to uphold (if not defend)

an office or religion with a mind to holiness and order.

In December (1724) I made a tentative decision to seek ordination and in January I confided in my father. I wrote to him asking his advice as to ordination and suitable commentaries on the Bible; thinking that this would please him greatly.[1] I must admit that I was a little surprised by his reply. He cautioned me against the very thing that had already been in my mind and judiciously warned me against looking for an easy life in the ministry—a means of simply providing a living. Would I pass my life, as did so many, in hunting for parish livings, without a thought for the souls I would be held responsible for at the judgment seat of God? He exhorted me to weigh the cost and then to *wait* until my mind was more determined.[2]

The result of all this was confusion. I hovered for a time at the point of depression. Then on February 23, 1725, my mother wrote: "Dear Jacky: The alteration of your temper has occasioned me much speculation. I, who am apt to be sanguine, hope it may proceed from the operations of God's Holy Spirit, that by taking away your relish of sensual enjoyments, he may prepare and dispose your mind for a more serious and close application to things of a more sublime and spiritual nature. If it be so, happy are you if you cherish those dispositions, and now, in good earnest, *resolve to make religion the business of your life;* for, after all, that is the one thing that strictly speaking is necessary, and all things else are comparatively little to the purposes of life. I heartily wish you would now enter upon a serious examination of yourself, that you may know whether you have a reasonable hope of salvation; that is whether you are in a state of faith and repentance or not, which you know are the conditions of the Gospel covenant on our part. If you are, the satisfaction of knowing it would abundantly reward your pain; if not, you will find a more reasonable occasion for tears than can be met with in a tragedy. This matter deserves great consideration by all,

---

[1]Samuel commented that the Bible was its own best commentary but apart from that, Grotius was the best for the most part, expecially on the Old Testament. See Whitehead, *John Wesley,* Vol. I, pp. 384f.

[2]See Green, *The Young Mr. Wesley,* p. 66, for the same period.

but especially by those designed for the ministry; who ought, above all things, to make their own calling and election sure; lest, after they have preached to others, they themselves should be cast away."[3]

Frankly, I think that if her letter had ended there, my depression would have continued. But then followed (in the same letter) the encouragement that I was seeking. She commented on the letter to my father concerning ordination. "I was much pleased with it, and liked the proposal as well; but it is an unhappiness almost peculiar to our family that your father and I seldom think alike. I approve the disposition of your mind, and think the sooner you are a deacon the better; because it may be an inducement to greater application in the study of practical divinity, which I humbly concede is the best study for candidates for Orders. Mr. Wesley differs from me, and would engage you, I believe, in critical learning, which, though accidentally of use, is in no wise preferable to the other. I earnestly pray God to avert that great evil from you of engaging in trifling studies to the neglect of such as are absolutely necessary. I dare advise nothing: God Almighty direct and bless you! I have much to say, but cannot write you more at present. I long to see you. I wish all be well. Adieu! Susanna Wesley."[4] Can you coubt for a moment the tremendous impact that this correspondence had upon my life during these formative months?

A rather careless proverb has it: "What woman wills, God wills." I was not surprised that my father, in a letter dated March 13, 1725, concurred with my mother and encouraged me to enter Orders as soon as possible, to devote myself to prayer and study, and to work especially on St. John Chrysostom and the Articles of the Church. It should also be stated (as it occurs to me now) that my father's change of disposition might have been motivated by more than my mother's "advice." He had just been granted the additional living of Wroot and could (to put it honestly) use my help. At any rate, my decision was made.

---

[3]Tyerman, *The Life and Times of John Wesley*, Vol. I, p. 32. Italics mine.
[4]Ibid.

In preparation for Holy Orders, I chose to remain at Oxford in order to fulfill the requirements for the Master's degree, living in the same rooms used in Christ Church. Perhaps a college Fellowship would become vacant providing the financial security necessary to free me from the temptation of accepting a parish for the wrong reasons. Then, however, things began to happen so quickly that it is difficult to remember the exact order of events over the next few months.

On April 5 I began my *Diary*.[5] Less than two weeks later I journeyed west from Oxford into the Cotswolds, a beautiful range of mountains pocked with quaint villages, rising up just north and east of Bristol. On April 15 I met Sally Kirkham whose father, the Rev. Lionel Kirkham, was rector at Stanton. Although there were at least five families in the three villages of Buckland, Broadway, and Stanton who were to influence me greatly over the next few years, I have singled out Sally since she was to become my *first religious friend*.[6] She would be my Varanese, the designated pseudonym used in our correspondence. She was both witty and sensible and I was so drawn to her that I quickly and freely shared with her the dilemma of my wanting to follow with integrity a calling to Christian ministry. I confessed my ambivalent feelings to her. On the one hand, I wanted to make (to use my mother's words) "religion the business of my life"; but, on the other, I wanted to enjoy what I thought to be much gayer times. So, I would go dancing one day and even play cards in the Common Room at Oxford, but then have those "transient fits of repentance" the next.

As I confided in Sally, she was so sympathetic (but never indulging) and helpful with her advice that I soon found myself comparing her with my mother. I remember think-

---

[5] A facsimile of page 1 of Wesley's *Diary* can be found in the *Journal* (Curnock ed.), Vol. 1, p. 37.

[6] The significance of this religious friend can be seen in the *Journal* review for May 24, 1738. The five families mentioned here (and there were others to a lesser degree) were the Tookers, the Granvilles, the Griffiths, the Kirkhams, and the Winningtons. See Green, *The Young Mr. Wesley*, pp. 202ff. for further details on these families.

ing to myself: "χύριε βοήθει (Lord, help me)! I'm in love!" I felt a sudden panic. My sister Emilia had written me from Wroot just one week earlier despairing of frustrated love. A part of that letter reads: ". . . whether you will be engaged before thirty or not I cannot determine; but if my advice is worth listening to, never engage your affections before your worldly affairs are in such a posture that you may marry very soon. . . . Were I to live my time over again and had the same experience I have now, were it for the best man in England I would not wait one year. I know you are a young man encompassed with difficulties that has passed through many hardships already . . . but believe me if you ever come to suffer the torment of a hopeless love all other afflictions will seem small in comparison of it."[7] Emilia's remarks seemed alarmingly appropriate. After all, what did I have to offer? My family was impoverished, and I was still in debt. Yet, in spite of mistrusted feelings, my friendship with Sally grew. I showed her my *Diary*. She approved, and placed in my hands a copy of Bishop Taylor's *Rule and Exercises of Holy Living and Dying* which so sealed my daily practice of recording my actions (which I have continued faithfully until this moment) that I later prefaced that first *Diary* with his "Rules and Resolutions."[8] This helped me to develop a style of introspection that would keep me in constant touch with most of my feelings, whether religious or otherwise.

Soon after this Sally encouraged me to read Thomas à Kempis's *Imitation of Christ*. This too found its mark. Consequently, both Taylor and a Kempis (although there was much in their writings that I called into question), along with countless conversations with Varanese and the correspondence with my mother, were responsible for my religious conversion. It was at this time that I determined that God should have me or I would perish.

---

[7]See Tyerman, *Life and Times*, Vol. I, p. 33, for this letter in full.

[8]See *Journal*, Vol. I, p. 48, for a copy of these "Rules and Resolutions." There were actually two books, *The Rule and Exercises of Holy Living*, and *The Rule and Exercises of Holy Dying*. Jeremy Taylor (1613-1667) was one of the classic writers of the Anglican Church.

When I returned to Oxford I initiated a significant correspondence with my mother. I was now reading both Taylor and à Kempis even more carefully, but still not without some reservation. Sally and I both thought them too strict at some points.[9] On June 18 I wrote to my mother: If Taylor's conception of humility (as despising oneself and always thinking of oneself as worse than others) and repentance (where forgiveness cannot be perceived) are essential to salvation, then "who can be saved"?[10] My mother replied: "Taylor seeks in humility an *habitual disposition* which is far more comprehensive than your narrow understanding. Our humility should be in contrast with God more than man. One who realizes his unworthiness before God will also realize (without thinking) his unworthiness before man."[11] This was helpful. I began to put many of Taylor's *Rules* into practice, taking a more exact account of the manner in which I spent my time, writing down how I used every hour.[12] I summarized the result of all this in my treatise *A Plain Account of Christian Perfection* where I noted: "In the year 1725, being in the 23rd year of my age, I met with Bishop Taylor's 'Rule and Exercises of Holy Living and Dying.' In reading several parts of this book, I was exceedingly affected; that part in particular which relates to purity of intention. Instantly I resolved to dedicate all my life to God, all my thoughts, and words, and actions; being thoroughly convinced, there was no medium; but that every part of my life (not some only) must either be a sacrifice to God, or myself, that is, in effect, to the devil."[13]

Taylor's influence was significant indeed. His *Rules* later

---

[9]Wesley writes: "I have heard one I take to be a person of good judgment (i.e. Sally Kirkham) say that she would advise no one very young to read Taylor . . . he almost put her out of her senses . . . because he seemed to exclude all from being in a way of salvation who did not come up to his rules, some of which are altogether impracticable." *Letters,* Vol. I, pp. 17-20.

[10]See *Letters,* Vol. I, pp. 17-20 for this letter in full.

[11]See Tyerman, *Life and Times,* Vol. I, pp. 39-40 for this letter in full.

[12]Wesley's cryptic phrase, "idleness slays," entered several times into the *Oxford Diary,* no doubt reveals a summary of Taylor's teaching on the same subject. Cf. *Journal,* Vol. I, p. 55, with *Holy Living,* I, i.

[13]*Works,* Vol. XI, p. 366.

formed the basis for the *Twelve Rules of a Helper*, and eventually the *Rules for the United Societies*. I liked his combination of outward observance with inward intention. He taught me that total self-discipline applies both to the body and to the soul. The religious axiom, "The body and soul make a man but the Spirit and discipline make a Christian" has become one of my favorite expressions. [14]

Thomas à Kempis, like Taylor, influenced me greatly although again, not without some reservation. I wrote to my mother on May 28, 1725: "I can't think that when God sent us into the world he had irreversibly decreed that we should be perpetually miserable in it. If it be so, the very endeavor after happiness in this life is a sin; as it is acting in direct contradiction to the very design of our creation. What are become of all the innocent comforts and pleasures of life, if it is the intent of our Creator that we should never taste them?" [15]

Much to my relief, on June 8, my mother replied that although she had à Kempis by her side she had not read him lately and could not recollect the passage to which I was referring. She then stated that à Kempis was undoubtedly "an honest weak man, who had more zeal than knowledge." Then sensing my anxiety about my "innocent pleasures," she applied this practical criterion: "Whatever weakens your reason, impairs the tenderness of your conscience, obscures your sense of God, or takes off the relish of spiritual things . . . that thing is sin to you, however innocent it may be in itself." I remember then a letter from my father, who apparently not fully satisfied with my mother's impressions, wrote to set the matter straight. After conceding that à Kempis might have been somewhat one-sided, he reiterated the indispensable duty of mortification. "The world is a syren, and we must have a care for her; and if the *young man* will *rejoice in his youth*, yet let him take care that his joys be innocent; and, in order to this remember that *for all these things* God will bring him into judgment." My father then concluded that his "friend

---

[14]*Sermons*, Vol. I, p. 468.
[15]*Letters*, Vol. I, p. 16.

and old companion . . . may be read to great advantage."

So what was the result of all this? Again, from my *Journal* review for May 24, 1738, I wrote that: "The providence of God directing me to Kempis's 'Christian Pattern,' I began to see that true religion was seated in the heart, and that God's law extended to all our thoughts as well as words and actions. I was, however, very angry at Kempis, for being too strict; though I read him only in Dean Stanhope's translation. Yet I had frequently much sensible comfort in reading him, such as I was an utter stranger to before. . . . I began to alter the whole form of my conversation, and to set in earnest upon a new life. I set apart an hour or two a day for religious retirement. I communicated every week. I watched against all sin, whether in word or deed. I began to aim at, and pray for, inward holiness."[16]

Now, before describing my early ministry, let's review the sequence of these last important events. My religious friend, Sally Kirkham, convinced me to read Taylor where I discovered that there was no medium in religion. My entire life must be given either to God, or the devil. Then à Kempis further convinced me of the nature and extent of inward religion. True religion was seated in the heart and therefore one must give not just his life, but also his heart to God. The conversations with Varanese and the correspondence with my parents then helped to put all of this into proper perspective. For me, "simplicity of intention and purity of affection" had become the "wings of the soul."[17]

It was settled! Although the issue of faith, whether mystic or reformed (this problem had been accentuated by both Taylor and à Kempis), would prolong my "evangelical" conversion for some thirteen years, the dilemma was over. On September 19, 1725, I was ordained deacon by John Potter, the Bishop of Oxford. It is strange how some moments live with you forever.

---

[16]*Works*, Vol. I, p. 99 *The Christian Pattern* is an alternate title for *The Imitation of Christ*. Wesley published his own translation in 1735 which is entitled *The Christian Pattern: Or a Treatise of the Imitation of Christ.*

[17]*Works*, Vol. II, p. 366.

The Analysis, Part I

Everyone is born either an Aristotelian or a Platonist; one or the other, but no one can be both simultaneously.
Samuel Coleridge

In an attempt to have Mr. Wesley tell his "own" story, I have been unable (except by footnote) to make the kind of personal comment so important for a relevant biography. We however do have the advantage of studying Wesley's life in retrospect. One needs, therefore (if we are properly to anticipate the rest of the biography), to make at this point some observations concerning matters that he might not have been aware of himself.

Consequently, the objective here is both reemphasis and overall perspective. Our purpose is not only to explain the dynamics of Part I, but also to prepare you for Part II. Admittedly, if the chapters at the end of each part are combined, they comprise a fairly complete evaluation of Mr. Wesley's theological and emotional development. If this development is not related to his life "in process," however, confusion sets in easily.

John Wesley was to become a great theologian, but theology was not his greatest strength. John Wesley was to become a great preacher, but preaching was not his greatest strength. Wesley's most significant contribution to the eighteenth century and to the church as a whole lies in his exceptional ability to organize people into the kind of body that would sustain both them and the movement called the eighteenth-century Evangelical Revival. With this clearly in mind, our task now is to examine the influences that would enable John Wesley to function as a theologian/evangelist so that his real strength could be manifest practically in the life of the church. What were his motivating principles? Where did he stand with regard to the basic doctrines of the church? In short, how did Wesley "do" theology so that he might become the man called by God to change the history of a nation?

If Wesley's greatest strengths were not to lie in his theology or preaching, it was simply because he would have even greater strengths which were tied closely to the needs of people. His practical theology rarely drew attention to itself, but was constantly geared to his own needs and then to the needs of those given into his care. The major problem with dealing with a practical theologian, however, is that his theology seems to shift as needs shift. Here, therefore, we will examine Wesley's theology within the context of his life in an effort to interpret just where the emphasis needs to be placed.

A word of caution. Some will be tempted to skip these analysis chapters as unnecessary interruptions in what might otherwise be considered a "pleasant" biography. *Do not do it!* Unless I can adequately demonstrate the interdependence of the biographical chapters and the analyses, the book as a whole misses its mark. Good biography is concerned with facts, but it is more than that. It also struggles with the soul of its character. As in the biographical sections, I have attempted to use language acceptable to most. Certainly the concepts here are involved and force us to stop and ponder; but, if you want to master John Wesley, here is the price you must pay. Here are the windows into the life of a man. So, with the story of his early years now fresh upon our minds, let's pause for the analysis.

The theological key for Part I is not to be found so much in Wesley's "religious" conversion (although this brought things into passionate focus) as in the eighteenth-century setting into which he was born and then, to an even greater extent, in the influence of his home environment.

The beginning of the eighteenth century was a breeding ground for theological schizophrenia. Basically there were two schools of thought. On the one hand there were those (to use the Aristotelian model) who thought that reality had to do only with those things perceivable by sense experience. Matter, since it could be touched, or smelled, or tasted, or heard, or seen, was real. Since matter was the only reality, one had to reason one's way inductively (by observation) to faith. In a phrase—*reason leads to faith.*

This had several spin-offs in the eighteenth century. Deism, for example, asserting the basic goodness of man, claimed (as we saw briefly in chapter 2) that man, if left alone, would reason his way to faith. In fact, it exalted reason to the place where faith was discoverable only by "natural" theology or things observable by sense experience.

The Church of England, although denying (at least by virtue of its Articles of Religion) that natural theology was the only route to faith, was nonetheless basically Aristotelian in its approach to God. Through its Arminian doctrine it taught that man (since original sin affected him only from the neck down, corrupting his heart but not his intellect) had the freedom to reason his way to faith.[1] Although his heart was prone to evil, his mind was left free to reason with the heart and respond to God by faith once the call was understood.

To a lesser extent, one branch of Puritanism followed the same model.[2] The Puritan appeal to reason was to use logic as a tool to make thought clear. Although faith (as in the Church of England) was a matter of divine revelation (where God completes natural theology through revelation not observable in nature alone), the intellect through practical theology sought to maneuver the heart into the disposition for faith.

The second school of thought included those (to use the Platonic model) who thought that reality had to do with ideals. Matter, though perceivable by sense experience, was an illusion. Since reality had to do with ideals, not perceivable by sense experience, understanding came (deductively) by faith. In a phrase—*faith leads to reason.*[3]

---

[1]Arminian theology, arguing for a degree of free will, over and against the tenets of strict Calvinism, found its greatest acceptance in the Church of England.

[2]Basically the Puritans were divided over their reaction to Quaker "enthusiasm" on the one hand and High Church Anglicanism on the other.

[3]"Reason" here actually means "understanding."

This too had several spin-offs in the eighteenth century. Mysticism, for example, was basically Platonic in its approach to God. Although there is some reason to believe that the mystics offered a third alternative shortcutting both reason and faith by direct access to God, they believed that reality was nonsensory and, therefore, accessible only by mystical experience. The essential part of man, a divine spark untouched by original sin, if unencumbered by creation would inevitably return to God by stages culminating in a kind of mystical faith.[4]

Again, still another branch of Puritanism (exemplified by the Cambridge Platonists on the one hand and the Puritan Divines contributing to the Westminster Confession on the other) tended to follow this second model. They believed that both

---

[4]Since "mysticism" belongs to that totally useful family of words whose meanings are more in their atmosphere and suggestions, than in their mathematical precision, we can prevent considerable confusion later on by taking some pains to define it here. The basis of mystical theology is "Orison" or meditation which is then methodically applied to the disposition of the soul that it might be elevated toward God. Several levels of mystical consciousness are involved, and while mystics in general are by no means unanimous in their description of these levels, an overall pattern does emerge. The pattern usually assumes three (but sometimes four or even five) stages. The first is the *purgative* stage (usually preceded by some sort of religious awakening similar to Wesley's religious conversion experienced in 1725) involving ascetical exercises and is roughly analagous to the training of an athlete. This rigid discipline, aimed at purifying the body, buffets the flesh that it might never inhibit the spirit. This stage has led some to describe mysticism on the whole as morbid, but one must carry on to judge the tree by its fruits, not by its roots. The first stage, characterized by mortification, must then lead to a second stage, the *illuminative* stage. Illumination, a somewhat misleading term involving mystical faith, requires one to concentrate all his faculties on God. This frequently involves a delicate balance between agony and ecstasy as one must ultimately learn to trust God further than he can see. During this illuminative stage God sends shafts of light into the soul which provide the mystic with "sensible comforts." At this point, however, most would insert an additional stage as the illuminative eye of faith leads into the all-important mystical "death," where (according to the mystic) God withdraws these shafts of light forcing the mystic to come to him by "naked faith." St. John of the Cross described this death as the "dark night of the soul" where a supreme moral crisis is constituted as the will of man completely surrenders to the will of God. The final stage in the mystical path is the *unitive* stage, which has been frequently misinterpreted. While much of the more unguarded language of mystical union has the odor of pathological deification, most mystics understand this "complete" union with God as an almost unreachable ideal. Even the greatest mystics were involved in an infinite process of growth in which they continued until death.

In chapter 8 Wesley will describe these stages as they apply to his own mystical experiment at Wroot.

the heart *and* the intellect were corrupted by sin and that only the grace of God, drawing us by faith, would lead to understanding.

So, the result is that we find here two divergent schools of thought; one insisting that faith comes by reason, the other that reason (or understanding) comes by faith. Coleridge claimed that we are all one or the other, but that no one can be both simultaneously. How did this affect John Wesley?

Maldwyn Edwards reminds us that John Wesley not only influenced the eighteenth century, but that the eighteenth century also influenced John Wesley.[5] Historically, the stage was set for Wesley with the Aristotelian model and deism as the prevailing philosophy on the one hand and the High Church, Puritan background of his parents, on the other.[6] If these had been the only influences, one could simply surmise that Wesley, apparently having a high appreciation for reason, came to a religious understanding in 1725 that led him to faith. It is not that simple, however. If Wesley was not to find faith (at least in the evangelical sense of the word) until Aldersgate, thirteen years later, what was happening now? Let's look a bit closer.

We mentioned earlier that Wesley was greatly influenced not only by the eighteenth-century but by his home environment as well. A significant part of the influence surrounding Wesley's home environment involved a tremendous amount of devotional reading. Since little devotional literature was coming out of the High Church tradition as such, and even less from the deists, the reading at the Epworth rectory consisted mostly of the Puritan Divines and mystics.[7] We should not be

---

[5]Maldwyn Edwards, *Wesley's Social and Political Influence on the Eighteenth Century,* see chapter 11.

[6]Remember that even though Samuel and Susanna were committed to the Established Church (in the High Church tradition) both their parents had distinguished themselves as Dissenters (in the Puritan tradition).

[7]We must be careful not to belabor this point. Frank Baker, for example, in an article, "Wesley's Puritan Ancestry," comments that since both Samuel and Susanna were converts from Dissent, "it is not surprising that they *did not* fill their children's heads with stirring tales of their predominantly Puritan forefathers." LQHR, p. 187 (italics mine). Yet, the fact remains that Richard Baxter, John Bunyan, George Fox, as well as Scupoli-Castaniza, and Henry Scougal were all read devotionally at the Epworth rectory while Wesley was a boy.

surprised, therefore to find that Wesley, while becoming a lover of reason (after the Aristotelian model) was also developing a real appreciation for mystic theology (after the Platonic model). If Coleridge was correct, then seeds of an impasse were being sown in the mind of John Wesley at an early and impressionable age.

The problem here can be demonstrated still further. Wesley's High Church/Puritan/mystical heritage was bringing still other influences to bear. There was in the High Church tradition, for example, a strong emphasis on asceticism as the "handmaid to reason." Since the intellect had not been corrupted by sin, it could instruct the believer through self-denial and mortification. Implementing this was a kind of rigorism focusing upon the sacraments as the means of grace. Likewise there was a strong emphasis on asceticism among the Puritans. In order to make their calling sure the Puritans focused upon disciplined living and moral rigorism. Being a Christian in earnest was of utmost importance. Furthermore, the mystics also exalted asceticism. As in the High Church and Puritan traditions, spiritual exercises, again focusing upon rigid discipline through self-denial and mortification, were the beginning of true religion. Understandably, ascetical exercises in the High Church tradition (so prevalent in the Puritan and mystical tracts read in the Epworth rectory) would become for Wesley the all in all.[8] So, his love for reason would eventually work itself out (in more or less degrees) through rigorism, moralism, and legalism. We should now concern ourselves with just how these influences came into play.

Few would question Wesley's intense desire to know and be known by God. His request for assurance of salvation became an obsession. The origins of this "need to know" are deeply rooted. Suffice it to say that from an early age Wesley was constantly reminded of the consequences of sin. It was simply that Wesley did not want to die a sinner since he greatly feared what he thought to be the inevitable result.

Some of this fear was obviously reinforced during his years at Charterhouse where he became well acquainted with death in the infirmary. He was a "sinner" constantly being reminded

---

[8]This is especially prevalent in chapter 7.

of his mortality.[9] The enemy, however, was not so much sin as *death*.[10] For nearly twenty-five years (1714-1738) Wesley would pursue the kind of assurance that would deliver him from his fear of death and dying. The pilgrimage would take some rather strange turns.

While at Oxford, for example, Wesley was plagued by such thoughts as: "What, if 'the generation of men be exactly parallel with the generation of leaves?' if the earth drops its successive inhabitants, just as the tree drops its leaves? What, if that saying of a great man be really true,—*Post mortem nihil est; ipsaque mors nihil* (Death is nothing, and nothing is after death)?"[11] Wesley then flirts with the stories of apparitions which seemed to imply some sort of life after death, but he was apparently too "logical" to find much relief there. Ultimately, as an undergraduate, his only escape from fear was to do what many of us do—not to think much about it.

Then toward the end of 1724 Wesley, now an Oxford graduate, is confronted with a dilemma—what to do? His decision to enter Holy Orders brings the divergent influences into conflict. Wesley's high sense of calling, a brand plucked from the burning, weighed heavily upon him and, for the most part, dormant influences awake with enormous impact. Although Wesley states at this point that he remembered little of holiness or inward obedience, opposing sides were mounting strength and his religious conversion (let's not argue as to whether this was a "Christian" conversion) brought these influences into play with such force that it took him thirteen years to sort them out.

Here is the problem. Wesley wanted assurance, the inward witness. His religious experience had revived his fear of death. He could no longer merely lay the issue aside. Two influences previously mentioned emphasized what Wesley interpreted as assurance—Puritanism and mysticism.[12]

---

[9]Although Wesley was no blatant sinner, he was certainly no saint (at least in the image of the Epworth rectory).

[10]It is interesting how throughout the Revival Wesley insists that the "people called Methodists" *fear sin more than death*.

[11]*Works*, Vol. VI, p. 356.

[12]It would be good to remember that assurance for the mystic was altogether different from that of the Puritan. Actually Wesley was confusing

The Puritans taught that faith itself (after the doctrine of the Reformation) was "the [assurance] of things hoped for, the evidence of things not seen." Repent and believe was their formula for faith where "the Spirit [of God] beareth witness with our spirit, that we are the children of God." So, at the time of his religious conversion Wesley might well have experienced something like the Aldersgate assurance by responding to God through faith in the Puritan (evangelical) sense, but at least two things prevented it.[13]

First, all of the variant influences had one common denominator—asceticism. To use the Wesleyan phrase: "The body and soul make a man, but the Spirit and discipline make a Christian." Wesley was duty bound. His appreciation for assurance of faith in the Puritan sense was momentarily overruled.

Second, the mystics spoke of a union with God where a person could have a constant awareness of God's presence in his life and in the world. This must have sounded too good to be true (in fact, it was, at least by mystical means). Here, thought Wesley, was assurance with a wall around it. This would make him invulnerable to fear. His troublesome doubts would vanish. The enemy would lose his hold, and who knows, if the mystical stories were true, death might even become a friend. The Puritan Christocentric mediated communion with God lost out to a "loftier" mystic theocentric unmediated union with God.

The discussion in Part II has to do with Wesley's futile search for an assurance that rigid asceticism could not produce. In fact, one might well conclude that Aristotelian means do not mix with Platonic ends. How can one achieve religious ends (mystical union) attainable only by faith (the Platonic model), by a philosophy (the Aristotelian model) that achieves religious ends only by reason (asceticism)? Again, Wesley could be one

---

assurance with the mystical union with God which contained what Wesley thought to be an element of assurance but was, in fact, achievable only by "blind trust in the absence of assurance."

[13]It is my opinion that although the Aldersgate experience was delayed, it was inevitable. Wesley's religious conversion was in earnest. Outler states that the change of heart in 1725 was a "conversion if ever there was one." Wesley was clearly *in process.*

or the other, but not both simultaneously.

In Part II we will observe Wesley attempting to put Platonic means with Platonic ends. In 1732, for example, he would opt for faith, not in the Puritan sense, however, but through the mystical understanding of faith as the "dark night of the soul" (simply a more subtle kind of inward asceticism) which plunged him even deeper into despair. The enemy loomed larger. The "sensible comforts" experienced by reading Taylor and à Kempis were a prelude not to union with God, but to darkness.

Interestingly enough, Part III then relates Wesley's reintroduction to faith in the evangelical sense. Wesley (by that time) had had "darkness" enough! Ironically the Aldersgate experience, which should have followed his religious conversion immediately, was delayed by the thing that would eventually lead him to greatness—a duty-bound conscience that feared a holy God. A philosophy deadly for the sinner became remedy for the saint. Fortunately, Wesley would preach faith with the same vigor that he preached works.

So, Wesley, in 1725, made religion the business of his life. He wanted to clean himself up that God might love him. Those who wait until they have "cleaned" themselves up before they let God love them, however, wait a long time. Wesley waited thirteen years, and then laid aside all pretense of self-righteousness in order "to follow naked, the naked Jesus." God then breathed into John Wesley the spirit of new life and the Revival was on! That is the beautiful story left to tell. Let's hear Wesley describe it himself.

Bibliography, Part I[1]

Primary Sources

John Wesley, *Journal*, Standard Ed., Nehemiah Curnock, ed. (1909-16), 8 vols.

———, *Letters*, John Telford, ed. (1931), 8 vols.

———, *A Concise Ecclesiastical History*, 4 vols. London: J. Paramore (1781).

———, *A Concise History of England*, 4 vols. London: R. Howes (1776).

Green, Richard, *The Works of John and Charles Wesley. A Bibliography* (1896).

The Union Catalogue of the Publications of John and Charles Wesley, Duke University Divinity School.

Secondary Sources

Abbey, C. J., *The English Church and Its Bishops, 1700-1800* (1887).

———, and Overton, J. H., *The English Church in the Eighteenth Century* (1878), 2 vols.

Baker, Frank, *Charles Wesley* (1948).

———, "A Study of John Wesley's Readings," LQHR, 168 (1943), 140-45.

———, "Wesley's Puritan Ancestry," LQHR, 187 (1962), 180-86.

Baxter, Richard, *Aphorisms of Justification With Their Explication Annexed* (1649).

Castaniza, Juan de, *The Spiritual Combat; or, The Christian Pilgrim in His Spiritual Conflict and Conquest*, trans. by Richard Lucas (1698) (also attributed to Lorenzo Scupoli).

Clark, George, *The Later Stuarts, 1660-1714*, 2nd ed. (Oxford, 1955). (Vol. X of the Oxford History of England.)

---

[1]Each of the four parts concludes with its own Bibliography. Though these lists are by no means exhaustive they should give the reader the flavor for the kind of sources available to those who want to pursue a given area in greater detail. The sources that reappear in the subsequent Bibliographies for parts II-IV will be in abbreviated form.

Clarke, A., *Memoirs of the Wesley Family*. London (1823).

Coke, Thomas and Moore, H., *Life of the Rev. John Wesley*. London (1792).

Edwards, M. L., *Family Circle*. A study of the Epworth Household. London (1949).

_____, *Sons to Samuel*. London (1961).

_____, *The Astonishing Youth*. London (1959).

Green, Richard, *John Wesley*. London (1882).

Green, V. H. H., *The Young Mr. Wesley*. London (1961).

_____, *John Wesley*. London (1964).

Harmon, Rebecca, *Susanna, Mother of the Wesleys*. Nashville (1968).

Jackson, Thomas, *The Life of the Rev. Charles Wesley, M.A.* London (1841).

Kempis, Thomas à, *De Imitatione Christi*. Translated by George Stanhope (1660-1728). New edition (1809). Wesley's own translation entitled *The Christian Pattern: or A Treatise of the Imitation of Christ*. London (1735).

Law, William, *Works*. New Forest (1893) or London (1702), 9 vols.

Léger, A., *La Jeunesse de Wesley*. Paris (1910).

Monk. R. C., *John Wesley: His Puritan Heritage*. London (1966).

Moore, Henry, *The Life of the Rev. John Wesley*. This includes the life of the Rev. Charles Wesley . . . and memories of the Wesley Family. London (1824/25), 2 vols.

Newton, John A., *Methodism and the Puritans*. London (1964).

_____, *Susanna Wesley and the Puritan Tradition in Methodism*. London (1969).

Overton, J. H., *John Wesley*. London (1891).

Rupp, E. Gordon, *Studies in the Making of the Protestant Tradition in the English Reformation*. London (1948).

Schmidt, Martin, *John Wesley, a Theological Biography*. Nashville (1962), Vol. 1.

Scougal, Henry, *The Life of God in the Soul of Man*, Winthrop H. Hudson, ed. Philadelphia (1948).

Southey, Robert, *The Life of Wesley and the Rise of Methodism*, 2 vols. London (1858). New edition (1925).

Stevenson, George, *Memorials of the Wesley Family*. London (1876).

Taylor, Jeremy, *The Whole Works*. London (1847-54). 10 vols.

Telford, John, *The Life of John Wesley*. London (1924).

Tuttle, Robert G., Jr., "The Influence of the Roman Catholic Mystics on John Wesley." An unpublished dissertation (University of Bristol, 1969).

Tyerman, Luke, *The Life and Times of Samuel Wesley*. London (1866).

_____, *The Life and Times of John Wesley*. London (1890).

Vulliamy, C. E., *John Wesley*. London (1931).

Wakefield, Gordon S., *Puritan Devotion; Its Place in the Development of Christian Piety*. London (1957).

Wesley, Charles, *Journal*, John Telford, ed. London (1909).

Wesley, Samuel, *A Letter From a Country Divine to His Friend in London, Concerning the Education of Dissenters in Their Private Academies in Several Parts of This Nation; Humbly Offered to the Consideration of the Grand Committee of Parliament for Religion, Now Sitting* (1703).

_____, *The Pious Communicant Rightly Prepared . . . . to Which Is Added a Short Discourse on Baptism* (1698).

Wesley Historical Society, *Publications* and *Proceedings* (Burnley, England, 1896--).

Whitehead, John, *The Life of Rev. John Wesley, M.A.* This includes the life of the Rev. Charles Wesley. London (1793-96), 2 vols.

Part II
His Early Ministry

6

Setting the Stage

Imposture and fanaticism still hang upon the skirts of religion. Weak minds were seduced by the delusions of a superstition, styled Methodism, raised upon the affectation of superior sanctity, and pretensions to divine illumination. Many thousands were infected with this enthusiasm by the endeavours of a few obscure Preachers such as Whitefield, and the two Wesleys, who found means to lay the whole kingdom under contribution.
Smollett's *History of England*

Tuesday, March 18, 1788 (9:00 P.M.), Gloucester, England. Again, Mr. Wesley is alone, but speaks to you, the reader, as though you were in the room with him.

We are presently in Gloucester, England. At 5:30 yesterday morning I left you in Bristol. I took to my chaise, which all insist that I must use, rather than travel by horseback, as I am now in my eighty-fifth year. I am a little surprised by this for "the old murderer" obviously has more power over my horses than he does over me.[1] Just last year I went through four in a single week while I keep running the race that is set before me. Although I am now getting old, bless God, "'the grasshopper is' not 'a burden,'" and I am still as capable of traveling as ever.[2]

At 8:30 I arrived at Newport in time for tea. After tea I conversed and prayed for nearly an hour with several who were there. Oh, let me redeem the time! How easily, in a few moments, to impress even the elegant when we strongly enforce the Word of God. I recall a few years ago that some rather careless people came to one of our meetings dancing and laughing as if to a theater; but their mood

---

[1]*Works,* Vol. IV, p. 378.
[2]Ibid., p. 442.

quickly changed and in a few minutes were as serious as my subject—Death. "I believe, if they do not take great care, they will remember it—for a week!"[3]

By 9:30 I was back in my chaise, stopping only once for half an hour (to visit with some who needed a word from God) before arriving at Stroud at half past noon.

Between 12:30 and 5:00 I wrote letters, first to Adam Clarke and then to others, breaking only to eat enough to strengthen me (twenty years ago I weighed 122 lbs. Today I weigh not a pound more or less. I doubt whether such another instance is to be found in Great Britain), converse with a few of the Society, and pray.[4] I mention Mr. Clarke by name since it will fall to him (and to others like him) to sustain the work of the Revival after I have been claimed by the One who has bought me at so great a price. Mr. Clarke is a man after my own heart. He retains a state of perfection (which is impossible in and of itself) by *growing* in pure love. He preaches with force (sometimes too much so, which has more than a little affected his health). His diligence (though I must keep him from killing himself) in maintaining the Society is an example for all to follow. He cares both for those *within* our movement through the classes, bands, and Select Society, and for those *without* through the Strangers' or Friend Society (still another fruit of Methodism instituted wholly for the relief of the poor, sick, or friendless strangers).

---

[3]Ibid., p. 106.

[4]The letter addressed to Adam Clarke (Stroud, March 17, 1788) reads: "Dear Adam,—I immediately answered the letter which brought the account of Sister Horn's case. I am afraid they will make wilful mistakes and carry your letters to the Isle of Wight.

I am glad you have spread yourselves through the islands and that Mrs. de Saumarez has had the courage to join you. I believe she has very good uprightness of heart and (if she goes on) will be a burning and shining light. You have reason likewise to praise God on account of Alderney. There is a seed which shall not easily be rooted up. Drink largely when need be of warm lemonade and no bilious complaint will remain long.

Our Conference Deed provided for what Dr. Jersey desires. I desire the very same thing; nay! I observe Mr. Walker too. The sooner it is done the better. Send your translation to London. My kind love to Miss Lempriere, Jenny Bisson (who owes me a letter), and the dear family at Mont Plaisir. Peace be with your spirits.—I am, dear Adam, Your

At 5:00 we had tea, during which time I again felt led to enforce the word of God and pray before preaching at 6:00 on 1 Peter 1:8-9 to so crowded an audience as I have not seen in Stroud for some years: "Whom having not seen (in the flesh), ye love; in whom, though now ye see him not, yet believing, ye rejoice with joy unspeakable and full of glory: Receiving the end of your faith, even the salvation of your souls." My own translation might read: "Receiving *now already, salvation—from all sin into all holiness,* which is the qualification for, the forerunner and pledge of eternal salvation."[5] I suppose a large part of this crowd had never heard this sort of preaching before. They now heard with inexpressible attention, and, I believe, not in vain. God opened, as it were, the windows of heaven, and sent a gracious rain upon His inheritance. I am in hopes a plentiful harvest will spring from the seed which was sown this hour.[6] In this I find the reason why the work of God does not gain ground in some of our circuits. Their preachers give up the Methodist testimony. Either they do not speak of perfection at all (the peculiar doctrine committed to our trust), or they speak of it only in general terms, without urging the believers to "go on unto perfection," and to expect it every moment. Wherever this is not earnestly done, the work of God does not prosper.[7]

After preaching, I met with the Society enforcing the necessity of Christian fellowship on all who desired either to awake or stay awake.[8] I make an honest attempt to visit all of our Societies each year and set apart three or four days to transcribe personally the London Society. This is a dull but necessary work which I have taken upon myself once a year for these fifty years.[9] No society can bear neglect. I continue in my resolve to have regular societies or none. I recall an incident in Norwich where the bands were al-

---

affectionate friend and brother. Direct to me at London, and your letter will come safe." *Letters,* Vol. VIII, pp. 46f.

[5]Wesley, *Notes on the New Testament,* p. 874.

[6]*Works,* Vol. IV, p. 360.

[7]Ibid., p. 83.

[8]Ibid., p. 222.

[9]Ibid., p. 356. To "transcribe" was to update the list by making a spiritual inventory of each society member.

lowed to fall into pieces and no care at all was taken of the classes, so that it mattered little whether they met or not. Going to church and observing the sacrament were forgotten. The people rambled here and there without direction or correction. So, I met the Society and read the Rules.[10] I desired everyone to consider whether they were willing to walk by these Rules or not, in particular in meeting their class every week unless hindered by distance or sickness (the only reasons for not meeting which I could allow), and being faithful at church and sacrament. "I desired those who were so minded to meet me the next night, and the rest to stay away. The next night we had far the greater part; on whom I strongly enforced the same thing. [The next morning] I spoke to every Leader, concerning every one under his care; and put out every person whom they could not recommend to me. After this was done, out of two hundred and four members, one hundred and seventy-four remained. And these points shall be carried, if only fifty remain in the society."[11]

After supper, I prayed the rest of the evening before retiring at 9:30, my usual hour.

This morning I was up again at 4:00 for prayers. I then wrote letters until 8:00, at which time I had tea and conversed before returning to my letters until nearly 11:00. At 11:00 I was back in my chaise, arriving at Painswick at noon in time to preach quite well before lunch. My text was the same as last Sunday: "And he said unto him, If they hear not Moses and the prophets, neither will they be persuaded, though one rose from the dead" (Luke 16:31). True repentance implies an entire change of heart, but a thousand apparitions (though extremely remarkable in some instances) cannot effect this. Only God can, applying His word.[12] I spoke more strongly than I am accustomed to doing, and I hope that my listeners were not sermon-proof.

Back in my chaise (reading), I arrived in Gloucester at 4:00 where nearly three quarters of a century ago my good

---

[10]For a full description of these Rules see *Works*, Vol. VIII, pp. 138-168.

[11]*Works*, Vol. IV, p. 36.

[12]Wesley, *Notes on the New Testament*, pp. 267f.

and dear friend George Whitefield was born. [13] It is difficult
to believe that it has been eighteen years since I preached
his funeral sermon. How mysterious the providence of
God that has thrown our names together in both good and
bad company. I remember, for example, reading Smollett's
History of England. He writes: "Imposture and fanaticism
still hang upon the skirts of religion. Weak minds were
seduced by the delusions of a superstition, styled
Methodism, raised upon the affectation of superior sanctity, and pretensions to divine illumination. Many
thousands were infected with this enthusiasm by the endeavors of a few obscure Preachers, such as Whitefield,
and the two Wesleys, who found means to lay the whole
kingdom under contribution." [14]

Poor Smollett! What must your readers think? "Thus to
transmit to all succeeding generations a whole heap of
notorious falsehoods!" [15] Let me put the matter straight.

There was no imposture and no fanaticism! "Neither
one nor the other had any share in the late revival of
scriptural religion, which is no other than the love of God
and man, gratitude to our Creator, and good-will to our
fellow-creatures. Is this delusion and superstition? No, it
is real wisdom; it is solid virtue. Does this fanaticism 'hang
upon the skirts of religion?' Nay, it is the very essence of it.
Does the Doctor call this enthusiasm? Why? Because he
knows nothing about it. Who told him that these 'obscure
Preachers' made 'pretensions to divine illumination?'
How often has that silly calumny been refuted to the satisfaction of all candid men? However, they 'found means to
lay the whole kingdom under contribution.' So does this
frontless man, blind and bold, stumble on without the
least shadow of truth!" [16]

On another occasion the *Scots Magazine* (for May, 1739)
was put in my hands. I was asked to read an essay entitled:
"Danger Attending Tumultuous Preaching; With Some

---

[13]George Whitefield (1714-1770) is discussed at some length later.
[14]Smollett's *History of England*, Vol. XV, pp. 121-122 (quoted in
Works, Vol. IV, p. 148).
[15]*Works*, Vol. IV, p. 148.
[16]Ibid., pp. 148f.

Queries Offered To and Some Observations Upon the Conduct of Mr. Whitefield." Toward the middle of this essay (and there were countless other similar essays) I read: "Now I never heard that Mr. *Whitefield*, the Mr. *Westleys*, or any other of these *gifted* Gentlemen, has as yet wrought, or pretended to a power of working *miracles*; though, very likely, they may soon arrive to that perfection of enthusiasm."[17] One comment: If ever we reach "perfection," it will not be "of enthusiasm," lest you condemn the gospel writers to the man. Farther along in the same essay I read: "The *Westleys*, indeed, have not yet gone so far as Mr. *Whitefield*; but they are wilful transgressors against the authority of *God and man*, against the orders of *church and state*, by holding congregations in *unlicensed* places, and after an unauthorized manner; and everyone that gives them any countenance by attending them, or who does not discountenance their proceedings, if they be in proper authority, is in some measure a partaker with them in their sins, and answerable for the mischievous consequences of them."[18] Again one comment: Their charges are utterly false, as incorrect as their spelling of my name. Those who gave us "countenance" lost nothing but misery. Furthermore, bless God, the day would come when the "Mr. Westleys" would not only go so far, but far surpass even Mr. Whitefield in preaching on perfection.

This afternoon I wrote another letter before tea. Following tea I spent a full hour in prayer before preaching at 6:00. At 6:00 I preached from Matthew 7:24: "Therefore whosoever heareth these sayings of mine, and doeth them, I will liken him unto a wise man, which built his house upon a rock." Realizing I had wealthy people to deal with, I attempted to stir them up. I showed them the various ways whereby the generality of good men (so called) usually build upon the sand. I recall the story of a late Marquis who reportedly received forty thousand pounds a year in England, and fifteen or twenty thousand in Ireland. And what has he now? Six foot of earth.

---

[17]*Scots Magazine*, May 1739, pp. 206f.
[18]Ibid.

A heap of dust is all remains of thee!
'Tis all thou art, and all the proud shall be.[19]

I then concluded the sermon by strongly showing what it is to build upon the rock Jesus Christ. How times have changed. Fifty years ago if I had preached here with such plainness I might have been stoned; but not a dog wagged his tongue.[20] "It seems the scandal of the cross (such is the will of God) is ceased. High and low, rich and poor, flock together, and seem to devour the word. Many, I believe, were cut to the heart; for it was a day of the Lord's power."[21] May they be not "almost persuaded." How sad that many half-awakened sinners will be wide awake when it is too late.[22]

I have just now finished supper, and before praying myself to bed, was considering how strangely the grain of mustard seed, planted about fifty years ago, has grown up. The Revival has spread through all of Great Britain and Ireland; the Isle of Wight, and the Isle of Man; then to America, from the Leeward Islands through the whole continent, into Canada and Newfoundland. And the societies, in all these parts, walk by one rule, knowing religion is holy temper; and striving to worship God, not in form only, but likewise "in spirit and in truth."[23] That story, however, is not yet to be told. First, there would be thirteen years of "preparation" (bless God, they were not in vain), including a pilgrimage to faith which might speak to the needs of your own life as well. Let me share it with you now.

---

[19]*Works*, Vol. IV, p. 340.
[20]Ibid., p. 339.
[21]Ibid., p. 409.
[22]Ibid., p. 372.
[23]Ibid., pp. 298f.

7

An Oxford Don

As we would willingly suffer a little pain or forego some pleasure for others we really love, so if we sincerely love God we should readily do this for Him. For this reason one act of self-denial is more grateful to our Master than the performance of many lesser duties.   John Wesley

For those who properly understand Christianity as a never-ending adventure (O how our very lives depend upon it), the race was on! From the time of my religious conversion in the spring of 1725, though the enemy seemed never far behind, the process had begun.[1]

During the summer months I prepared for ordination. I remember an interesting conversation which occurred toward the end of June. I have had several close friends these past years. John Griffith was such a friend. We were attending the funeral of one with whom we were both acquainted, a young woman named Eliza Carter.[2] Whenever the enemy confronted me openly I sought, as if by reflex, to make my own way sure by some act of religion. As John (or Robin as he was affectionately called) and I turned into one of the aisles of St. Mary's Church, Oxford, "I asked him if he really thought himself my friend; and if he did, why he would not do me all the good he could. He began to protest; in which I cut him short by desiring him to oblige me in an instance which he could not deny to be in his own power—to let me have the pleasure of making him a whole

---

[1]Keep in mind that the "enemy" referred to here is Wesley's fear of death.

[2]Eliza Carter is actually the best choice of several possibilities for identifying this young woman. See *Letters*, Vol. I, p. 364.

Christian, to which I knew he was at least half persuaded already; that he could not do me a greater kindness, as both of us would be fully convinced when we came to follow that young woman."[3]

God, not counting my motive, effectively used that encounter, so much so that Robin turned very serious and kept something of that disposition ever since. Yet, my own way was still not clear.

I recall a comment from my *Journal:* "Now, 'doing so much, and living so good a life,' I doubted not but I was a good Christian."[4]

Yet, on the eve of my ordination I confided to my *Diary* what I then felt to be my most serious faults. Due to impossible standards (impossible apart from true faith in Christ), I continually broke my self-imposed resolutions. This kept me at the brink of despair. Nonetheless, on September 26, 1725, I managed to preach my first sermon at South Leigh near Witney (a few miles from Oxford), this being the first Sunday following my ordination. I remember the anticipation as I rode along through the Oxfordshire lanes toward the quaint little church with frescoed walls. From my text, Matthew 6:33: "Seek ye first the kingdom of God and his righteousness," I sought to enforce (however inadequately) the rule of God and *his* righteousness.[5] Using the additional words from 2 Kings 17:41: "These nations feared the Lord, and served their graven images," to dramatize a "higher" righteousness (which transcended that commonly so-called), I established that whoever seeks this *first,* will soon come to seek this only.[6]

Actually it was not a bad sermon (not altogether unuseful even today), although it was poorly delivered. Even then I worked by the light that I had. I was pleased that my brother Samuel made favorable judgment on the manu-

---

[3]*Letters.* Vol. I, p. 40.
[4]*Journal,* Vol. I, p. 467.
[5]The text mentioned here for this first sermon is not conclusive. Cf. Schmidt, *John Wesley: A Theological Biography,* p. 93, N. 2; *Journal,* Vol. I, pp. 59-60; *Sermons,* Vol. II, p. 496.
[6]*Notes on the New Testament,* p. 22.

script (though not without some objection).[7] Yet I, who would call sinners to repentance, had little knowledge of genuine repentance myself. I realize that some of this may cause perplexity for the historians of our movement, so let me put my position simply and plainly to you now. During the years 1725 to 1729 I had no foundation of repentance (at least not the sort that leads to faith, properly so-called. Repentance for those who were influencing me most (especially Taylor and à Kempis) was self-abasement, and continued self-condemnation. Consequently, self-righteousness (after all, did not I, more than any of those around me seek to follow diligently the whole counsel of God?) was mixed with self-condemnation—thus ambivalence.

I was a student in transition—from layman to clergyman; from Christ Church to Lincoln College. These next few years would be packed with intense struggle, and it was, in fact, this terrific struggle which drew me (at least in part) almost irresistibly to like-minded "Christians" who apparently struggled much in the same way. These, however, instead of decreasing my anxiety, increased my frustration. My confusion would now be exaggerated even more by the squabble among these divines (particularly the mystics) as to whether the pursuit of holiness lay more in bodily austerity (after the Jesuits and Jansenists) or in the inward temper (after the Carmelites and Quietists).[8]

At any rate, after my ordination I was obsessed by the notion of moral imperfection and was continually dissatisfied with my efforts in the pursuit of the holy life. Consequently, in order to do battle with idleness, boasting, lying, heat in arguing, levity, detraction, intemperate sleep, unclean thoughts, and the like, aceticism in the form of "rules" *initially* won out.[9]

The rules which now preface my first *Diary* are a "collection" of some of Jeremy Taylor's noblest paragraphs.

---

[7]See *Letters*, Vol. I, p. 32.

[8]The issue with regard to the Jansenists and the Quietists was similar to that depicted among the Aristotelians and Platonists described in the Analysis, Part I.

[9]Green, *John Wesley*, p. 15.

They are entitled "A General Rule in All Actions of Life" with two subtitles: "General Rules of Employing Time" and "General Rules as to Intention." Under "General Rules of Employing Time" we read: 1) Begin and end every day with God, and sleep not immoderately. 2) Be diligent in your calling. 3) Employ all spare hours in religion; as able. 4) Make all holidays, holy days. 5) Avoid drunkards and busybodies. 6) Avoid curiosity and all useless employments and knowledge. 7) Examine yourself every night. 8) Never on any account pass a day without setting aside at least an hour for devotion. 9) Avoid all manner of passion. Under "General Rules as to Intention" we read: 1) In every action reflect on your own end. 2) Begin every action in the name of the Father, the Son, and the Holy Ghost. 3) Begin every important work with prayer. 4) Do not leave off a duty because you are tempted in it.[10]

For the next two years self-denial became the all in all. A memorandum from my *Diary* reads: "As we would willingly suffer a little pain or forego some pleasure for others we really love, so if we sincerely love God we should readily do this for Him. For this reason one act of self-denial is more grateful to our Master than the performance of many lesser duties." Early rising, endless resolutions, self-examination, fasting, ejaculatory prayers, and many other mystical means of purging the soul now became my common practice, so much so, as hard as I tried I could not, without some periodic remorse (those transient fits of repentance), enjoy even the most innocent pleasures.

So, I stayed on in Christ Church, anticipating my election to a Fellowship at Lincoln College in the spring. Following the advice of those who directed my progress, I elaborated even more on my rules. An inquisition was held every Saturday night. Like a country boy taking his weekly bath, I wanted to be "clean" on Sunday morning. God and I banded together that He might more effectively root out those things that were separating me from Him and those around me. So, I would inquire: have I loved

---

women or company more than God? and resolve: never to let sleep hinder me from going to prayers. Inquire: have I taken God's name in vain? Resolve: never to mention it but in religion. Inquire: irreverent behaviour at church? Resolve: never to laugh or talk idly there. Inquire: indevotion? Resolve: prayer and humility. Inquire: pride? Resolve: consider death, the Scriptures. Inquire: idleness? Resolve: six hours every day. Inquire: intemperate sleep? Resolve: at five. Inquire: unclean thoughts? Resolve: God's omnipresence.[11]

Between September 1725 and March 1726 I took several trips into the Cotswolds to visit my friends, though I did not lodge with them (but hired a room) until the following year. Just after Christmas Sally married the local schoolmaster. I remember writing in my *Diary:* "May God give her the happiness she deserves." Our relationship did not end, however. Although I worried that I had loved women more than God, Sally put matters into perspective during our tender, sentimental moments; though void of passion. My sister Hetty chided that I "loved women for being women." Perhaps she was right.

On March 27, 1726, I was elected Fellow of Lincoln College, a position I maintained until my marriage a quarter of a century later. Although some thought me too serious about religious discipline, this opposition had been overruled by a word from my brother Samuel.[12] My Fellowship introduced me to a cultured and congenial society which came somewhat into conflict with the intent of my resolutions. At the same time, the immensely spiritual, though delightful atmosphere, of the Cotswold scene came as close as anything I am aware of to blending the religious and the social so that I might (had not the demands of a nation gone mad with irreligion pressed so heavily upon me) have become for the rest of my days a happy, though useful, Oxford Don or even a country parson.

---

[11]*Journal,* Vol. I, p. 52.

[12]See *Letters,* Vol. I, p. 27. John expresses appreciation to Samuel for his assistance in securing the Fellowship.

Although I was small (not much over five feet) and too frail for vigorous athletics, I did manage to hold my own reasonably well on the tennis court. I also enjoyed pulling an oar on the river, swimming, riding, and hunting. I frequently walked long distances, sometimes the entire route between Oxford and Epworth, in order to save money.

Although I had changed my way of life considerably, I had not (as some might suppose) become an austere, prematurely developed, world-denying pharisee. I was eager and enthusiastic, gay without being frivolous. I remember noting in my *Diary* the steps of a new dance: "A grip and a gink with the other foot . . . walk a little faster . . . First salute her, then bow, and hand her to a chair."[13]

Furthermore, I liked the friendly climate at Lincoln College. I was happy, my parents were proud; my father kept addressing me as "Dear Mr. Fellow Elect of Lincoln."[14] I was finally in a position to reduce my debt. I was not wealthy but the Fellowship meant that I shared in the common revenues of the college and for those in residence (which was not required) there were additional provisions including rooms, a share in the common table, obit and gaudy money, and even some allowances for the laundress and barber, and access to the buttery and kitchen.[15]

Since the Fellows (there were eleven in all) did not have to maintain residence (at least not until 1729 when some restrictions were laid upon Junior Fellows), I was entitled to a share in the common revenues which occurred annually whether in residence or not. This gave me the freedom to ask for a leave of absence which I was granted on April 9. Since my appointment was attached to a region (as most Fellowships were), I felt it appropriate to spend some time in the county that had sponsored my election—

---

[13]Green, *The Young Mr. Wesley*, p. 101. This was in cipher, a common practice Wesley used extensively along with shorthand. See *Journal*, Vol. I, pp. 71f.

[14]Tyerman, *Life and Times*, p. 399. Telford, *Life of John Wesley*, p. 43. These include a letter from Samuel to John which is full of both pride and self-pity.

[15]"Obit and gaudy money" refers to that money to be used for necessities (obit) and recreation (gaudy).

Lincolnshire. I walked to Epworth, arriving on April 23. I was pleased to find my family well (though my father had grown old). The next day, being Sunday, I read prayers for my father twice. The summer months were spent in transcribing my father's work for a book on Job, serving as curate at Wroot, visiting with my mother, swimming, shooting (I once bagged three plovers), and reading. It might have been a totally pleasant experience but for my father, who was on occasion unrelenting.

I remember evenings spent with a young Epworth woman, Kitty Hargreaves. I might easily have fallen in love except for my father who, suspecting romance, attempted to frustrate our meeting. Once he actually sent her away. I was so unnerved that I rather impulsively vowed never to touch her hand again.

Another incident of the summer also stands out. My sister Hetty was bright, cultured, and sensitive, but a bit rebellious. She fell in love with a young lawyer who once kept her away from the rectory an entire night. My father was inconceivably exasperated with her. No one dare come to Hetty's defense. I resorted to preaching a sermon on the unconditional duty of love in order to demonstrate that some tenderness was still due her, but my father was so offended that he appealed to a canon of the Established Church which forbade a doctrine that had previously been preached to be attacked in the same or adjoining church. When my brother Charles informed me that my father, holding to his strong High Church principle, came near to filing official charges, I went to him and promised never to contradict him again. We both shed tears and he replied that he had always known that I "was good at bottom." My penance was to transcribe his book on Job several days running. Hetty's was not nearly so easy. She was forced to marry a drunken plumber and her marvelous spirit was effectually crushed. She and my father were never fully reconciled. May God be more merciful to him than my father was to those given into his care.[16]

---

[16]*Letters*, Vol. I, p. 39. John describes the incident in a letter to his brother Samuel.

On September 21, 1726, I returned to Oxford in order to prepare for my statutory sermon to be delivered at St. Michael's on September 29. Life at Lincoln College promised to be leisurely, peaceful, and with few teaching demands in a comparatively scholarly and gentlemanly society. I desired to remain. On November 7, although I was not to receive the M.A. degree until February, 1727, I was elected by my colleagues to responsibilities as class moderator and Claviger along with tutorials in Greek.[17] Second only to religion were serious studies. Until the completion of my M.A., Monday and Tuesday were given to Greek and Roman classics; Wednesday to Logic and Ethics; Thursday to Hebrew and Arabic; Friday to Metaphysics and Natural Philosophy; Saturday to Rhetoric and Poetry, including my own efforts; and Sunday to Theology.[18]

During the Christmas holidays, 1726, I again went to the Cotswolds. Sally, now married a year and very much in love with her husband, was still my spiritual guide. Though much of our time was spent entertaining ourselves, Sally and I managed to discuss spiritual matters at great length. I remember about this time transcribing for her Fénelon's *Discourse on Simplicity*. We both admired it greatly. Simplicity for me, as with Fénelon, came to mean "that grace which frees the soul from all unnecessary reflections upon itself."[19] One's love toward God must be *simple and pure*. Fénelon's understanding of love, defined as "the love of God and man filling the heart and governing the life," came to represent true religion for me.[20]

It should also be mentioned that soon after this I first encountered William Law's *Christian Perfection*. Law completed the celebrated triumvirate (along with Taylor and à Kempis) which had such a powerful impact on the early stages of my doctrine of perfection.

Then, on January 10, 1727, Robin Griffith died. The

---

[17]"Claviger" is a term for warden or custodian and originally refers to the "keeper of the keys."

[18]Telford, *Life of John Wesley*, p. 49; cf. *Journal*, Vol. I, pp. 65 and 66 for a list of the books read during this time.

[19]*Letters*, Vol. VI, p. 128.

[20]*Works*, Vol. VII, p. 162 (a sermon, *On Former Times*).

enemy was back at my throat. In preparing Robin's funeral sermon, I sought to detach myself of all sentiment and personal feeling. Had I done otherwise, I would have revealed to all my nagging fear of death. As such a lack of faith would have been comfort to none (save the enemy), I chose what I felt to be the lesser of two evils: rather than confess my doubts I hid behind a rather odd interpretation of 2 Samuel 12:23: "But now he is dead, wherefore should I fast? can I bring him back again? I shall go to him (so I had hope), but he shall not return to me." In concise, unpretentious sentences, I attempted to repress feeling by emphasizing the utter uselessness of mourning and grief. I commented: "Grief, in general, is the parent of so much evil and the occasion of so little good to mankind, that it may be justly wondered how it found a place in our nature." Supposing that the enemy was in fact a friend (vain words) I stated further: "Be it my comfort . . . that I shall soon awake from this tedious dream of life." I then exhorted my listeners not to weep for the dead but for the living, "who still want that happiness."[21]

I did not leave it there, however. I sought to comfort with these words from 1 Thessalonians 4:14: "For if we believe that Jesus died and rose again, even so them also which sleep in Jesus will God bring with him." (Bless God for ointment soothing to those smarting wounds.) Even as I spoke, however, I feared that these words were not meant for me. As I expressed soon afterward in a letter to my mother: "I never gave more reason to suspect my doctrine did not agree with my practice; for a sickness and pain in

---

[21]This sermon appears in *Works*, Vol. VII, pp. 63-68. Although Wesley's pre-1738 sermons were brilliantly calculated to convince the sinner and stimulate the believer, they do not present the "way of salvation." Perhaps this can be seen most clearly in the fact that the concept of a *personal justifying faith* does not even remotely exist in any of the eight extant sermons from this period, nor in fact does the term "faith" appear in the evangelical sense. In fact, the word "faith" itself occurs less than a dozen times in all eight sermons (outside the few quotations from Scripture, which were used incidentally to faith). For anyone who enters the study of John Wesley convinced that Wesley was more or less an evangelical Christian from 1725 on (as I did), it is an enormous shock to see the vast difference in Wesley's sermons before and after Aldersgate. The full significance of this will become more apparent later on.

my stomach, attended with a violent looseness, which seized me the day he was buried, altered me so much in three days, and made me look so pale and thin, that those who saw me could not but observe it."[22]

On February 14, 1727 I received my master's degree. I gained considerable reputation by my disputation delivering statutory lectures in natural philosophy on the soul of animals; in philosophy on Julius Caesar; and in theology on the love of God.

I had seemingly matured physically, intellectually, and socially, but emotionally and spiritually I was still very much in process. Robin's death had an unnerving effect. So much so that the intellectual and social demands became too much for me. They took more from me than I could give in return. I decided to busy myself. Rising an hour earlier and going to company an hour later helped some, but I was still not satisfied. I found myself being drawn into mysticism. The mystics' pursuit of holiness appealed to my innate sense of morality, but their love of contemplation aroused my natural inclination for solitude. With Fenelon fresh upon my mind I wrote to my mother: "And I am so little at present in love with even company, the most elegant entertainment next to books, that unless they have a peculiar turn of thought I am much better pleased without them. I think 'tis the settled temper of my soul that I should prefer, at least for some time, such a retirement as would seclude me from all the world to the station I am now in."[23]

I began reading more extensively among the mystics, mostly (although not exclusively, as they were being recommended by several friends as well) those recommended by my mother. Still plagued by doubt, I plunged deeper and deeper into the mystical writings. I became convinced that I had to find some environment where I, at least for a time, could put mysticism to the test without interruption.

---

[22]*Letters*, Vol. I, p. 43, where John discusses with his mother the funeral at Broadway.

[23]*Letters*, Vol. I, p. 42.

8

My Father's Curate

Although it is always consistent with reason, reason cannot produce faith in the scriptural sense of the word. Faith, according to Scripture, is "an evidence" or conviction, "of things not seen." It is a divine evidence, bringing a full conviction of an invisible eternal world. It is true, there was a kind of shadowy persuasion of this, even among the wiser heathens; . . . but this was little more than faint conjecture: it was far from a firm conviction; which reason, in its highest state of improvement, could never produce in any child of man.   John Wesley

In August, 1727, anticipating another leave of absence from the college (granted on November 6, and subsequently on May 6 and November 6 of the following year), I returned to Epworth (by way of London, visiting my brother Samuel) in order to assume the curacy of my father's second living in Wroot. Apart from brief trips to the Cotswold villages of Broadway, Buckland, and Stanton, and several journeys to London (to visit Samuel) and to Oxford (on business and to visit Charles), I remained in Wroot until November, 1729.[1]

I wanted a remote setting. I had previously applied for the headmastership of a school in Skipton, an isolated little market town in Yorkshire. The endowment was good and I should have been out of debt within a year. Yet I liked most of all its "frightful description." Even today, "the town lies in a little vale, so pent up between two hills that it is scarce accessible on any side; so that you could expect little com-

---

[1] Charles had left Westminster for Christ Church in 1726.

pany from without and within there was none at all."[2] I was disappointed when that position passed to someone else.

There might have been the possible alternative of a college living, but this was highly unlikely since I was still a Junior Fellow, not long in Orders. Besides, I was not ready for a university parish. I was small in stature and relatively weak. Although later I would "readily trace the wisdom of Providence in allotting me these imperfections" (under the merciful guidance of God, good would be extracted from evil), I could not yet happily accept the rather odious Common Room smiles prompted by my seriousness toward religion.

So, in August, 1727, if I could not have Skipton, I accepted what I believed to be the next best thing. I yielded to the pressing desires of my father (who was increasingly infirm) and took up residence at Wroot, four-and-a-half-miles west of Epworth. Nearly as remote as Skipton, it was well-suited for my intentions.

The road between Epworth and Wroot was rough and unpredictable at best (being frequently flooded), making it difficult to travel by foot or on horseback. The "surest" way was by boat to Scawsit Bridge, then walking across the Common to Epworth. I recall that my father, upon my arrival, was still ill due to a soaking contracted during such a crossing by the water washing over the sides of the boat. I was pleased to relieve him from so unpleasant a passage, although the next year he narrowly escaped drowning while crossing in a strong wind.

My parents, who had lived at Wroot since 1725, now had an opportunity to return to the rectory at Epworth where they remained until 1735 (except for occasional exchanges with me during the period now under consideration). For all practical purposes Wroot was mine. This proved to be my first and last experience as a parish clergyman. Commonly known as "Wroot-out-of-England," it had less than three hundred inhabitants whom Hetty rather unsympathetically described as "asses dull on dung hills born." My

---

[2]*Letters*, Vol. I, p. 43.

father had made some progress with these good people, but precious little. He had managed to raise them from a level of ignorance and brutality to a level of depressing dullness, but certainly no higher.

I settled into my routine quickly with few interruptions. I performed my duties with regularity and order. I rose early for prayer, and spent most mornings either reading, sermon writing, sorting my father's papers, looking up references, or drawing up a list of subscribers to his work on Job. The evenings I frequently spent with my mother, discussing my friends (especially my relationship with women), plotting my ongoing spiritual struggle, or reading aloud an occasional novel or more serious work. On Sunday I usually read prayers at Wroot, but also preached at Flixborough and Burton.

During the long summer months I had some time for working in the garden, gathering flowers, as well as some shooting and swimming, but most of my efforts were spent in sorting out my inner spiritual life. Much of this centered around my mother. We exchanged devotional tracts and read to each other from the mystical authors. I read a great deal from the works of the Cambridge Platonist, John Norris, who had come under the influence of Nicholas Malebranche.[3] George Herbert, Anton Horneck, and Dr. Heylyn were also favorites of mine during this time, all three of them having flirted with mysticism in one form or another.

About this time I first encountered William Law's second treatise, *A Serious Call to a Devout and Holy Life.* Although this served to reinforce Taylor, à Kempis, and his earlier work, *On Christian Perfection,* and brightened the fire of my spiritual ambition, I was drawn even more to the mystical works. I carefully read *The Holy Life of Monsieur de Renty.*[4] De Renty, a wealthy French marquis, under the

---

[3]Wesley later included Malebranche's *Search for Truth* in several courses for study. *Letters,* Vol. IV, p. 249; cf. *Letters,* Vol. III, p. 163; Vol. V, p. 110; Vol. VII, p. 228.

[4]Wesley later abridged this work and circulated it among the Societies. It is entitled *Extract of the Life of M. de Renty,* first published independently in 1741.

influence of Vincent de Paul gave away most of what he had and went to the bread lines of Paris in order to feed the hungry. I studied this great and good man closely. I especially liked his attitude toward death. I remember his comment regarding the death of his beloved wife: "Were it not for common decency, I could have danced at her funeral." Still plagued by fear and doubt, de Renty's "experimental verity" (an assurance of God's presence) and his imperviousness to death, kept (at least for a while) the enemy on a leash. I recall also reading to my mother Fontenelle's *New Dialogues of the Dead* and Taylor's *The Rule and Exercises of Holy Dying* which gave some assistance; but most comfort came from the mystics.

I found myself becoming morbidly individualistic. The more I read, the more I wanted to pass my time solely in the company of the mystical authors. It was during this experimental period that I "perfected" the practice of ejaculatory prayers. The use of devout ejaculations was common among the eighteenth-century English mystics. In fact, some mystics frequently abandoned all forms of prayer except for these periodical ejaculations. Since their entire lives were spent in the attitude of prayer, they saw no real need for formal prayers. I remember writing at the foot of my *Diary:* "No hourly prayer like ejaculations."[5] I had been using this form of prayer for some time. In all my examination work, for example, whether for ordination, or degree, or fellowship, I used it freely, sometimes profusely.[6] Although the practice dwindled during the earliest years after my return to Oxford, "as the Holy Club became more and more highly organized, it revived in greater force than ever."[7] In January, 1734, I began to mark the regularity of these prayers with the letter "e" at the beginning of every hour followed by a corresponding number (5, 6, or 7) indicating the length of the prayer. It is safe to say that I

---

[5]*Diary,* December 9, 1735 (see *Journal,* Vol. I, p. 127). The first Oxford Diary proves that Wesley adopted the habit of using these prayers long before the formation of the Holy Club. These were emphatic prayers, lasting usually from five to eight minutes.

[6]*Journal,* Vol. I, p. 127.

[7]Ibid.

esteemed ejaculatory prayer more than any other type of prayer. I used it extensively and was reluctant to give it up. Although the practice dwindled again after my return from Georgia, I included these mystical prayers in my *Scheme of Self-Examination* along with a strong exhortation toward love and simplicity.[8]

This kind of prayer (emanating from a type of self-examination that was an obsession with me now) was all a part of a larger form of mysticism. It was an interesting (though I now realize deceptive) kind of classical mysticism involving five stages in one's approach to God. Since these stages were to become so much a part of my "in process," let me describe them to you.

The first stage, called *awakening,* is a moral or ethical awakening such as I had experienced in the spring of 1725, just three years earlier. The second stage, called *purgation,* involved purging the flesh so that it required little or nothing of the spirit. This was my constant struggle. I sought to condition my body to function without much sleep or food so that, little by little, it required less and less of the spirit. The third stage, called *illumination,* involved the witness of God's Spirit. Just for a moment, the Holy Spirit would bear witness with my spirit that I was a child of God. These "sensible comforts," however, were precious few. The fourth stage was called *the dark night of the soul.* Here, according to the mystic, God withdrew even the occasional comfort forcing the mystic to come to Him by naked faith. This I did not fully comprehend since such blind trust seemed to me contrary to the illusive assurance I had always believed to be a part of saving faith. The fifth stage, called *union with God,* involved a *constant* awareness of God's presence in the world and in the life of the believer. This I wanted (and still do, but alas, it is not meant to be) with all my heart!

I still had no understanding of justification by faith in the personal sense. I was well on my way to being utterly duped by the self-saving delusion of mystical theology. Taylor, à Kempis, Law, and the mystics (though not for the

---

[8]*Works,* Vol. XI, p. 521.

same reasons) rarely used the word "faith," and when they did, it was far from evangelical. Faith, on the one hand (for Taylor, à Kempis, and Law), was a lifeless "ascent to any truth upon rational grounds"; and on the other (for the mystics) a blind obedience to God involving the dark night of the soul. [9]

Before I could respond by faith in the evangelical sense, *both* these philosophies had to be purged away. Reason was the first to go. Up to now reason had maintained the upper hand in my search for real scriptural assurance, but this was about to change. In a sermon entitled *The Case of Reason Impartially Considered,* written many years later, I sought to demonstrate (and I think adequately for candid men) the complete inability of reason to produce faith. [10] I stated: "Although it is always consistent with reason, yet reason cannot produce faith in the scriptural sense of the word. Faith, according to Scripture, is 'an evidence,' or conviction, 'of things not seen.' It is a divine evidence, bringing a full conviction of an invisible eternal world. It is true, there was a kind of shadowy persuasion of this, even among the wiser Heathens . . . but this was little more than faint conjecture: It was far from a firm conviction; which reason, in its highest state of improvement, could never produce in any child of man."

To use some of the same words I cited earlier: "Many years ago (during my stay at Wroot) I found the truth of this by sad experience. After carefully heaping up the strongest arguments which I could find, either in ancient or modern authors, for the very being of a God, and (which is nearly connected with it) the existence of an invisible world, I have wandered up and down, musing with myself: 'What, if all these things which I see around me, this earth and heaven, this universal frame, has existed from eternity?' What, if 'the generation of men be exactly parallel with the generation of leaves?' if the earth drops its successive inhabitants, just as the tree drops its leaves? What, if that

[9]Cf. *Letters,* Vol. I, p. 20 and *Letters,* Vol. II, p. 264. It is important to remember that William Law was not yet into his more mystical phase.
[10]*Works,* Vol. VI, pp. 350f.

saying of a great man be really true,—

Death is nothing, and nothing is after death?

How am I sure that this is not the case; that I have not followed cunningly devised fables?—and I have pursued the thought, till there was no spirit in me, and I was ready to choose strangling rather than life.

"But in a point of so unspeakable importance, do not depend upon the word of another; but retire for a while from the busy world, and make the experiment yourself."[11] In fact, I had done just that, but the victory was not yet won. I still had no understanding of the Scripture notion of faith as the "conviction of things hoped for, the evidence of things not seen." So, I plunged even deeper into mysticism, still plowing with their own wicked "heifer." Mystic faith (swallowed and digested so deceptively by the dark night of the soul) was no better than "rational" faith. Yet, I was to pursue it (as if to the end of the earth) for another ten years. Even then I marveled at my ineffectiveness. My soul had no life. My sermons were fruitless. Let me illustrate.

Although I preached many sermons during this period (including those on Holy Communion, election, and reprobation), I remember one in particular, a sermon entitled, *On Corrupting the Word of God.*[12] I emphasized the need for sincerity in preaching the Word of God. One must never adulterate or intermingle the gospel with one's own opinions or traditions. I criticized those who add to the gospel by blending it with human inventions. Although I later cited the "mystic foxes" (the chief offenders at this very point) for spoiling the Word of God with a "new gospel," not yet understanding the simple gospel of justification by faith myself, there was no exhortation to faith in Christ nor any criticism of the mystic writers.

On July 27, 1728, I journeyed to Oxford by way of London. On September 22, I was again ordained by Dr. Potter, then bishop of Oxford who had also been a Fellow of

---

[11]*Works,* Vol. VI, pp. 355f.
[12]*Works,* Vol. VII, pp. 468-473.

Lincoln, this time to Priest's Orders. The examining chaplain, Dr. Hayward (who subscribed to my father's book on Job and later contributed to the funds of the Holy Club), left an indelible impression upon me by stating: "Do you know what you are about? You are bidding defiance to all mankind. He that would live as a Christian priest ought to know that, whether his hand be against every man or no, he must *expect* every man's hand should be against him."[13]

As I returned to Wroot I was not certain that my experiment was a success. I still felt unprepared (in spite of the mystic advice) to receive happily the abuse which the priesthood would undoubtedly bring. Further complicating matters were the disputes with my father. I was sad, and chided myself for such an unworthy emotion.

Early in 1729, a serious man, Mr. Hoole, rector of Haxey, and my father's friend and nearest neighbor, said to me: "Sir, you wish to serve God and go to heaven? Remember that you cannot serve him alone. You must therefore find companions or make them; the Bible knows nothing of solitary religion."[14] Accordingly I began to increase my excursions into the Cotswolds.[15] Then on June 16, 1729, I journeyed once again to Oxford and observed for the first time the little society begun by my brother the previous month.[16] I met with them for about two months before returning to Wroot. In August I was surprised by the fact that I was acquiring a new taste for company. Wroot was losing its hold. Toward the end of September I remember still another dispute with my father. I was weary of my experiment. My *Diary* is filled with the ejaculations: κύριε ἐλεῆσον(Lord, have mercy!) and κύριε βοήθει(Lord, help me).

On October 21, 1729, I received a letter from Dr. Morley informing me that the College had decided that the Junior

---

[13]See Green, *The Young Mr. Wesley,* p. 119 (italics mine).

[14]Although the identification of this "serious man" is not certain, Curnock argues convincingly for Mr. Hoole. See *Journal,* Vol. I, p. 469.

[15]The *Diaries* which have been lost for most of this period are resumed on April 30, 1729.

[16]*The Holy Club,* see chapter 10.

Fellows who had been nominated to the moderatorships were now expected to fulfill their offices in person. Surely this was answer to prayer. On November 22, I happily returned to Oxford where I was not to receive another leave of absence for some years.

As I conclude this part of my story I do not want to give the impression that the time spent at Wroot was totally fruitless. I was now convinced, for example, that the effects of our parent sin extended not only to the heart, but to the intellect as well, inhibiting one's reason from leading him to faith. Yet there was still another victory to be won. Interestingly enough parts of the second battle had already been waged. Although I still did not understand the principle of faith, sinking even deeper into mysticism during the days to follow, I was now convinced that my experiment in mystic solitude (at least as such) was a failure.

9

The Holy Club

I went to the weekly sacrament, and persuaded two or three young students to accompany me, and to observe the method of study prescribed by the statutes of the university. This gained me the harmless name of Methodist. In half a year (after this) my brother left his curacy at Epworth, and came to our assistance.   Charles Wesley

I remember a feeling of near exhilaration as I saw the spires of Oxford. I must have seen them a hundred times before, but somehow this was different. As I turned my horse (which I had purchased the previous summer) into the lane at Lincoln College I felt almost as if I was returning home, not leaving it. I have experienced a few such moments since, but this still stands out in my mind. It was November 22, 1729. I was now to act as tutor to the undergraduates.

Although my experiment at Wroot no doubt heightened the contrast, I was back into society. I immediately became an active member of the Senior Common Room where I frequently gathered with the Fellows, their guests, and the gentlemen commoners after dinner. Perhaps my colleagues, realizing the Junior Fellows now had to remain in residence, determined to make the best of me. In spite of the fact that many of these later lost their resolve and chose to remain apart, initially, life was at least congenial.

While I was learning to enjoy once again some of the normal recreations—dancing, attending an occasional concert or play, visiting London and the Cotswolds—I was also redoubling my efforts to purge away all "superfluities." I had been concerned for Charles when he first came up from Westminster. Then, while I was at Wroot, he had fairly well established himself at Christ Church. He had been diligent enough in his studies (no doubt remembering the advice of our brother Samuel, his former tutor) and led a regular, harmless life; but when I pressed him about religion, he would reply, "What, would you have me to be a saint all at once?"[1]

Charles wanted to become a proper gentleman. He feared being "dull as a dog and twice as broke." He would sit by a fireless grate in his Oxford rooms writing to himself somewhat dolefully:

> . . . *'tis in the power of a few Epworth or Wroot guineas and clothes to give things the favorable turn and make a gentleman of me. Come money then and quickly to rescue me from my melancholy maxim "ex nihilo nihil fit".* [2]

Then, during the previous January, Charles experienced what he termed his "reformation" as his religious life began to take a definite turn. I have a letter he wrote to me at Wroot, dated January, 1729: "I verily think I shall never quarrel with you again 'til I do again with my Religion, and that I may never do *That* I am not ashamed to desire your prayers."[3] I remember praying instantly: "If this be true, let him not return as a dog to his vomit."

Charles was himself uncertain as to exactly when he first awoke out of his lethargy. I recall my mother (upon my return to Wroot in 1727) expressing some concern regarding his apparent idleness, and she corresponded with him frequently, no doubt with some consequence. Yet, there were additional factors at work effecting this change.

By 1729 Charles had become increasingly concerned with the state of religion at Oxford. Apart from general apathy, Arianism and Deism had crept in, attracting enough attention to alarm the university officials. Upon one of my visits I noted with some interest that several of these officials were disturbed that infidelity had become so fashionable, many of the students who had thus far re-

---

[1]Green, *The Young Mr. Wesley*, p. 145.
[2]Ibid., p. 146.
[3]Ibid., p. 147.

mained nominal in their religious observances had now abandoned them altogether. The result was that Dr. Butler, the vice-chancellor, under some pressure, issued a circular letter to be posted in the majority of the college halls urging college tutors to inform their pupils of their Christian duty by "explaining to them the articles of religion which they professed, and are often called upon to subscribe," and by "recommending to them the frequent and careful reading of the Scriptures, and such other books that may serve more effectually to promote Christianity, sound principles and orthodox faith."[4]

I was so encouraged by word of this notice that I asked Charles to send me a copy immediately. He quickly obliged, also expressing alarm that the Dean of Christ Church (no doubt resisting the impulse of outside authority, even from the vice-chancellor himself) had refused to display it in Christ Church Hall. As Providence would have it, the Dean's obstinance prompted Charles (in like manner) to follow the notice's directives to the letter. It is against this background that Charles wrote later: "I went to the weekly sacrament, and persuaded two or three students to accompany me, and to observe the method of study prescribed by the statutes of the university. This gained me the harmless name of *Methodist*. In half a year (after this) my brother left his curacy at Epworth, and came to our assistance."[5]

So, in May, Charles joined with William Morgan and Francis Gore (both of Christ Church) in order to establish the study habits which he had once found so difficult to sustain and which Mr. Morgan and Mr. Gore had found unpalatable.[6] Then in November I took the advice of my "serious friend," Dr. Hoole, against solitary religion and quickly joined these young men who had united together. In fact, being somewhat more mature and stronger-willed

[4]Ibid., pp. 147f.

[5]Ibid., p. 148.

[6]Wesley later identifies Robert Kirkham, not Francis Gore, as the third student along with Charles and Morgan, but this is surely an error since Kirkham did not join the Holy Club until February, 1730. Cf. Green, *The Young Mr. Wesley*, p. 155 and n. 1.

(Charles lacked stability and was constantly plagued by ill health), I soon emerged as the leader of our "little company," serving as tutor both to my brother and his friends.

The "Holy Club," as it was commonly called, began by concentrating only on the study of the Greek New Testament. Under my direction, however, it soon progressed to include other exercises as well. My devotional life, for example (due to my experiment at Wroot), had already established a pattern which adapted easily to the objectives of my brother's society. In turn, I found the influence of the society benefited me. On weekdays I rose at an increasingly early hour (usually between 5:00 and 6:00), went to prayer, and read my Greek New Testament along with some devotional work. Weighing the seriousness of my vocation, I used a Collect at 9:00 in the morning, at noon, and at 3:00 in the afternoon, interspersed with fervent ejaculations every hour. My *Diary* began to portray much more consistently the fruits of regularity; my resolutions seemed to have more bite.

We made steady progress. In February, 1730, we were joined by Robert Kirkham, of Merton College, who had taken the fancy (I would to God the whole of mankind would follow his example), "that he would lose no more time or waste no more money." Somewhat to my surprise he "left off tea, struck off his drinking acquaintance to a man, gave the hours above specified to Greek Testament and Hugo Grotius, and spent the evenings either by himself or with my brother and me."[7]

Although my responsibilities with the members of the Holy Club could properly be termed tutorials (I read with them Milton, Lucas, Norris, Bonnel, de Renty, and the *Second Spira*), I still had no private pupils.[8] So, on February

---

[7]*Letters*, Vol. I, pp. 48f.

[8]Green, *The Young Mr. Wesley*, p. 131, describes the works of these authors in some detail. Cf. p. 196n. on the *Second Spira*. The full title was *The Second Spira, being a Fearful Example of an Atheist, who had apostated from the Christian religion, and died in despair at Westminster, December 8, 1692.* This was one of John's favorites. The victim, lamenting his faithlessness, cries out: "Oh that I was to broil upon that fire for a thousand

27, 1730, I accepted a temporary curacy at Pyrton near Wallingford, eight miles from Oxford. The salary was thirty pounds a year which prevented me from having to sell my horse. Then in June, the rector, Dr. Morley (a great and good man), allotted eleven men into my care. Since these were younger men (just entering Oxford), I felt a responsibility beyond the obligations of a tutorial nature. Although none were coaxed into the Holy Club, I regularly invited them to breakfast and prayers. None had any doubt as to what I expected of them concerning either academic or religious observances. Weekdays I met with them at 10:00 in the morning and then at 2:00 or 5:00 in the afternoon, and on Sunday I frequently saw them for religious instruction.[9]

Up until now the Holy Club had gone relatively unnoticed. As our activities increased, however, this changed. During the summer of 1730, William Morgan assumed responsibility for various works of charity. By the end of the summer we not only studied the Scriptures, took weekly communion, and observed every order of the Church, but also took time from sleep and amusements for religious exercises: to attend the sick and dying, the poor and illiterate, to conduct prayer meetings (a practice resumed later in the Revival), and to visit the prisons. The latter was especially significant.

The prisons had long been a problem. The keepers were both corrupt and lewd. The new prisoners were frequently abused by the older prisoners. Drunkenness, swearing, and gambling were epidemic. Finally, these conditions brought about a parliamentary committee in 1729. The enthusiasm of young Mr. James Oglethorpe, first for improving the lot of poor debtors (a project of particular interest to me as a result of my father's imprisonment some years earlier), and then for conditions on the whole,

---

years, to purchase the favor of God, and be reconciled to him again. But it is a fruitless wish! Millions and millions of years will bring me no nearer to the end of my tortures than one poor hour." His last words were, "Oh the insufferable pangs of hell and damnation." Wesley evidently thought this was suitable material for his young friends.

[9]Ibid., p. 132, gives a rather complete list of the books read by both Wesley and his students during this period.

secured for him a seat on this committee which exposed a horrid story of laxity and corruption.[10] I remember reading their initial report while still at Wroot and a later report the previous May. On August 24, 1730, Charles and I accompanied Mr. Morgan to Oxford Castle. The result was that we determined, provided we could get the approval of the prison governor and the bishop (a courtesy insisted upon by my father when I wrote asking his advice on the matter), to set aside some time each week for this service.

Our prison work advanced so during the next two years that by 1732 this occupied most of our time. Our members held services at the Castle and the Bocardo regularly. We held prayers most Wednesdays and Fridays, a sermon on Sunday, and Holy Communion once a month. We put aside every penny we could spare for legal advice, to pay the debts of those who had been confined for relatively trivial sums, to provide medicines, books, and a few necessities. We even hired a schoolmaster to instruct the debtors' children.[11] Although not all the prisoners were grateful for our intervention, most of the ridicule came from our colleagues at Oxford who frequently accused us of being "righteous over much." By then we were known not only as the Holy Club, but also were called individually "Bible moths," "Bible bigots," "supererogation men," "enthusiasts," as well as "Methodists." Since the latter did not greatly offend us, we soon accepted it as our badge of cause.[12]

This was not a badge easily carried, however. As Methodists, we were not to be content with just solemn devotions or early rising, but "at all times and at all places make fervent returns to the mind of God." Was this carrying things too far? Were we spending strength on unneces-

---

[10]Parliament appointed this committee on February 25, 1729. Samuel, Jr. was so moved by their first report that he wrote *The Prisons Open'd:*

> Yet Britain ceased my Captives' Woes to mourn,
> To break their Chains, see Oglethorpe was borne!

[11]*Journal,* Vol. I, p. 467.

[12]*Letters,* Vol. I, pp. 53f. See Schmidt, *John Wesley,* Vol. I, p. 102, for a good study of the origin of the term "Methodist."

sary burdens? I think not, but there was so little support. Although we were not actually persecuted (the rumors that the disciplinary officials of Christ Church were going to "blow us up" were greatly exaggerated), several discouraging things began to happen.

On November 6, 1730, I had been appointed moderator in philosophy. I quickly developed an expertise for argument (a skill to be greatly used during the Revival), establishing a reputation as a reasonable tutor in logic. I was gaining confidence. Although I was shaken a bit by the death of Dr. Morley on June 13, 1731, this seemed to present no real problem since I played a significant role in the election of the new rector, my friend, Euseby Isham, one month later. Dr. Isham seemed sympathetic and generous (he donated money for our work at the Castle), but then apparently developed some later concern for my religious zeal. By 1732 he entrusted me with fewer and fewer students. This in itself would not have caused much anxiety, but for the fact that even members of my own family began to question our actions. My brother Samuel, for example, after a visit to Oxford wrote:

> *Does John beyond his strength presume to go?*
> *To his frail carcass literally a foe?*
> *Lavish of health as if in haste to die,*
> *And shortened time to ensure eternity?*[13]

Samuel could be excused, but surely my mother would understand. I wrote to her concerning those who had accused us and was quite surprised when she replied by cautioning me against glorying in temptation. She wrote that I should pray to avoid temptation rather than conquer it. I was near despair. My only real confirmation concerning my present activities came from my devotional reading, again, mostly among the mystics. This seemed to rekindle my affection for solitude, however.

Then a crowning blow. In August, 1732, William Morgan died.[14] The Holy Club in general, and Charles and I in

---

[13]George Stevenson, *Memoirs of the Wesley Family* (London: S. W. Partridge and Co., 1876), p. 245.

[14]William Morgan died after a long illness which was thought by some to have resulted from the excessive fasting imposed by Wesley.

particular, were blamed for his death. The enemy was back at my throat. This time he would strike at the root. Presenting our defense in the now well-known series of letters to Morgan's father, I described the intent and purpose of our works of charity, even our spiritual exercises, with so much satisfaction that the senior Morgan sent his younger son to me upon his matriculation in Oxford some two years later. I, however, was the one who most needed convincing. I felt lonely and abandoned. The enemy had done his work well. So much so, that I delivered my soul to Mr. Morgan and promptly withdrew into the quietness of my own rooms for a period of reexamination.

Although I was still mildly social, with occasional visits to the Cotswolds and to London during the winter months, I spent less and less time with anyone apart from the Holy Club, avoiding the Common Room almost altogether. The Holy Club itself continued with remarkable regularity, although I considered for a time resigning, at least as its leader.[15]

It was about this time that I was drawn to William Law. In July, 1732, I first visited him at Putney and he was so favorably impressed with us that he chose to write in our defense.[16] I was soon to realize, however, that he was defending our religious asceticism (especially as related to mysticism), not our works of charity. Again in my *Journal* review for 1738 I wrote: "A contemplative man convinced me more than ever that outward works are nothing and instructed me how to pursue inward holiness, or a union of the soul with God."[17] Although I would not abandon these

---

Since Wesley himself had been fasting for only six months and Morgan had not fasted for eighteen months prior to his death this accusation is certainly false. The letter that John wrote to Morgan's father in defense of the Holy Club is an interesting study of early Methodism. The letter along with a poem written by Samuel Wesley, Jr. in memory of William Morgan serve as an introduction to the *Journal* (Vol. I, pp. 87-105).

[15]See Green, *The Young Mr. Wesley,* p. 58.

[16]The title of Law's paper was: *The Oxford Methodists Being Some Account of a Society of Young Gentlemen in that City so Denominated.* See John S. Simon, *John Wesley and the Religious Societies,* pp. 97ff. for extracts from this paper.

[17]Curnock (*Journal,* Vol. I, pp. 468f) wrongly identifies this contemp-

works of charity altogether, my interest in the inner life of the contemplatives was once again reinforced. Perhaps I should try my hand at writing. I had obviously demonstrated some gift for the pen in my correspondence with Mr. Morgan. I began my first book, *A Collection of Forms of Prayer for Every Day in the Week,* which was written for my students. It was published the following year.

In the meantime, William Law was to become my mentor (Charles once referred to him as our "John the Baptist"). He quickly overruled the painful lesson I had learned at Wroot and once again I was back on the mystic way. Since the days of his *Christian Perfection* and his *Serious Call,* Law had combined his ethical idealism with a high degree of mystical detachment. I was persuaded to read the *Theologia Germanica* and other mystical works, and while I failed to understand all that Mr. Law was saying, I was nonetheless a willing student.[18] Law put me on a kind of inner penance. Although my rigid asceticism had continued (my health was a bit precarious at this point, and my rigorous self-discipline imposed a severe strain on my constitution), I was once again inclined to seek solitude and to abandon social service. Like Wroot, Oxford became another mystical experiment involving a withdrawal from the world. At Oxford, however, I would sink even deeper into the esoteric world of mysticism. As at Wroot, the inner approach to God again got the upper hand. This time, however, it was not over and against reason, but against any form of outward works-righteousness. I remember writing that Mr. Law "spoke so incautiously against trusting in outward works, that he discouraged me from doing them at all."

---

lative man as Dr. Hoole. Dr. Hoole, you will remember, had exactly the opposite effect.

[18]The eminent Putney physician and mystic, Dr. Cheyne, fired Law's enthusiasm for mysticism with the works of Jacob Boehme. Law did not stop there, however. He knew the desert fathers, especially Macarius. He was also greatly attracted to the fourteenth-century mystics: Tauler, Eckhart, Suso, and Ruysbroeck. Likewise, Wesley's *Diary* for 1732 and 1733 reveals his own interest in the mystical authors: Rodriguez (*On Humility*), François de Sales (*Introduction to a Devout Life*), Monsieur de Renty, Fénelon (*Maxims of the Saints and Pastoral Letters Concerning*

There is a subtle, but extremely important, turn here. Although Law discouraged me from outward works, his *Mental Prayer and the Like Exercises* were "as much one's own works as visiting the sick or clothing the naked."[19] Law's effectual means of purifying the soul, the uniting of it with God, were as much "my own righteousness as any I had before pursued under another name. In this refined way of trusting my own works and my own righteousness (so zealously inculcated by the mystic writers), I dragged on heavily, finding no comfort or help therein til the time of my leaving England."[20]

William Law was not the only one influencing me at this time. Nor was I the only member of the Holy Club influenced by mysticism. Mr. Law's friend and physician, Dr. Cheyne, first introduced me to the well-known mystic, Count Marsay. Similarly, John Byrom, another friend of Mr. Law, who contributed much to the revival of mystical studies during the first half of the century, directed my attention to several mystical treatises as well.

Furthermore, our entire "company" developed an interest in the ascetical aloofness of mysticism. I remember writing to Miss Bishop in November, 1774. After warning her against mystic solitude, I was forced to admit that "most of our little flock at Oxford were tried with this, my brother and I in particular." Undoubtedly the majority of our members were impregnated with a certain degree of mysticism, especially Charles and I, John Clayton, John Gambold, Westley Hall, and George Whitefield. Of course, it affected different members in different ways.

In spite of the controversy surrounding young Morgan's death, the Holy Club continued to attract others. We rarely had fewer than four nor more than seven. In the spring of 1732, John Clayton, a Fellow and tutor of Brasenose, be-

the Love of God), Castaniza, Ephraem Syrus *(On Repentance),* Malebranche, A. H. Francke, Norris Horneck, Heylyn, Taylor, à Kempis, Law, and even the *Bull Unigenitus* all find their way into Wesley's theological/devotional reading.

[19]*Journal,* Vol. I, p. 469.
[20]Ibid., pp. 469f.

came a member of our society. His orthodoxy was unquestionable, but he soon drifted into mysticism. He wrote to me the following August that "it meant a great deal to him that he was beginning to understand what was meant by the union of souls, so much talked of by Malebranche and Antoinette Bourignon."[21] I believe that this was my first encounter with Madame Bourignon. Under her influence Mr. Clayton not only heightened our quest for union with God, but soon had us praying and fasting after the mystical plan.

John Gambold also joined our company in 1732. A self-styled religious seeker, living a sequestered, secluded, and introspective life, Mr. Gambold made no secret of the fact that he had read widely among the mystics and encouraged us to do the same.

There were still others. Westley Hall, one for whom I had great hope, wandered into Quietism (both he and Gambold were later drawn to the Moravians). You can imagine my remorse when Mr. Hall became a smooth-tongued hypocrite, and was unfaithful in his marriage to my sister Martha.

Even George Whitefield, one of our most distinguished members, dabbled in mysticism. He unashamedly claimed that his reading in the mystic Henry Scougal's *Life of God in the Soul of Man* led to his conversion.

Before describing the events of 1735, a climactic year in many respects, let me put some of this into perspective. Perhaps the one thing that stands out as a result of the time spent with William Law (especially during the years 1732 to 1735) and my resurgence into mysticism was the realization that faith does not come by outward works. Although, as I have already mentioned, the mystic inward journey was simply a more subtle form of works-righteousness, I was not to see the truth in this for some three or four years to come. The issue now was (though I did not know it at the time) that my works of charity, though noble, were the result, not the cause, of saving faith. Holiness was a matter of the heart. This should not, however, lead you to believe

---

[21]Tyerman, *Life and Times*, Vol. I, pp. 83f.

that I or any of our company abandoned works in a lump. Although Law and mystics discouraged works in *theory*, we, like many of the mystics, continued several of the acts of charity in *practice*. Although many of these mystics exaggerated the effects of their *theology*, it was the mystic *lives* that attracted as well. Even then, in many ways, that which was least mystical about the mystics—a way of life which frequently demonstrated a high degree of social concern along with a serious vein of piety aimed at Christian perfection—impressed us most. With this in mind, I used these mystical lives as a pattern for instructing those under my care.[22]

Perhaps a brief review of my sermon, *Circumcision of the Heart* (first preached in 1733), will reveal something of the mood of the time. Here sanctification is achieved largely through self-denial. Although I state clearly that love is the sum total of the perfect law, I cite the phrase (so often quoted in mysticism): "Let the spirit return to God that gave it, with the whole train of its affections, 'unto the place from whence all the rivers came,' thither let them flow again."[23] We must give God all our affections. We must surrender our whole heart to God in love. "This is the way wherein 'those children of God' (our mystic friends) who being dead still speak to us: 'Desire not to live, but to praise his name; let all your thoughts, words, and works tend to his glory. Set your heart firm on Him, and on other things only as they are in Him, that you may love nothing but for his sake.'"[24] This concept of "purity of intention" emerged as one of the mystical mainsprings in the pursuit of holiness and taught me once again that true holiness involves the heart.

In fact, I remember writing to my father about this time that "by holiness I mean not fasting or bodily austerity (as

---

[22]An excellent illustration demonstrating the extent to which Wesley went to oversee the spiritual lives of his flock is provided in a letter to Law, *Letters*, Vol. I, pp. 161ff. In 1734, Wesley read Scougal, Norris, Malebranche, Francke, de Sales, Taylor, Law, and *The Life of Ebenezer Yokton, an Exact Entire Mystic.*

[23]*Sermons*, Vol. I, p. 279.

[24]Ibid.

he seemed to suppose) or any other external means of improvement, but the inward temper, to which all these things are subservient, a renewal of the soul in the image of God."[25]

In December, 1734, my father tried once again to persuade me to return to Epworth as he would soon need someone to replace him in the work of the parish. I then believed that I could best pursue God's holiness at Oxford. Although I was soon to change that decision, it was too late, for a few months later he was dead. Just prior to his death he had told me that the "inward witness was the strongest proof of Christianity." Had I convinced him while still remaining unconvinced myself? I was a haunted man. If reason or outward works would not lead to a sense of divine acceptance, then perhaps I was on the right track. Perhaps the quickest way to secure this inner assurance was through mysticism.

About five months after my father's death, I wrote a sermon entitled "The Trouble and Rest of Good Men." This was the first sermon I ever committed to the press (bless God, it was never reprinted). It undoubtedly represents my theological nadir. I still did not understand "by grace through faith." If fellowship with God was not secured by reason or outward works, then surely it was by the various mystical means. The text for the sermon was Job 3:17: "There the wicked cease from troubling; and there the weary be at rest." I demonstrated the efficacy of pain as remedial and spiritually therapeutic. I assumed that the body was the moral seat of evil and that death alone delivers perfectly from sin. By insisiting that wicked men are good men's "needful food" I disregarded the fact that all bad men are potentially good men. The entire sermon was more of an attempt to justify the actions of the Holy Club in the face of persecution, rather than an exhortation to holiness. May a merciful God not hold this sermon against me.

Before moving on I should say that my jealous care for the Holy Club was somewhat justified. Our number con-

---

[25]*Letters*, Vol. I, p. 168.

tinued to influence the Oxford community for several years to come. In spite of my leaving shortly afterward, the little band of Oxford Methodists provided the nucleus for the beginning of revival just four years later. Before that story can be told, however, there is yet another chapter in my pilgrimage to faith that must be described.

The belated decision to accept my father's offer to go to Epworth served to break the spell of the Oxford cloister and it enabled me, a few months later, to move to a different environment altogether. Just how different, let me describe to you.

10

Georgia

In the midst of the Psalm wherewith their service began, the sea broke over, split the main-sail in pieces, covered the ship, and poured in between the decks, as if the great deep had already swallowed us up. A terrible screaming began among the English. The Germans calmly sung on. I asked one of them afterwards, "Was you not afraid?" He answered, "I thank God, no." I asked, "But were not your women and children afraid?" He replied, mildly, "No; our women and children are not afraid to die." The Journal of John Wesley

Suddenly "the sea broke over us from stem to stern; burst through the windows of the state cabin, where three or four of us were, and covered us all over, though a bureau sheltered me from the main shock. About eleven I lay down in the great cabin, and in a short time fell asleep, though very uncertain whether I should wake alive, and much ashamed of my unwillingness to die. Oh, how pure in heart must he be, who would rejoice to appear before God at a moment's warning! Toward morning, 'He rebuked the winds and the sea, and there was a great calm.'"[1] But, once again the enemy had showed his teeth.

"We returned God thanks for our deliverance, of which a few appeared duly sensible. But the rest (among whom were most of the sailors) denied we had been in any danger. I could not have believed that so little good would have been done by the terror they were in before. But it cannot be that they should long obey God from fear, who are deaf to the motives of love."

A few days later another storm began. "In the morning it

---

[1]This and the following six paragraphs are taken from Wesley's *Journal. Works*, Vol. I, pp. 20ff.

increased, so that they were forced to let the ship drive. I could not but say to myself, 'How is it that thou hast no faith?', being still unwilling to die. About one in the afternoon almost as soon as I had stepped out of the great cabin-door, the sea did not break as usual, but came with a full, smooth tide over the side of the ship. I was vaulted over with water in a moment and so stunned that I scarce expected to lift up my head again, till the sea should give up her dead. But thanks be to God, I received no hurt at all. About midnight the storm ceased.

"At noon the day following our third storm began. At four it was more violent than before. Now, indeed, we could say, 'the waves of the sea were mighty, and raged horribly. They rose up to the heavens above, and' clave 'down to hell beneath.' The winds roared round about us, and (what I never heard before) whistled as distinctly as if it had been a human voice. The ship not only rocked to and fro with the utmost violence, but shook and jarred with so unequal, grating a motion, that one could not but with great difficulty keep one's hold of anything, nor stand a moment without it. Every ten minutes came a shock against the stern or side of the ship, which one would think would dash the planks in pieces. At this time a child, privately baptized before, was brought to be received into the Church. It put me in mind of Jeremiah's buying the field when the Chaldeans were on the point of destroying Jerusalem, and seemed a pledge of the mercy God designed to show us, even in the land of the living.

"We spent two or three hours after prayers, in conversing suitably to the occasion, confirming one another in a calm submission to the wise, holy, gracious will of God. And now a storm did not appear so terrible as before. Bless be the God of all consolation!

"At seven I went to the Germans. I had long before observed the great seriousness of their behaviour. Of their humility they had given a continual proof, by performing those servile offices for the other passengers which none of the English would undertake; for which they desired, and would receive no pay, saying, 'it was good for their proud hearts,' and 'their loving saviour had done more for them.' And every day had given them occasion of showing a meekness which no injury could move. If they were pushed, struck, or thrown down, they rose again and went away; but no complaint was found in their mouth. There was now an opportunity of trying whether they were delivered from the spirit of fear, as well as from that of pride, anger, and revenge. In the midst of the Psalm wherewith their service began, the sea broke over, split the main-sail in pieces, covered the ship, and poured in between the decks, as if the great deep had already swallowed us up. A terrible screaming began among the English. The Germans calmly sung on. I asked one of them afterwards, 'Was you not afraid?' He answered, 'I thank God, no.' I asked, 'But were not your women and children afraid?' He replied, mildly, 'No; our women and children are not afraid to die.'

"From them I went to their crying, trembling neighbors, and pointed out to them the difference in the hour of trial, between him that feareth God, and him that feareth him not. At twelve the wind fell. This was the most glorious day which I have hitherto seen." It was January 25, 1736, on board the *Simmonds* bound for America.

The previous September, Dr. John Burton, a tutor at Corpus Christi College, had suggested that I leave Oxford for a time and consider the SPG (The Society for the Propagation of the Gospel) chaplaincy in the newly established colony of Georgia.[2] I had long admired the work of several missionaries and since I still understood salvation in terms of spiritual exercises and withdrawal from the world (although I was now more determined to follow closely the Word of God in an effort to restore what I believed to be primitive Christianity), this seemed an ideal situation.

On October 10, 1735, the Georgia trustees approved my appointment. I was ready to leave. I had only to keep an audience with the Queen in order to present her with a copy of my father's book on Job (bless God my father was

---

[2]A letter to Dr. Burton (October 10, 1735) describes Wesley's motives for accepting this assignment (Dr. Burton was overjoyed). Wesley wrote that he hoped "to learn the true sense of the gospel." See *Letters*, Vol. I, pp. 187-91.

not alive to hear her rather casual comment commending only the pretty binding) and attend my brother's ordination on October 12 (Charles had been ordained deacon only eight days earlier and would have refused Priest's Orders had he not planned to make the journey with us and needed to have full authority in his new endeavor).

Georgia was still in its infancy. It had received its first settlers only three years earlier under the leadership of Mr. Oglethorpe, a man I already held in great esteem as the result of his efforts in prison reform. Oglethorpe had founded Savannah and concluded a treaty with the Creek Indians soon afterward.

I presented myself to Mr. Oglethorpe in person. I had already had the pleasure of his acquaintance some years past while visiting Mr. Law at Putney. Before deciding, however, I consulted my brother Samuel, my friend Mr. Clayton, and finally my mother, who replied: "Had I twenty sons, I should rejoice that they were all so employed, though I should never see them more."[3]

Although the advice received was not unanimous (William Law, for example, called our plans the scheme of a "crock-brained" enthusiast), I felt the way was clear. Less than a week after my appointment we (my brother Charles, his friend Benjamin Ingham, and Charles Delamotte, the son of a London merchant whose father was displeased with the prospect of such an adventure, and I) began our journey. I immediately identified with some of my mystic friends. Gregory Lopez, for example, answering the mystic call to the desert, had gone himself at the age of twenty from Spain to Mexico, where he spent the rest of his life among the Indians. Before losing sight of land, I found myself reading his biography and thinking to myself: Now I shall have a desert and Indians of my own. Lopez experienced an uninterrupted communion with God and I desired, more than anything, the perfect love that enables a person to dwell continually in the presence of God. Yet, I was still dissatisfied with my religious life. I continued my inner struggle. I did not love God with my whole heart.

---

[3]Henry Moore, *Life*, Vol. I, p. 234.

Nor did I understand the way of grace through faith. So, I determined to preach, to follow after, and to trust in "that righteousness whereby no flesh can be justified."[4] The twenty-six German Moravians on board (among whom I made several strong acquaintances) instantly tried to show me a better way, but I "understood it not at first," for I was "too learned and too wise."

Nonetheless, as I continued to observe these Moravians (they were kind enough to teach me German), I became even more impressed with the seriousness of their behavior, their humility, and their peace of mind in all circumstances. I watched them closely, especially during the storms. While I shook with fright and while others were screaming, they were either singing or praying as if they were safely secure within the hallowed walls of St. Paul's. If my enemy, my tormentor, my fear of death, was truly no respecter of persons, then they knew something that I did not yet know.

On board ship I took my pastoral duties (as prescribed by the SPG) seriously. I read both to myself and to any who would listen, for the most part among the mystics, though I must admit that my chief motive was to save my own soul even more than the souls of those given into my care.

February 6, 1736, I first set foot on American soil, an uninhabited island called Tybee from which Mr. Oglethorpe then proceeded on to Savannah. We had been on the open seas nearly two months.

Before Charles journeyed on to Frederica (a small community one hundred miles south of Savannah, where he became secretary to Mr. Oglethorpe and priest to the settlers), and I to Savannah, we were introduced (while still on the little island) to Mr. Spangenberg, one of the Moravian pastors whom Oglethorpe had brought back from Savannah. It would be difficult for me to estimate the impression he made on me. Just a year younger than myself, he instantly pressed us with questions regarding the witness of the Spirit. I remember his asking: "Have you the witness within yourself? Does the Spirit of God bear

---

[4]*Journal*, Vol. I, p. 470.

witness with your spirit that you are a child of God?" I must admit that I was surprised, and did not know what to answer. He then asked: "Do you know Jesus Christ?" After a pause, I replied: "I know he is the Savior of the world." "True," he said, "but do you know that He has saved you?" I answered: "I hope He has died to save me." He only added: "Do you know yourself?" I said: "I do," but I fear they were vain words. The significance of that encounter would soon come to light. In Georgia, as at Wroot and Oxford, I believed that discipline wrapped in self-denial, *not faith in Jesus Christ,* was still the means of obtaining religious ends, and I fought hard and long for a full self-mastery which might lead to conscious union with God.

Interestingly enough, there was yet another side to Spangenberg that held my attention. He had a profound interest in mystical divinity which we frequently discussed. He was also a great admirer of à Kempis and, in fact, acknowledged himself to be a mystic.[5] The Moravians in general, and Spangenberg in particular (although not mystics in the ordinary sense of the word), managed to combine a degree of mystical Quietism with a strong doctrine of assurance. Spangenberg continued to press me with regard to my assurance of salvation. Already impressed by the Moravian display of inner peace I observed while on board ship, I was primed for this encounter. Then, Spangenberg introduced me to several mystical treatises. On February 27 we spent the afternoon discussing mysticism. That evening, after a period of meditation, we discussed the mystics and the conversation turned to my mystical friend, John Gambold. The next morning we again discussed mysticism and that afternoon I began Madame Bourignon's *Light of the World.* Since I already had invested so much, I wanted to believe that mysticism was the key to Spangenberg's assurance. That same day I read Scougal to Mrs. Hawkins, one of our company from on board ship. In March I read *The Life of Tauler.* In April and May, Madame Bourignon *(Treatise on Solid Virtue),*

---

[5]*Journal,* Vol. I, p. 169,

Fleury, Francke, de Renty, and à Kempis, all figured prominently. On March 14 I meditated in my garden, à Kempis in hand. On my first trip to Frederica, à Kempis and Bourignon *(Light of the World)* went with me. On Easter I refreshed my spirit with Fleury. All of these Roman Catholic mystics were encountered or reencountered in fairly rapid succession during my first few months in Georgia.

Following that first meeting with Mr. Spangenberg, while still moored off Tybee Island prior to our arrival at Savannah, I had yet another meeting which I felt was both providential and symbolic. Some of the Indians sent us word of their intention to come down to us. About 1:00 in the afternoon on February 14, Chief Tomochachi, his nephew, Theenouhee (the Crown-prince), his wife, Sinauky, with two more women, and two or three Indian children, came on board. As soon as we came in (wearing our surplices and Oxford hoods, as some of the Indians were in costumes), they all rose and shook us by the hand. Tomochachi (being interpreted by a Mrs. Musgrove) spoke as follows: "I am glad you are come. When I was in England (Oglethorpe had taken him to England two years previously), I desired that some would speak the great Word to me; and my nation then desire to hear it, but now we are all in confusion. Yet I am glad you are come. I will go up and speak to the wise men of our nation; and I hope they will hear. But we would not be made Christians as the Spaniards make Christians: We would be taught, before we are baptized."

I answered, "There is but One, He that sitteth in heaven, who is able to teach man wisdom. Though we are come so far, we know not whether He will please to teach you by us or no. If He teaches you, you will learn wisdom, but we can do nothing." We then withdrew.

Although I was somewhat encouraged by this initial encounter, my ministry among the Indians would, for the most part, be thwarted. Mr. Oglethorpe (who shortly returned to take my brother to Frederica where they joined Mr. Ingham, who had gone ahead, while Mr. Delamotte and myself went on to Savannah) intended that I should build up the colony by ministering only to the English inhabitants. In addition, the Indians were frequently warring among themselves. So my repeated efforts to initiate some kind of mission to the heathen were continually blocked by either Mr. Oglethorpe or the Indians. It seemed that whenever I made plans to approach the Indians, either Oglethorpe would disapprove, or Indian warfare created an almost insurmountable obstacle.

It should be stated that Mr. Oglethorpe was not without some cause. Upon my arrival at Savannah I soon found that the colonists needed just as much attention as any heathen. Although my predecessor, Mr. Quincy, had been with them some three years, there was little or no religious discipline even among the most serious-minded. As Mr. Quincy had not yet left the house where we were afterward to live, Mr. Delamotte and myself happily took lodging with the Germans. "We now had an opportunity, day by day, of observing their whole behavior. For we were in one room with them from morning to night, unless for a little time I spent in walking. They were always employed, always cheerful themselves, and in good humor with one another; they had put away all anger, and strife, and wrath, and bitterness, and clamour, and evil-speaking; they walked worthy of the vocation wherewith they were called, and adorned the Gospel of our Lord in all things."

I watched closely as they met to consult concerning the affairs of their church. "After several hours spent in conference and prayer, they proceeded to the election and ordination of a bishop. •The great simplicity, as well as solemnity, of the whole, almost made me forget the 1700 years between, and imagine myself in one of those assemblies where form and state were not; but Paul the tentmaker, or Peter the fisherman, presided, yet, with the demonstration of the spirit and of power."

I recall a particular conversation with their bishop, Mr. Nitschmann (a simple, straightforward gentleman of about sixty, who had accompanied his flock on the crossing), concerning one who was seriously ill. I shall never forget his reply as he smiled and said: "He will soon be well; he is ready for the Bridegroom."[6] "Oh death, where *is* thy sting? O grave, where *is* thy victory?" I would to God I had then understood the words following that verse, for surely, "the strength of sin *is* the law."

Both Mr. Spangenberg and Mr. Nitschmann soon left Georgia. One went to Pennsylvania and the other back to Germany. I determined to settle into some kind of routine. My days were properly occupied. As a rule I got up at 5:00, sometimes at 4:00. I frequently took part in morning prayers with the Germans and afterward read the Anglican Office of Morning Prayer myself in the courthouse. I then conversed with one or another about religion, frequently during walks. I usually breakfasted with the Germans, had further pastoral talks, or read. I remember being fascinated by a book on anatomy which I read with Dr. Reinier, a physician. Most of my reading, however, was devotional. The remainder of the afternoon was spent either working in the garden or praying with Mr. Delamotte. After tea I read and took evening prayers, with an exposition of Scripture for the congregation. I then went to the Germans and, if in time, took part in their singing-meeting. Otherwise I meditated on my own. After evening prayer I went to bed at 10:00.

While in Georgia fasting became the rule. I took only such nourishment as was absolutely necessary. Reminiscent of Charterhouse, Mr. Delamotte and myself found that we could live for several days on only one kind of food with excellent results. We drank no wine and frequently ate no meat. Like the mystics, I continued my ascetical life in other ways as well. We slept in the parsonage upon the bare board floor, rather than in beds. We chose to eat the simplest dishes, though we could have had the best food from the storehouse. Once when the Germans wanted to give us something better, we declined it, believing that they had already given us food enough of another sort.

On March 7, I preached my first sermon in Savannah entitled, *On Love*. I began with the warning that "some, having no root of humility, or self-denial, when persecution ariseth because of the word, will, rather than suffer for it, fall away."[7] The essence of Christianity presented here, however, was not faith in Christ, but humility and self-denial. I then believed that too much care for the world, not the absence of faith, prevented one from going on to perfection. Little wonder that I had to admit that I, too, was vulnerable to temptation and confessed "an evil heart of unbelief." I still believed that persecution was the fire that tested true faith. Little did I realize that that persecution was soon to be upon me.

Soon afterward I received word from Mr. Ingham concerning Charles. Charles was proving inadequate as a secretary and disastrous as a priest at Frederica. Taking his commission seriously, he sought diligently to hold the insensitive, if not licentious, colonists accountable for their sins. When I first visited him, I found him dangerously sick with a fever, huddled in a corner of his hut, without so much as a board for a bed. He had taken an oath to starve rather than ask for food. To make matters worse, those against Charles had convinced Mr. Oglethorpe (though only for a while, as he and my brother were later reconciled) that he was a fool. As if that were not enough, two designing women then confessed to Charles that they had had adulterous relations with Mr. Oglethorpe, and Charles knew no better than to take them seriously.

Somewhat confused as to what matter of course I should take, I decided to replace my brother at Frederica while he went to Savannah. Thorougly disillusioned, Charles returned to England in July, with dispatches from Mr. Oglethorpe for the Board of Trade.

I was soon to find that my efforts at Frederica were not much better received than those of Charles. One of the women who had deceived Charles actually tried to shoot me for telling the truth plainly. Nonetheless, I lingered on. After all, I had been preaching "the reasonableness of those precepts of self-denial, daily suffering, and renouncing the world, which are so peculiar to Christianity, and which are *the only foundation* whereon the other virtues,

---

[7]*Works*, Vol. VII, p. 493.

recommended in the New Testament, can be practiced or attained."[8] Had I not exhorted those who would hear to hate their own lives and to suffer?[9] If one would take any step at all toward the countenance of God, "to dislike your present self must be the first."[10] Furthermore, "There is a way to rescue ourselves, in great measure, from the ill consequences of our captivity; and our Saviour has taught us that way. *It is by suffering.*"[11] One must suffer to "get above our corruption at present, and enjoy the Holy Spirit."[12]

Expecting to gain some entry with the Indians, I returned to Savannah weeks later. Although this was not to be, I followed the example of Mr. de Renty and managed to consider a matter which we found most useful to the little flock at Savannah. We agreed: 1. "To advise the more serious among them to form themselves into a sort of little society, and to meet once or twice a week, in order to reprove, instruct, and exhort one another." 2. "To select out of these a small number for a more intimate union with each other, which might be forwarded, partly by our conversing singly with each other, and partly by inviting them all together to our house; and this accordingly, we determined to do every Sunday in the afternoon."[13]

I determined also to become a teacher. I established a school where I catechized the children, both in church and in private. In the evening I taught the more gifted students and some even seemed to profit, but my own religious state of mind remained much the same. I was still convinced that I was not yet a son of God. Even the thunder and lightning (no small thing in Georgia) frightened me terribly. My absolute rule of religion, so instilled in me by the mystics, was not holding up under the test of practical experience.

---

[8]*Works*, Vol. VII, p. 517

[9]Ibid., p. 517

[10]Ibid., pp. 517f.

[11]Ibid., p. 518.

[12]Ibid., p. 518.

[13]*Works*, Vol. I, p. 310. Wesley later cites this as an important step in the development of his thought and practice on societies. *Works*, Vol. VIII, pp. 138-168.

That same month (May, 1736), I determined to join the Herrnhuters. After the departure of Mr. Spangenberg and Mr. Nitschmann, Johann Töltschig was left in charge. We talked at length about ground for my admission. For some days I had been translating their hymns for use among the English-speaking colonists. I was again impressed by their mystical cast. Unfortunately, this was not enough. I still did not have the faith that brings peace with God. I was denied membership. True, there were ecclesiastical differences as well, but on the whole, my heart was not right. I remember writing in my *Journal* following a thunderstorm: "This voice of God, too, told me I was not fit to die; since I was afraid, rather than desirous of it. Oh, when shall I wish to be dissolved and to be with Christ? When I love him with all my heart."[14] Although Töltschig invited me to share in their sacrament, I declined.

In a word, I was despondent. The old enemy seemed always near. I sought on a number of occasions to take him head on. I remember writing a poem, "On Death," and introduced it to my congregation.[15] Yet, whenever one of my parishioners would die, I was deeply affected. During a particularly painful episode later, I was so possessed with thoughts of death that I actually wrote my will.[16] I came to believe that shortness of life imperiled the process of sanctification.[17]

So, during the summer I turned once again to the mystics. I studied carefully both Law and Scougal, but even more important, I began to pin my faith on Macarius and Ephraem Syrus. Macarius emphasized a highly individualistic Christian ideal. Like many of the mystics, he taught one to expect the fulfillment "of being born from on high" and that this would lead to a measure of Christian perfection. Especially significant at this point, however, was the fact that he also added a strong doctrine of *progress* in the Christian life. In September, Macarius extended my

---

[14]*Works*, Vol. I, p. 37.
[15]*Journal*, Vol. I, p. 272.
[16]*Journal*, Vol. I, p. 337. The crisis here was the day of Sophy's marriage (see on p. 141).
[17]*Letters*, Vol. I, p. 120.

rigid, static concept of perfection (*disciplined* love) to include a more dynamic progressive concept of perfection (*aspiring* love).

At the same time I was plagued by backsliding. I was especially troubled by those parishioners, who, in my presence and under my leadership, responded to my discipline, but, in my absence their conviction quickly wore off and they soon fell away. I began to see how the mysticism of Macarius and Ephraem would stand in the gap. Here the emphasis was upon growth and perseverance. I studied Ephraem on September 19, in preparing for the pulpit. On September 23, I wrote in my *Journal* on the mystics. On September 24, after morning prayers and coffee, I spent six hours with the mystics. On September 25 the mystics absorbed most of the morning. And, on September 27, my day's study again began with the mystics. In my *Diary*, Ephraem then reappears on October 16, 17, 19, and 20, and on November 1, 2, 3, and 22. As I began to understand his concept of perfection as a continuous process, I felt my spirit somewhat revive. Unfortunately, I was building upon a foundation which had not yet been laid. Such a noble superstructure needed to be founded upon a rock. So, matters got worse.

My frustration as a missionary and pastor climaxed at Frederica. "Being ignorant of the righteousness of Christ, which, by a living faith in him, bringeth salvation 'to everyone that believeth,' I sought to establish my own righteousness; and so labored in the fire all of my days."[18] My own works-righteousness (both external and internal) was revealing its lack of power to transform. Frederica would teach me a painful lesson. The mystic "form of godliness" (remember I carried both à Kempis and Bourignon's *Light of the World* with me on my first visit to Frederica) revealed its impotency clearly there. I grew to *expect* my parishioners to backslide. On October 17, for example, I wrote in my *Diary* that I reached Frederica at half past three in the afternoon. I then noted despairingly that I "met Mark Hird, 'in trouble, alas! in trouble. O, my

[18]*Journal*, Vol. I, p. 470.

Frederica!'"[19] Again after a later visit to Frederica I wrote: "Most of those we met with were, as we expected, cold and heartless. I could not find one who had retained his first love."[20] My attitudes began to change. On November 22, 1736, I laid Ephraem Syrus, my constant companion for nearly three months, aside for more than a decade. His rule and law needed life and root.

The following day I wrote to my brother Samuel: "I think the rock which I had the nearest made shipwreck of the faith was the writings of the mystics: under which term I comprehend all, and only those, who slight any of the means of grace."[21] Although this was far from a final break with mysticism, one corner had been turned. Although my objection to mysticism had deepened from my earlier concern for its "strictness," to a concern for its "slighting the means of grace," a much deeper problem had not yet surfaced, and would not surface for some eighteen months. That is the story of Aldersgate.

At this point I want to drop back and give you firsthand the account of the much publicized (if not completely distorted) romance with Sophy Hopkey, the niece of the wife of Mr. Causton, chief magistrate of Savannah.

I met Miss Sophy March 13, 1736. She was young (not yet nineteen, while I was nearly thirty-three), impressionable, and seemingly serious about her religious instruction. I readily accepted her as one of my students.

By October things had progressed to the place where I began to consider a proposal of marriage. We discussed the possibility on a number of occasions during that month and the months following. I was certain that I loved her though I still feared loving women more than God and confessed this in my *Diary*. I sought the counsel of Mr. Delamotte and Mr. Ingham, the priests who had made the journey with us the previous year. They questioned her sincerity.

I then sought the advice of my Moravian friends who suggested that I retire to the woods in order to pray, which

---

[19]Ibid., p. 282.
[20]Ibid., p. 310.
[21]*Letters*, Vol. I, p. 207.

I did for more than a week. Upon my return, I informed Miss Sophy that if I did marry, I would not do so until I had been among the Indians, at least for a while. Obviously hurt, she determined not to come to my house any more, but quickly invited me to hers. When I reminded her how I disliked a crowd, she affectionately replied: "We needn't be in it."

So, I struggled on, as I was prone to do even about the most trivial matters, for nearly a month. These were difficult days.

Then, on March 9, I was informed of her engagement to a Mr. Williamson, a dull, irreligious man, whom Sophy said she would marry, if I had no objection. Obviously trying to force my hand, what she meant was, "I will marry him, if you will not marry me."

This was my dilemma. I feared for Sophy's soul if I did not marry her, yet I could not take fire into my bosom and not be burned. Two days later she married Mr. Williamson (a narrow escape) and within weeks had lost nearly all the grace she had. On July 5 I wrote her a mild and friendly letter objecting to her neglecting the worship, the fast, and the communion.

On August 7 I was forced by conscience to refuse her communion since she would not inform the curate regarding her intentions to commune (a rule of the church) and she further refused to confess her sins openly. A lawsuit (recorded by her uncle) resulted, which dragged on to no conclusion for better than four months. On December 22, rather than prolong the matter still further, I took a rather hasty (though openly published) leave of America, as some would have made an attempt (however feeble) to prevent it.

To summarize, therefore, I went to Georgia expecting to find a spiritual climate conducive to yet another mystical experiment. My disappointment, rather than leading me to alter my methods, caused me to redouble my efforts in an almost frantic attempt to achieve a constant awareness of God. Out of my subsequent frustration I unleased an attack on my mystic masters (remember the letter to

Samuel), thinking them to be the source of my failure as a pastor and missionary. Although my general diagnosis was correct, I still failed to understand the true nature of my lack of power. The disease went far deeper than I had imagined. I still had no faith, no peace, and no assurance. My journey home would prove this conclusively. I had learned precious little from my "trial by fire." I left America a dejected man.

The Analysis, Part II

How ought you then never to desist from seeking after God? For the damage which you sustained by your neglect is exceeding great tho' you may even seem to be established in the mystery of grace.   Macarius

John Wesley, during the years 1725-1737, led a futile search for an assurance, an awareness of God's presence, that asceticism (remember that this was the one common denominator prevalent in all the variant influences of his youth) could not produce.

In the first theological analysis we attempted to establish that Platonic ends do not mix with Aristotelian means.[1] Asceticism, for a time Wesley's all-in-all (1725-1727), even coupled with the solitude of Wroot (1727-1729), the outward works of the Holy Club (1730-1732), and the interior, but more subtle works of Law (1732-1735), did not produce for Wesley that elusive assurance of salvation. All this became painfully clear in Georgia (1735-1737). He left there a dejected man, still lacking the witness of the Spirit that would deliver him from his fear of death. This is the almost pathetic pilgrimage that needs to be described here.

Although his evangelical conversion at Aldersgate was, by the time he left Georgia, less than six months away, Wesley still did not understand faith as "the assurance of things hoped for, the conviction of things not seen." His own abbreviated analysis for the period reads: 1725-1729—no foundation of repentance; 1729-1734—a little repentance but no faith in the

---

[1]Wesley would later build his own case against outward works (including asceticism) producing inward holiness in an interesting letter to John Smith. *Letters*, Vol. II, pp. 68ff.

blood of the covenant; 1734-1738—a little faith but still no fruit.[2]

Before we begin our own analysis in greater detail, perhaps a brief word about sources would be appropriate. Although the *Journal* does not begin until his departure for Georgia, his *Diary* begins ten years earlier, in April, 1725. Consequently, at several points we can and should confirm or document our conclusions with the *Diary* itself. The story now becomes strikingly personal.

Wesley's *Diary* is brutally honest. In fact, it tends toward self-condemnation if not properly understood. Take the romance with Sophy Hopkey, for example. She appears to be the victim of a remarkably insensitive man, but if we had equal insight into Miss Sophy, the truth would probably lie somewhere in between.[3]

In addition to the *Diary*, two secondary sources are particularly helpful for the student of Wesley's life during this period.[4] First, V. H. H. Green's *The Young Mr. Wesley*, reveals a great deal of information about Wesley's years at Oxford. He takes good advantage of his access to the unpublished *Diaries* (1725-1735), as well as the archives at Oxford relevant for such a study. Then, Martin Schmidt's *John Wesley, A Theological Biography*, Vol. I, draws heavily upon the Herrnhut archives available to him for the study of the Moravian influence, especially in Georgia.

For the mystical influence I draw upon my own dissertation, "The influence of the Roman Catholic Mystics on John Wesley," presented to the University of Bristol in partial fulfillment of the requirement for the Doctor of Philosophy Degree in theology. Although the material here is by no means a review

---

[2] *Letters*, Vol. II, p. 264.

[3] Even the "champion" of Victorian morality, William Gladstone, in his recently published *Diaries* (Oxford: University Press) writes that he was so guilt stricken over what he regarded as shameful sexual thoughts, that he frequently went home after his "rescue" meetings with the prostitutes and whipped himself (it was public knowledge that he was committed to saving prostitutes from their sins). *Time* magazine, 3/24/75.

[4] There are numerous other books (see Bibliography, Part II) which are perhaps equally helpful, but these have been selected as representative works published within the last twenty years.

of that work, some of the conclusions are a result of that study.[5]

Just as the chapter headings suggest, Wesley's early ministry contains four major phases, all focusing upon *aceticism*. As a young Oxford tutor (1725-1727) this spells itself out through self-denial. As a curate at Wroot (1727-1729), an emphasis upon solitude sets the stage. Under the influence of the Holy Club, works of charity (1730-1732), and the interior life as exemplified by William Law and the mystics (1732-1735), provide the key. The journey to Georgia then confirmed the futility of Wesley's ascetical exercises to produce faith either in himself or in others and left him utterly confused.

As we turn to the analysis, several persons figure prominently in each of the successive stages. Let us take Mr. Wesley back through these past twelve years and examine individually the effects of these important influences.

During Wesley's first two years as an Oxford tutor he was a man obsessed (to use the description from chapter 7) by the notion of moral imperfection and was continually dissatisfied with his efforts in the pursuit of holiness.[6] Consequently it was during this period of Wesley's life (1725-1727) that the more ascetical side of his character gained ascendency. Taylor and à Kempis had convinced him that "faith is either in dead earnest or just dead." William Law (who completes the celebrated triumvirate referred to in Wesley's *A Plain Account of Christian Perfection*) would reinforce their emphasis upon "simplicity of intention and purity of affection." Furthermore, Wesley's previously casual acquaintance with the mystics would now be accentuated by his intention to give his *all* to God.[7]

Neither Taylor nor à Kempis, nor even his spiritual director for the time, Sally Kirkham, provide the theological key for this period, however. Taylor and à Kempis had already made their

---

[5]Additional works are listed in the Bibliography at the end of this chapter, but again, these have been singled out for the degree of competence they display for the period now under consideration.

[6]In his *Diary* for December 1, 1725, January 29 and March 12, 1726, Wesley condemns himself for "unclean thoughts," etc. Cf., Green, *The Young Mr. Wesley,* pp. 81-83.

[7]Unfortunately, the *Diary* is missing from February, 1727 to May, 1729. If we had that diary there would no doubt be much more data, but it is significant that Fénelon appears close to where the *Diary* ends and Monsieur de Renty appears soon after the *Diary* begins again.

mark (though it was a lasting one and needs to be taken seriously throughout). Sally Kirkham's theological influence (though she contributes significantly to the biographical sections due to her influence on Wesley's personal and spiritual life) was, for the most part, through the books that she recommended and was, therefore, indirect. Most of the theology that accrues during this period must be traced to other sources *epitomized* by William Law and François Fénelon.

Although Law's influence was not nearly so prominent here as it was during his mystical years (when both the Wesleys were visiting him personally), much of Wesley's theological perspective can be identified in Law's *Christian Perfection*.[8] Wesley writes: "A year or two after (meeting with Taylor and à Kempis), Mr. Law's 'Christian Perfection' and 'Serious Call' were put into my hands. These convinced me, more than ever, of the absolute impossibility of being half a Christian; I determined, through His grace (the absolute necessity of which I was deeply sensible of) to be all-devoted to God, to give him all my soul, my body, and my substance." Although Law's *Serious Call* was actually not encountered until Wesley was at Wroot, his *Christian Perfection* added integrity to Wesley's ascetical practices and enabled him to articulate theologically his various religious exercises.

The second influence which should be mentioned can be demonstrated by François Fénelon. Wesley knew at least some of Fénelon's works by the winter of 1726/1727. By February, 1727, we find him transcribing Fénelon's *Discourse on Simplicity* for Varanese. Wesley read a great deal of Fénelon and a surprising number of his books still can be found in John's personal library.[9] Wesley was especially fond of Fénelon's concept of "simplicity," and refers to it on numerous

---

[8]Wesley tells us that he first read Law after eight years at Oxford. Since the *Diary* is missing, however, the exact date is unknown. The spring of 1727 is a fairly good guess, but it could be a little later.

[9]The following works appear in the catalogue to Wesley's personal library under Fénelon: *Letters* (1718), *Dialogues sur L'Eloquence* (1718), *Oeuvres Philosophiques ou Demonstration de L'Existence de Dieu* (1721), *Histoire de la Vie et des Fourages* (1729, trans. 1738), *Extract from a Discourse on Humility* (1758), and *A Discourse Upon Christian Perfection* (1759). Wesley also read Fénelon's *Telemachus* (*Journal*, January 7, 1760).

occasions.[10] Simplicity for Wesley, as with Fénelon, came to mean "that grace which frees the soul from all unnecessary reflections upon itself."[11] One's love toward God must be simple and pure. Fénelon came to represent "true religion" for Wesley, defined as "the love of God and man filling the heart and governing the life."[12] Although most of the mystics read during these years (and there were many) were studied more for their ascetical practices, their theological influence was beginning to surface.

Significantly, soon after Fénelon was encountered, Wesley began looking for a place where he could pursue his religious goals without interruption. The next two years (1727-1729) were spent, for the most part, at Wroot.

In chapter 8 we noted that Wesley had considerable theological insight into his own situation during these years. The analysis here will serve as a brief review with a few additional comments concerning the influence of William Law and the mystic, Monsieur de Renty.

At the outset, Wesley's experiment with solitude served one immediate purpose. The route to faith upon purely rational grounds would soon lose its appeal. His fear of death (recently aroused by the death of his friend, Robin Griffith) would not give way to reason. This did not mean, however, that he would now opt for Platonic means to accommodate Platonic ends. The appeal of mystical union with God delayed this still further. Wesley, at this point, sought faith as a blind obedience to God, dominated by ascetical exercises (a more subtle kind of *interior* works), exalting solitude. This can be demonstrated by Law's second treatise, *A Serious Call to a Devout and Holy Life,* and even more importantly, by another mystic, the Marquis de Renty.

Wesley's father, and more especially his mother, figure prominently in his personal and spiritual life, but as with Sally Kirkham, their theological influence was more through the books they recommended. Although it is open to question as to who recommended what to whom, much of their reading

[10]Cf., *Letters,* Vol. V, p. 193 and Vol. VI, pp. 8,128,281.
[11]*Letters,* Vol. VI, p. 128.
[12]*Works,* Vol. VII, p. 162, sermon, *On Former Times.*

during this period focused upon Law and de Renty.

Law's *A Serious Call* represents a transitory stage between a highly ethical period and a highly mystical one beginning in 1732. Although scholars differ as to the degree of mysticism in this second treatise, the fact remains that *A Serious Call* heightened Wesley's sensitivity to the influence of de Renty.[13]

In the extract of de Renty's *Life*, published by Wesley in 1741 and included in the first edition of his *Works*, we find: "For the things done in community, I often cannot rest there: I perform indeed the exterior for the keeping of order; but follow always my interior, because when a man hath God, there is no need to search for him elsewhere."[14] He continues: "For the interior, therefore, I found this attractive; and for the exterior, I see the divine will, which I follow, with the discernment of his spirit, in all simplicity; and so I possess by his grace, in all things, silence of spirit, a profound reverence, and solid peace. I communicate almost every day, perceiving myself strongly drawn thereto. I continually give up myself to God through Jesus Christ, . . . I enter into a heat and into a fire, and even to my finger ends, feel that all within me speaks for its God, and stretched itself forth in length and breadth in his immensity, that it may there dissolve and there lose itself, to glorify him."[15]

Although there was much in de Renty that Wesley would continue to appreciate, even long after Aldersgate, the attraction here to solitude (Wesley's interpretation of the "interior") would, like reason before it, soon lose its appeal. It simply did not produce the assurance that would deliver him from his fear of death. Faith was still an illusion. Consequently, when his father's friend, Dr. Hoole, insisted that there was no solitary religion, Wesley (at the direction of Dr. Morley recalling all

---

[13]Bishop Cannon sees no apparent mystical element in the stern but practical view of religion presented in this work. On the other hand, Dunn Wilson (in an unpublished dissertation, Leeds University, 1968, entitled "The Influence of Mysticism on John Wesley") argues that Law's idea of partaking of the mysterious sacrifice of Christ lies at the heart of Christian mysticism (Law's *Works*, Vol. IV, pp. 174-175). Wilson also cites Law's mention of the "transports of devotion" (Law's *Works*, Vol. IV, p. 135).

[14]*Extract*, pp. 5f. Wesley mentions de Renty in two of his sermons in light of his mysticism (*Works*, Vol. VII, p. 44; Vol. VIII, p. 77).

[15]*Extract*, pp. 5f.

Junior Fellows) willingly returned to Oxford where he immediately joined the "little company" organized six months earlier by his brother Charles.

In spite of his disillusionment with mystic solitude, Wesley continued to read de Renty during the years of the Holy Club (1729-1735). For the careful reader, de Renty poses an interesting marriage between the interior and exterior life. Asceticism, for Wesley, would still supply the common ground, but the interior life would no longer be interpreted in terms of solitude, but mystic prayer (a near obsession with him now), and the activities of the Holy Club (especially between 1730-1732) would provide a proper stage for the exterior life through works of charity.

Again de Renty simply epitomizes the best of those read at this time, but William Morgan's social sensitivity must have reminded Wesley of de Renty. Several similarities can be noted between de Renty and Wesley with reference to this love manifesting itself in works of charity. Both attended the needs of the poor.[16] De Renty frequently had the poor in to dine, as did Wesley at the Foundery.[17] Both lived economically in order to give to the poor. Both visited the sick and took a considerable interest in the medical art. Both spent much time ministering to the imprisoned: de Renty assisted the English prisoners captured during Buckingham's expedition to Rochelle and Wesley ministered to the French prisoners captured during the Seven Years' War. De Renty undoubtedly interested Wesley in the *practical effects* of the mystical life with God which combined an "internal evi-

---

[16]*Extract,* p. 10. "During the war at Paris, he went himself to buy bread for the poor, and carried through the streets as much as his strength would permit. . . ." Remember that de Renty was in frequent communication with Vincent de Paul. De Renty not only cooperated with Vincent in works of charity, but on occasion directed the saint's special attention to them. De Renty, "a worthy co-labourer" animated with the same spirit, was always sensitive to those in need and was actually the one who brought to de Paul's attention the relief of the refugee nobility of Lorraine and the relief of the Catholic *and* Protestant refugees from England (those loyal to Charles I). Cf., *The Life of the Baron de Renty or, Perfection in the World Exemplified* (London: Burns and Oates, 1873), pp. 197ff.

[17]Wesley refers to this practice at the Foundery as "a comfortable earnest of our eating bread together in our Father's Kingdom."

dence firm and unshaken" with an external life of constant service.[18]

We will discuss de Renty's influence later (especially with regard to his ideas on religious societies), but for now suffice it to say that Wesley was vulnerable to the more speculative mysticism of William Law. Between 1732-1735 Law, a recent convert to the German mysticism of Tauler and Boehme, would serve as Wesley's spiritual director. In chapter 9 we see that Law, the "contemplative man," put Wesley on an inner penance. Ironically, Law nullified the more positive influence of de Renty by seeking to discourage Wesley's works of charity altogether.

Although Wesley continued these works at an abbreviated pace, William Morgan was dead. The enemy was back at full strength, and Wesley pursued his own righteousness under another name, "dragging on heavily" until he left for America.

Aldersgate at this point was still three years off. During the past ten years this is what he had learned: reason alone would not produce faith; mystic solitude would not produce faith; works of charity (the exterior life) would not produce faith; inner penance (the "interior life" reinforced by his father's dying words concerning the inward witness) would not produce faith. All of these, even wrapped in asceticism, produced nothing. What was left? Before that story is to be told, Wesley journeys to Georgia (1735-1737).

Wesley must have been thinking: "Surely my religious endeavors count for something." After all, was he not "a brand plucked from the burning"? Perhaps the right opportunity had not yet presented itself. Georgia could well have been that opportunity. He rushed in! Four days after his appointment was approved, his journey began. He reveals the extent of his determination by looking the enemy full in the teeth. There was a good possibility that such an adventure would cost him his life. If the sea did not surrender him to the murderer, then

---

[18]From Wesley's *Extract*, p. 36, we read: "The grand exercises of M. de Renty was, to apply and unite himself to our Saviour, and from that union, an example, to derive all his virtues and good works. To mold himself after him was his general course, both in his inward tempers and outward behaviours."

the Indians would. If need be, the "brand plucked" would return to the fire in order to fulfill its greatness.

We have seen that Wesley, although committed to mysticism intellectually, lacked some of the basic mystical characteristics. Indeed, one is forced to ask at times whether he ever really understood the mystics. For example, Wesley had studied Fenelon enthusiastically, but his love for God was far from "disinterested." Furthermore, Wesley was anything but indifferent to salvation and the one thing he wanted most the mystics could not give—assurance. Yet Wesley's understanding of the goal of religion was essentially mystical. His negative view of the world, his misconception of faith, and his determination to achieve a conscious relationship with God, were all mystical ideas. Wesley, at this point, seems to have inherited many of the mystics' "vices," but few of their virtues. His experience in Georgia, however, began to put things more in perspective.

As the *Simmonds* leaves England, the mystic Gregory Lopez is pictured as a possible model for Wesley's extended pilgrimage. Although Wesley briefly describes Lopez's influence in chapter 10, there are still other influences that need to be mentioned. Spangenberg, Macarius, Ephraem Syrus, and the November, 1736, letter to his brother Samuel, have been selected as representative.

Spangenberg (and later Peter Bohler) exhibited a kind of synthesis between mystical piety on the one hand and the theology of the continental reformers on the other.[19] Spangenberg's self-styled "mysticism" must have appealed to Wesley. He recommended a completely passive attitude extremely close to the mystical writers.[20] The internal witness of the Spirit, however, was to be appropriated through faith in Jesus Christ. There was no dark night. This was Wesley's first real opportunity to gain insight into the impasse relative to works and faith (between the Aristotelian means and the Platonic ends) but he was "too learned and too wise." Again he might have responded by faith in the evangelical sense, but his bouts with

---

[19]This will be demonstrated at some length in Part III.

[20]The Moravians dotted all the "i's" in Lutheran theology and consequently taught that there could be no salvation by any action or work.

the enemy on board ship had done him little good. He seized upon Spangenberg's mystical Quietism, but then substituted his own "inner" works-righteousness for the Moravian faith in Christ. As we anticipate the reversal of that order a few years later, we are encouraged, but for the time being, Georgia was just another mystical experiment.[21]

Georgia was not a total loss, however. Several of the mystics would teach Wesley much about his doctrine of perfection (especially as it related to perseverance). This would carry through to the Revival even after the "final" break with mysticism was made. Both Macarius and Ephraem Syrus, for example, provided him with significant insight into the concept of *dynamic*, or ongoing, perfection.

Macarius' doctrine of progress in the Christian life (closely linked with his insistence on moral purification) hinged on the efficacy of the experiences of struggle against sin, and sought to make strong spiritual warriors out of mere struggling Christians.[22] A significant spinoff from this relates to the influence of Macarius regarding the discipline of perseverance. Macarius taught that after receiving the Holy Spirit one needed to improve the gift imparted in order to persevere.[23] Macarius speaks of the degrees or stages of perfection. He writes that "sometimes the love flames out and kindles with greater strength; but at other times more slow and gentle."[24] Eventually, however, the humble soul is received into the "mystical fellowship in the fullness of grace."[25] This filling of the Holy Spirit implies an entire redemption from sin, but perfection is gradual: "there are heights which the soul does not reach all at once; but through many labors and conflicts,

[21]By February, 1738, Wesley would be ready to listen to the other side of the Moravian synthesis, but it would take someone like Bohler, who understood Wesley's mystical mind, to lead him from it.

[22]Macarius was born in Egypt in A.D. 301. He became well-acquainted with the Scriptures at an early age, and his seriousness earned him the title of "the young old man" by the time he was thirty. Following his banishment to an island, he practiced the exercise of religious solitude for the next sixty years, until his death in A.D. 391.

[23]Most of the references here to Macarius are taken from Wesley's *Extract* in the *Christian Library,* entitled: *Primitive Morality: or the Spiritual Homilies of St. Macarius the Egyptian,* Vol. I.

[24]Wesley, *Christian Library,* Vol. I, p. 102.

[25]Ibid., p. 106.

with variety of trials and temptations, it receives spiritual growth and improvement."[26] Although Wesley on occasion spoke of "instantaneous sanctification" (that is, one grows gradually to the *moment* of full delivery), he certainly appreciated Macarius' emphasis on continual growth. Macarius taught that no matter how high the state of perfection, one could always grow in grace.[27] In short, it was foolish to boast that one has no sin (even if sinless), since one must grow to persevere.

Macarius' caution against backsliding (remember Wesley was also reading Macarius before the crisis at Frederica) also greatly appealed to Wesley. Although he strongly emphasized the grace of God, this grace was clearly not irresistible. Macarius answers the questions as to whether one can fall from grace in this manner. "If he (the Christian) grows careless, he certainly falls. For his enemies are never idle, or backward in the war. How ought you then never to desist from seeking after God? For the damage which you sustained by your neglect is exceeding great tho' you may even seem to be established in the mystery of grace."[28] What better treatise could Wesley use to remedy the backsliding in Georgia?

As we noted in chapter 10, Macarius was reinforced along these same lines by Ephraem Syrus. Wesley read Ephraem's *A Serious Exhortation to Repentance and Sorrow for Sin, and a Strict and Mortified Life* (written about the middle of the fourth century and translated into English in 1731) to Sophy and to several of his parishioners with the intention of reawakening their relish for spiritual things.[29] Ephraem's logic can best be seen in several characteristics of his mystical theology. This theology and his own particular mode of life is described in his comments on Elijah were he gives three reasons why God commanded Elijah to flee, to seek the cave, and to hide himself in a valley known by no one. First, he must suffer in order to

---

[26]Ibid., p. 107.

[27]Ibid., pp. 112ff.

[28]Ibid., p. 109. Wesley's *Extract* is almost verbatim.

[29]This 1731 edition of Ephraem is discussed in Nichol, *Literary Anecdotes*, i, 472; Mosheim, *Ecclesiastical History*, p. 135; and Mosheim, *History of the Christian Church*, Vol. 2, p. 88.

understand the suffering of others. Second, after the turmoil of the "ambassador's office," he needed the silence of contemplation in the wilderness in order to reevaluate his life relative to the times of prayer and labor. And finally, he must learn the need of prayer and supplication with labor, the need of entreaty with zeal.[30] Ephraem spent a considerable time in the desert of Egypt drinking deep from the cup of self-inflicted suffering. Morris states that it is the prerogative of Christianity to blend the active and contemplative life "and nowhere do they seem more thoroughly blended than in the mind of St. Ephraem."[31] The whole of Ephraem's works anticipates a style of devotional contemplation. His mysticism, however, extends beyond an attraction to suffering and contemplation. Take his *Rhythms*, for example. The word "rhythm" is a word in the Syriac frequently employed to express "a mystical commentary" on the text of Scripture, and Wesley's mention (May 21, 1761) of Ephraem's story about Abraham and Mary is no doubt a reference to an example of this type of commentary. Ephraem also spoke of days past and future as if they were present time. He believed that since one's mystical union with God enabled him to view things as God views them (and for God time is as nothing), he should view the unabidingness of time.[32] Wesley's opinion of Ephraem at this time is expressed in his *Journal* for October 16, 1736: "I read to them (the backsliders of Frederica) out of the exhortations of Ephraem Syrus—the most awakened writer, I think, of all the ancients."[33] Both Ephraem and Macarius continued to have an influence on Wesley long after Aldersgate.[34] For the present, however, Wesley, although no doubt intrigued with many aspects of their mysticism, was most impressed with the "picture of a broken and contrite

---

[30]Ephraem Syrus, *Rhythms of Saint Ephraem the Syrian* or *Select Works of Saint Ephraem the Syrian,* translated out of the original Syriac with notes and indices by J. B. Morris (1847), pp. xiiiff.

[31]Ibid., p. xv.

[32]Ibid., pp. 1f.

[33]*Journal,* Vol. I, p. 284.

[34]The *Minutes* of the first Methodist Conference recommended Ephraem to the assistants. *The Rules of the United Societies* also carry the mark of Ephraem and Macarius (Outler, *John Wesley,* pp. 143ff.). Outler also emphasizes the role of Macarius and Ephraem in the development of Wesley's doctrine of perfection (p. 9n; pp. 250-52). Cf. Wesley's *Address to the Clergy* (1756, in the *Works,* Vol. X, p. 484).

heart" linked with a thoroughly dynamic concept of perfection.[35] It is no coincidence that these two desert Fathers should appear just at this time emphasizing this particular point of view. Wesley's absolute rule of religion was breaking down under the "trial by fire." His static approach to Christianity was not standing the test of practical experience. His parishioners, in his presence and under his leadership, responded to his rigid discipline, but, in his absence the conviction soon wore off and they fell away. The mysticism of Macarius and Ephraem, therefore, gave him a brief glimmer of hope.

Albert Outler believes that Macarius and Ephraem probably first interested Wesley in perfection (they were certainly known long before Georgia). Ephraem appears in the *Oxford Diary* for 1732 and Wesley surely knew Macarius by this time, if not through William Law (who was strongly influenced by Macarius), then through someone else. At any rate, Macarius and Ephraem were the mystics to whom Wesley now pinned his faith. *Both* are vitally important at this particular time.

Before leaving the Analysis for Part II, a word of clarification needs to be said regarding the important letter to his brother Samuel, dated November 23, 1736, in which Wesley's condemnation of the mystics as the "rock upon which he nearly made shipwreck" should *not* be interpreted as his *final* break with mysticism. He continued to read and study them carefully (although with some declining interest) until his return to England some fourteen months later. The issue here is one of degree. Earlier his only objection had been against their strict ness, but more recently that had been rescinded. Now ne challenges their neglect of the means of grace (especially the German mystics expounded by Law, since the Roman Catholics like de Renty did not have this problem) amidst their inner exercise.[36] A passive dark night was too much for a man duty-bound. Faith in Christ, however, was still misunderstood. Although he had begun to move in the right direction, the crisis and victory was yet to come. That is the story of Part III.

---

[35] *Journal,* Vol. III, p. 284.

[36] By means of grace, Wesley means particularly the Lord's Supper. Since the Roman Catholic mystics continued to hold a high regard for these means, this would explain the relative consistency of their continued influence later on.

Bibliography, Part II[1]

Primary Sources

John Wesley, *Journal,* Curnock, ed.

———, *Letters,* Telford, ed.

———, *The Works of the Rev. John Wesley, M.A.* (Printed by William Pine, Bristol, 1771-74), 32 vols.

———, *The Works of John Wesley, A.M.,* 3rd ed., with last corrections of the author; Thomas Jackson, ed. (1829-31); (see also *Works* [Grand Rapids, Mich., 1958-59], a reprint of the Jackson ed.). 14 vols.

———, *A Concise Ecclesiastical History,* 4 vols.

———, *A Concise History of England,* 4 vols.

———, *A Collection of Forms of Prayer for Every Day in the Week.* London (1733).

Green, Richard, *Bibliography.*

Union Catalogue of Publications.

Secondary Sources

Abbey, C. J., *The English Church and Its Bishops.*

———, and Overton, J. H., *The English Church in the Eighteenth Century.*

Baker, E. W., *Herald of the Evangelical Revival.* London (1948). This is an interesting study of William Law.

Baker, Frank, *Charles Wesley.*

———, "Study of Wesley's Readings," LQHR.

———, "Wesley's Puritan Ancestry," LQHR.

Baxter, Richard, *The Practical Works.* London (1830). (Bibliography by A. G. Matthews, Oxford, 1932).

Cannon, William R., *The Theology of John Wesley.* New York/Nashville (1946).

Castaniza, Juan de, *The Spiritual Combat.*

Coke, Thomas and Moore, H., *Life.*

Coulter, E. Merton, and Saye, Albert B., *A List of the Early Settlers in Georgia.* Athens, Ga. (1949).

Cyprian, *The Writings of Cyprian* in the *Ante-Nicene Christian Library.* Edinburgh (1868).

---

[1]Those works that appear here in abbreviated form are given in full in the Bibliography, Part I.

Edwards, M. L., *Family Circle.*

———, *Sons to Samuel.*

———, *The Astonishing Youth.*

Fénelon, François de Salignac de La Mothe, *Dissertation on Pure Love.* London (1735).

———, *The Maxims of the Saints, Explained Concerning the Interior Life* (1698).

———, *Pastoral Letter Concerning the Love of God,* Robert Nelson, ed. (1715).

———, *On Simplicity.*

Fries, A. L., *The Moravians in Georgia.* Raleigh, N. C. (1905).

Francke, August Hermann, *Pietas Hauensis; or, An Abstract of the Marvellous Footsteps of Divine Providence . . . to Which Is Added a Short History of Pietism,* 2nd ed. (1707).

———, *Nicodemus: Or a Treatise Against the Fear of Man, Done Into English* by A. W. Boehme, Ed. (1731).

Godley, A. D., *Oxford in the Eighteenth Century* (1908).

Green, Brazier, *John Wesley and William Law.* London (1945).

Green, Richard, *John Wesley.*

Green, V. H. H., *The Young Mr. Wesley.*

———, *John Wesley.*

Harmon, Rebecca, *Susanna, Mother of the Wesleys.*

Jackson, Thomas, *Life of Charles Wesley.*

Kempis, Thomas à, *The Christian Pattern.*

Law, William, *Works.*

Léger, A., *La Jeunesse de Wesley.*

Monk, R. C., *John Wesley: His Puritan Heritage.*

Moore, Henry, *Life.*

Newton, John A., *Methodism and the Puritans.*

———, *Susanna and the Puritan Tradition.*

Orcibal, Jean, "Les Spirituels francois et espagnols chez John Wesley et ses contemporains," in *Revue de l'Histoire des Religions,* Vol. 139 (1951), pp. 50-109.

Overton, J. H., *John Wesley.*

———, *William Law, Nonjurer and Mystic.* London (1927-30), 2 vols.

———, *The Nonjurers.* London (1902).

Rupp, E. Gordon, *Making of the Protestant Tradition*.

Saint-Jure, John Baptist de, *The Holy Life of Monsieur de Renty*. Translated by E. S. Gent. London (1657).

Schmidt, Martin, *John Wesley*, Vol. I.

Scougal, Henry, *The Life of God in the Soul of Man*.

Simon, J. S., *John Wesley and the Religious Societies*. London (1921).

Southey, Robert, *Life*. 2 vols.

Stevenson, George, *Memorials of the Wesley Family*.

Syrus, Ephraem, *Rhythms of Saint Ephraem the Syrian*. Translated by J. B. Morris (1847).

_____, *Devotional Tracts Concerning the Presence of God and Other Religious Subjects*. London (1724).

_____, *On Repentance*.

Taylor, Jeremy, *Works*.

Telford, John, *Life*

Theologia Germanica, Pfeiffer ed. London (1907).

Tuttle, Robert G., Jr., "Influence of the Roman Catholic Mystics on Wesley."

Tyerman, Luke, *Life of Samuel Wesley*.

_____, *Life of John Wesley*.

_____, *The Oxford Methodists*. New York (1873).

_____, *The Life of the Rev. George Whitefield*. London (1890).

Vulliamy, C. E., *John Wesley*.

Wakefield, Gordon S., *Puritan Devotion*.

Wesley, Charles, *Journal*. Telford, ed.

Wesley, Samuel, *Letter From a Country Divine*.

_____, *The Pious Communicant*.

Wesley Historical Society, *Publications* and *Proceedings*.

Whitehead, John, *Life*.

Wilson, D. Dunn, "The Influence of Mysticism on John Wesley." An unpublished dissertation (Leeds University, 1968).

Woodward, Josiah, *An Account of the Rise and Progress of the Religious Societies in the City of London . . . and of Their Endeavours for the Reformation of Manners*, 3rd ed. (1712).

Part III
Aldersgate

11

Setting the Stage

Brethren, I count not myself to have apprehended: but this one thing I do, forgetting those things which are behind, and reaching forth unto those things which are before, I press toward the mark for the prize of the high calling of God in Christ Jesus.
Philippians 3:13,14

This evening I am in Birmingham. It is Saturday, March 22, 1788. Tomorrow is Easter. I last left you in Gloucester where Wednesday morning I was up at 4:00 and, after prayer, wrote letters until 8:00. I then had tea and conversed, after which I seized a few precious moments for prayer before transacting some business.

By 9:30 I was in my carriage heading north to Tewkesbury. As I approached the town, I could see the meadow where years earlier I had preached under a tall oak tree.[1] For some years now, this has been one of the liveliest places on the circuit.[2] These people are remarkably teachable.[3] I arrived at 11:30, and by 12:00, in spite of the noon market, the preaching house, built just over ten years ago, was overfilled so that many could not get in. However, those who did were deeply attentive so that more and more are continually convinced and converted to God.[4]

The text for my sermon on that occasion was John 9:4: "I must work the works of him that sent me, while it is day: the night cometh, when no man can work." Christ, the light of the world, looked down from heaven and "his

---

[1]*Works*, Vol. IV, p. 25.
[2]Ibid., p. 40.
[3]Ibid., p. 267.
[4]Ibid., p. 409.

arrows went abroad."[5] I have seldom seen persons more sensibly struck. They gathered closer together, until there was not one inattentive hearer and hardly one unaffected.

After dinner I conversed, but was back in my carriage by 2:00. I arrived at Worcester at 4:30 where, after tea, I conversed and prayed before preaching at 6:00 from the same text I had used at noon. I once preached there in a friend's barn, as it was too cold for the people to stand outdoors. Now we have a preaching house, this one built about sixteen years ago, but it is too small to hold the congregation as the Methodists there have "by well doing put to silence the ignorance of foolish men; so that they are now abundantly more in danger by honour than by dishonour."[6] This was not always the case. Time is as an arrow passing through the air. For a while our work might have been hindered by riotous mobs. I remember nearly twenty years ago our brethren in Worcester had chosen a place for me, in a broad street not far from the cathedral, where there was room for thousands of people. We soon had company enough, part serious, part like the wild ass's colt; but in a while the serious part prevailed and they silenced or drove away the rabble until we had a degree of quietness, and we concluded in peace.[7] Each time it seems trouble brewed Satan could come so far, but no farther. The time came when I was accepted with some ceremony (how fickle the eyes of men). During my northern journey in 1784, for example, "I preached to a crowded audience, in St. Andrew's Church. The Vicar read Prayers, and afterwards told me I should be welcome to the use of his church, whenever I came to Worcester," which I did again some months later.[8] Perhaps the time has arrived when the whole of England, like the rector of this parish, no doubt with some surprise "having never dreamed before that there was such a thing as common sense among the Methodists," will acknowledge the finger of God. The

---

[5]*Works*, Vol. III, p. 405.
[6]*Works*, Vol. IV, p. 409.
[7]*Works*, Vol. III, p. 440.
[8]*Works*, Vol. IV, p. 268; cf. p. 285.

society there, "by patient continuance in well-doing, has quite overcome evil with good; even the beasts of the people are now tame, and open not their mouths against them. They profited much when the waves and storms went over them: May they profit as much by the calm!"[9]

Immediately following the sermon in Worcester, I met with our Society. For several years the Select Society had been all of one heart and one mind; they were so closely united together that I have scarce seen the like in the kingdom. How swiftly God deepened His work in them! They are a loving people of about one hundred members demonstrating that God has saved them from inward as well as outward sin. "I have seen very few, either in Bristol or London, who are more clear in their experience. The account all whom I had time to examine gave, was scriptural and rational: And, suppose they spoke true, they are witnesses of the Perfection which I preach. Yet, that they *may* fall therefrom I know; but that they *must*, I utterly deny."[10] After supper at 8:00, I prayed myself to bed.

On Thursday, I was not up until 5:00, but before 8:00 I had preached a sermon on Isaiah 40:1: "Comfort ye my people, saith your God," transacted some business, and had written a letter to Charles' daughter, Sarah, with some remedies for her father.[11] The sermon itself, as was the practice of the prophet Isaiah, was both warning and promise. The *warning* was the example of morning preaching, which they had left for some months causing consid-

---

[9]*Works*, Vol. IV, p. 104.

[10]*Works*, Vol. III, p. 388.

[11]A copy of the letter is included here both to demonstrate Wesley's manner of writing as well as his interest in medical cures.

My dear Sally: Worcester, March 20, 1788
    Mr. Whitefield had for a considerable time thrown up all the food he took. I advised him to slit a large onion across the grain and bind it warm on the pit of his stomach. He vomited no more. Pray apply this to my brother's stomach the next time he eats. One in Yorkshire, who was dying for want of food, as she threw up all she took, was saved by the following means: boiled crusts of white bread to the consistence of a jelly; add a few drops of lemon juice and a little loaf sugar; take a spoonful once or twice an hour. By all means let him try this. If neither of these avail (which I think

erable damage.[12] The *promise* was from the Scripture text which sought to comfort those who determined to give up sin and continue in the way of perfect love.

I had tea at 8:00, and then conversed, prayed, and prepared a sermon on Hebrews 10:31: "It is a fearful thing to fall into the hands of the living God." After dinner, at 1:00, I found time to meditate and pray before reading over the biographical notes I want to share with you in a moment. At 4:30 I took tea, conversed, and prayed before preaching at 6:00 the sermon prepared earlier on Hebrews 10:31. We again considered the warning (the avenging justice of God), and the promise (the forgiveness available to all who diligently call upon Him). After the service, I met with our bands (smaller groups within the Society), supped at 8:00 and again prayed myself to bed.

Yesterday I was up at 4:00, prayed, and began a sermon on Hebrews 9:13,14: "For if the blood of bulls and of goats, and the ashes of an heifer sprinkling the unclean, sanctifieth to the purifying of the flesh: how much more shall the blood of Christ, who through the eternal Spirit offered himself without spot to God, purge your conscience from dead works to serve the living God?" At 7:00 I snatched a few moments for meditation before tea and a short visit with friends concluding with a prayer for the unity of the Spirit in the bond of peace. By 9:00 I was back in my carriage, arriving at Stourport (a small, newly built village) at 11:00 in time to spend an hour completing the sermon on Hebrews 9:13,14 which I preached at noon to a large congregation. We considered the merit of Christ's sufferings who, through the Spirit, offered Himself sinless to God.

---

will not be the case), remember the lady at Paris who lived several weeks without swallowing a grain by applying thin slices of beef to the stomach. But above all, let prayer be made continually; and probably he will be stronger after this illness than he has been these ten years. Is anything too hard for God? On Sunday I am to be at Birmingham; on Sunday Se'nnight, at Madeley, near Shifnal, Salop. My dear Sally, Adieu!

To Miss Wesley, in Chesterfield Street
    Marylebone, London.

Although these remedies seem quite primitive, many of Wesley's cures have been proven to be quite helpful.

[12]*Works*, Vol. IV, p. 145.

"The work of redemption being the work of the whole Trinity. Neither is the Second Person alone concerned even in the amazing condescension that was needful to complete it. The Father delivers up the kingdom to the Son; and the Holy Ghost becomes the gift of the Messiah, being, as it were, according to his good pleasure."[13] You might have thought that some of those present were as ignorant of the nature of religion as a Hottentot. "They seemed to be all serious and attentive as long as I was speaking; but the moment I ceased, fourscore or one hundred began talking all at once. I do not remember ever to have been present at such a scene before. This must be amended; otherwise (if I should live) I will see Stourport no more."[14]

My, how this little village has grown. Twenty years ago there was but one house, whereas now there are two or three streets. Almost a decade ago, Mr. Cowell, a local coal merchant, built us a preaching house which was then taken over by the Calvinists, so that the Arminian Methodists were turned out. In the name of Jesus we kill each other. I remember writing to a friend a few years past: "You have admirably well expressed what I mean by an opinion, contra-distinguished from an essential doctrine. Whatever is 'compatible with love to Christ, and a work of grace,' I term an *opinion*. And certainly the holding Particular Election and Final Perseverance is compatible with these. 'Yet what fundamental errors,' you ask, 'have you opposed with half that fervency as you have these opinions?'—I have printed nearly fifty sermons, and only one of these opposes them at all. I preach about 800 sermons in a year; and, taking one year with another, for twenty years past, I have not preached eight sermons in a year upon the subject."[15]

Rather than go to law over the matter, Mr. Cowell built another house, larger and more convenient, where after an afternoon meditating, dining, conversing, sermon-writing, at prayer and at tea, I preached again at 6:00 on I

---

[13]Wesley, *Notes on the New Testament*, p. 835.
[14]*Works*, Vol. IV, p. 482.
[15]*Works*, Vol. III, p. 211.

Corinthians 1:24: "But unto them which are called, both Jews and Greeks, Christ the power of God, and the wisdom of God." With these words I sought to mend our walls. Several clergymen were present and were as attentive as any. There remains throughout the kingdom a core of honorable clergymen both candid and sensible, who would listen, at least in part; whereas others would still have Methodists to the man hoisted from the nearest scaffold. "It would be excusable, if these menders of the Bible would offer their hypotheses modestly. But one cannot excuse them when they not only obtrude their novel scheme with the utmost confidence, but even ridicule that scriptural one which always was, and is now, held by men of the greatest learning and piety in the world. Hereby they promote the cause of infidelity more effectually than either Hume or Voltaire."[16] No matter, God is still God, and if we were not plowing in the sand, I anticipate a deep work of the Spirit in Stourport.

Immediately after preaching, I served communion, then had supper, conversed, and prayed before bed at 9:30. Just before dropping off to sleep, I meditated on Philippians 3:13,14: "Brethren, I count not myself to have apprehended: but this one thing I do, forgetting those things which are behind, and reaching forth unto those things which are before, I press toward the mark for the prize of the high calling of God in Christ Jesus."

This morning I was up at 4:00, praying and writing a sermon on Philippians 3:13,14 (the verses given to me the night before) before taking to my carriage, arriving at Kidderminster at 7:15, in time for tea at Mr. Pochimlister's. After tea, I meditated and prayed with a few serious and pious friends, genuine Methodists.

At 9:00 I was back in my carriage, arriving at Quinton (five miles from Birmingham) at 11:30, where I paused (at our new preaching house) to call upon the name of God for an outpouring of His eternal Spirit upon these needy people.

Back in my carriage, I arrived at Birmingham where

---

[16]*Works*, Vol. III, p. 504.

there is a glorious increase in the work of God. The Society here has grown to more than 800, so that it is at present inferior to none in England, except those in London and Bristol. For a time this was a dry, uncomfortable place where I expected to do little good.[17] Even the old preaching house was dreary, plagued by a thin, dull congregation; but I should have known that "I did not go a warfare at my own cost."[18] In time, the power of God was imminently present so that there was not a scoffer, not a trifler, not an inattentive person (so far as I could discern) left among them. Eventually God caused even this barren wilderness to blossom and bud as the rose.[19] Who knows, if God is here, it may continue!

After dinner, I conversed and wrote letters. Much of my work I do by letter because I frequently do not have the opportunity of talking with many face to face; because "I can write more freely than I could speak; because I can by this method say all I have to say at once; whereas, if we were talking together, I might probably forget some part; and because you may by this means have the better opportunity of calmly considering [my advice]."[20]

This afternoon (at 4:15) I felt the need for prayer before tea. After tea I conversed and prayed before preaching the sermon on Philippians 3:13,14. I sought to enforce those words: *"I do not account myself to have apprehended* this already; to be already possessed of perfect holiness. *Forgetting the things that are behind*—Even that part of the race which is already run. *And reaching forth unto*—Literally, *stretched out over the things that are before*—Pursuing with the whole bent and vigor of my soul perfect holiness and eternal glory."[21] The intent of this sermon was twofold. One, that "it is impossible that any should retain what they receive, without improving it."[22] The good people here, though God has bared His arm and they have beheld

---

[17]*Works*, Vol. II, p. 165.
[18]*Works*, Vol. III, p. 504; cf. Vol. IV, p. 231.
[19]*Works*, Vol. II, p. 165.
[20]*Works*, Vol. III, p. 368.
[21]Wesley, *Notes on the New Testament*, p. 735.
[22]*Works*, Vol. III, p. 204.

His strength (as well as His glory), must persevere or perish. Two, much of the seed which has been sown for these many years has been sorely tempted by the fierce, unclean, brutish, blasphemous Antinomians. The mystic foxes have also taken pains to spoil what remains.[23] What havoc would these two opposite extremes, Mysticism and Antinomianism, make among this earnest and simple people! It would have been better for those men not to have been born, by whom these little ones have been offended.[24] I will set down here the conversation (some forty years later) with one so deceived that every serious person may see the true picture of Antinomianism full grown; and may know what these men mean by their favorite phrase, of being "perfect in Christ, not in themselves."

"'Do you believe you have nothing to do with the Law of God?' 'I have not: I am not under the Law: I live by faith.' 'Have you, as living by faith, a right to every thing in the world?' 'I have: All is mine, since Christ is mine.' 'May you, then, take anything you will any where? Suppose, out of a shop, without the consent or the knowledge of the owner?' 'I may, if I want it: For it is mine: Only I will not give offence.' 'Have you also a right to all the women in the world?' 'Yes, if they consent.' 'And is not that a sin?' 'Yes, to him that thinks it is a sin: But not to those whose *hearts are free*.' . . . Surely these are the first-born children of Satan!"[25] Bless God, such matters are now laid to rest. That such wild boars may never again root up that which God has planted, I preach perfect holiness now as I always have these fifty years.

I am alone with my thoughts for I now want to take some time with you to pick up our narrative left off in Gloucester. Supper has just this moment been completed and tomorrow is Easter. Not until an experience at Aldersgate, however, did I realize fully that He had risen for *me*.

---

[23] *Works*, Vol. II, p. 324.
[24] *Works*, Vol. II, p. 397.
[25] Ibid., p. 11.

12

The Journey Home

I went to convert others, who will convert me. Who, what is he that will deliver me from this evil heart of unbelief: I have a fair summer religion. I can talk well; nay, and believe myself, while no danger is near. But let death look me in the face, and my spirit is troubled. John Wesley

After nearly fifty years, the experience at Aldersgate is almost legend. Since legends are so prone to abuse, let me tell you the story as I remember it, making a few comments (for interpretation) along the way to put it into proper perspective.

Let me begin by recounting the events of my return journey from Georgia to England. On Thursday, December 22, 1737, I went on board the *Samuel.* Two days later we sailed over Charlestown bar, and about noon lost sight of land. I took my leave of America, fully expecting to return, but such has not been the providence of God.

These were torturous days. Almost immediately I was stricken by a sickening fear of some unknown danger since the wind was light and the sea smooth. How true that wise maxim of Solomon: "The wicked flee when no man pursueth: but the righteous are bold as a lion." I knew in my head (to use the words of St. Paul) that "to die is gain" and "that all things work together for good to them that love God," yet my heart (usually a decade or so behind) made mockery of these cardinal Christian doctrines. I remember asking myself: "Do I, in fact, love God enough?"[1] I certainly did not have that "perfect love" written about by the mystic authors but who offered (apart from their religious exercises) little or no means for achieving it.

Christmas Day I was seasick, so much so that I could find relief only by lying down. The next day, however, I resolved to return to my old simple diet of no wine nor meat; and after I did so, neither my stomach nor my head complained of the motion of the ship.

Then soon after New Year's, in the fullness of my heart, I wrote the following words: "By the most infallible of proofs, inward feeling, I am convinced, 1. Of unbelief; having no such faith in Christ as will prevent my heart from being troubled; which it could not be, if I rightly believed in God. 2. Of pride throughout my life past; inasmuch as I thought I had what I find I have not. 3. Of gross irrecollections; inasmuch as in a storm I cried to God every moment; in a calm, not. 4. Of levity and luxuriancy of spirit, recurring whenever the pressure is taken off, and appearing by my speaking words not to edify.

"Lord, save, or I perish! Save me: 1. By such a faith as implies peace in life and in death. 2. By such humility as may fill my heart from this hour forever, with a piercing uninterrupted sense that, *nihil est quod hactenus feci* (what I have hitherto done is nothing); having evidently built without a foundation. 3. By such a recollection as may cry to thee every moment, especially when all is calm: give me faith, or I die; give me a lowly spirit; otherwise, *mihi non sit suave vivere* (let life be a burden to me). 4. By steadiness, seriousness, σεμνότες (holiness), sobriety of spirit; avoiding, as fire, every word that tendeth not to edifying; and never speaking of any who oppose me, without all my own sins set in array before my face."[2]

---

[1] Wesley was continually plagued by this thought long after Aldersgate. On June 27, 1766, for example (nearly thirty years later), he wrote to his brother, Charles: "[I do not love God. I never did.]" He then adds: "[I never] believed in the Christian sense of the word. Therefore I am only an honest heathen, a proselyte of the Temple, one of the φοβούμενα τόν θέον" (those that fear God). He continues: "I want all the world to come to " ὅν οὐκ οἶδα " (what I do not know.) *Letters*, Vol. V, pp. 15ff. The words in brackets were in shorthand.

[2] *Journal*, Vol. I, pp. 415f. The punctuation has been slightly altered.

Such was my condition. I hovered between two worlds. I desired a faith that would prosper even under the prospect of death; but, again, my instinctive reaction (not yet overcome) was to turn to the mystics.[3] By January 6 I had completed the abridgement of Mr. de Renty's *Life*.[4] Following his advice, I wanted to withdraw that God might somehow *find me*. So, when I went to speak to the sailors, I could not. Yet, what little relief I did experience came from enforcing God's Word. I finally managed to read and explain some passages to the cabin boy, and then to a young Negro, then to a Frenchman who could speak with no one but me since he knew no English, and eventually preached to all my fellow travelers so that my spirit revived.

This, then, was my dilemma. It was apparent that I still suffered from a lack of faith complicated by almost constant ridicule from my enemy—the fear of death. I wrote in my *Journal* some weeks later: "I think, verily, if the Gospel be true, I am safe: For I not only have given, and do give, all my goods to feed the poor; I not only give my body to be burned, drowned, or whatever God shall appoint for me; but I follow after charity, (though not as I ought, yet as I can,) if haply I may attain it. I *now* believe the Gospel is true. 'I show my faith by my works,' by staking my all upon it. I would do so again and again a thousand times, if the choice were still to make. Whoever sees me, sees I would be a Christian. Therefore 'are my ways not like other men's ways.' Therefore I have been, I am, I am content to be, 'a by-word, a proverb of reproach.' But in a storm I think, 'what if the Gospel be not true? Then thou art of all men most foolish. For what hast thou given thy goods, thy ease, thy friends, thy reputation, thy country, thy life? For what art thou wandering over the face of the earth?—a dream, 'a cunningly-devised fable!' O! Who will deliver me from this fear of death? What shall I do? Where shall I fly from it?

[3]Unfortunately the *Diary* is missing from September 1, 1737 to March 31, 1738, although the fact that Fleury (a mystic) appears at the point where the *Diary* leaves off and de Renty appears soon after it begins again is indicative.

[4]It has been mentioned that this was to be published in 1741.

Should I fight against it by thinking, or (as during my days at Oxford prior to my religious conversion) by not thinking of it?"[5]

Where was I to find peace? Had I not sought diligently to obey every commandment? Why this agony? I had the option of accepting the mystic explanation that God was withholding His Spirit intentionally in order to insure an ultimate union dependent upon pure love; or, of admitting that everything I had done thus far was for nothing. To put it another way, should I be content with my misery and hold on to the fleeting hope (I who had so much invested) that I was on the brink of divine union where light would flood my soul and give me the coveted awareness of God (de Renty's "experimental verity")? Or, should I go back and start afresh? Some years since "a wise man" advised me to "be still, and go on."[6] Once again (an amazing fact), I considered sinking wholly into mysticism; but then, a second major crisis was reached.[7]

On Monday, January 9, I decided that that which had pursued me for so many years, of being in solitude in order to be a Christian, was vain desire. I had had then, I thought, after Wroot and Georgia and to an extent even the cloisters of Oxford, *solitude enough.* Had solitude brought me nearer to being a Christian? Not if Jesus Christ was the model! "I doubt, indeed, I was much nearer that mystery of Satan which some writers affect to call by that name. So near that I had probably sunk wholly into it had not the great mercy of God just now thrown me upon reading St. Cyprian's works. 'Oh my soul, come not thou into their secret!'"[8] Cyprian had a sobering effect. He combined much of the gold found in both à Kempis and Taylor— ecclesiastic order, a high regard for the sacraments, even a rigid asceticism—with none of the dross. There was no room here for the dreamy speculative genius of the East. As I

[5]*Works*, Vol. I, pp. 74f. The words in the second pair of parentheses are not a part of the original text.

[6]*Journal*, Vol. I, p. 418. This "wise man" was no doubt William Law.

[7]The first crisis was the letter to Samuel, November, 1736.

[8]*Journal*, Vol. I, p. 416. "Mystery of Satan" refers to the mystical scheme involving "solitude" and the "dark night of the soul."

deliberated as to whether my misfortune was due to some "dark night" divinely imposed or to some transgression that lay within myself, I read the words of St. Cyprian: "We must confess that this calamity riseth chiefly of our own wickedness, while we walk not in the way of the Lord."[9] Here was my answer! There was no vision, the battle had not been won, but I was beginning to understand. From this moment I would see more and more clearly that mystic "darkness" had its roots in *sin,* not in God.

"On Friday, January 13, we had a thorough storm, which obliged us to shut all close, the sea breaking over the ship continually. I was at first afraid (the enemy would hardly have missed an opportunity such as this), but cried to God, and was strengthened. Before ten I laid down; I bless God, without fear. About midnight we were awakened by a confused noise of seas and wind and men's voices, the likes of which I have never heard before. The sound of the sea breaking over and against the side of the ship, I could compare to nothing except large cannon or American thunder. The rebounding, starting, quivering motion of the ship much resembled what is said of earthquakes. The captain was upon deck in an instant. But his men could not hear what he said. It blew a proper hurricane; which beginning at southwest, then went west, northwest, north, and, in a quarter of an hour, round by the east to the southwest point again. At the same time, the sea running (as they term it) mountain-high, and that from many different points at once, the ship would not obey the helm; nor indeed could the steersman, through the violent rain, see the compass. So he was forced to let her run before the wind, and soon the stress of the storm was over.

"About noon the next day it ceased. But first I had resolved, God being my helper, not only to preach it to all, but to apply the word of God to every single soul on the

---

[9]This quotation is found in Wesley's own extract, *Acts of the Christian Martyrs,* included in the *Christian Library,* Vol. II, pp. 272ff. Wesley was especially taken by Cyprian's heroism during the Diocletian persecution and by his exhortation to works of mercy, prayer, and fasting. Cf. the *Writings of Cyprian in the Ante-Nicene Christian Library,* Vol. I, pp. 1-20.

ship; and if but one, yea, if not one of them will hear, I know 'my labour is not in vain.'"[10]

I had no sooner executed this resolution than my spirit was once again revived. I wrote in my *Journal:* "I am a sensible one who thinks the being *in orco* [the mystic darkness], as they phrase it, an indispensable preparative for being a Christian, would say, I had better have continued in that state; and that this unseasonable relief was a curse, not a blessing. Nay, but who art thou, oh man, who, in favor of a wretched hypothesis, dost blasphemest the good gift of God? Hath not he himself said, 'This also is the gift of God, if a man hath power to rejoice in his labour?' Yea, God setteth his own seal to man's weak endeavors, while he thus answereth him in the joy of his heart."[11]

On Wednesday, February 1, at 4:00 in the morning, we landed at Deal. It was then almost two years and four months since I had left my native country in order to teach the Georgia Indians the nature of Christianity. I remember writing at that time what I have already briefly confessed to you before: "I went to convert others, who will convert me? Who, what is he that will deliver me from this evil heart of unbelief? I have a fair summer religion. I can talk well; nay, and believe myself, while no danger is near. But let death look me in the face, and my spirit is troubled."[12]

Friends, I am even today uncertain as to how best to interpret those words. I am sure (as you shall soon see) that God would not have left me in such a state, having even then the faith of a servant though not of a son.[13] These were not the thoughts of a mad man, however. These were the words of truth and soberness and I share the following with you now that some who still dream may awake, and see, that as I was, so are they.

---

[10]*Works*, Vol. I, p. 73. The words in the first pair of parentheses are not a part of the original text.

[11]Ibid., p. 74.

[12] Ibid.

[13]Wesley changed his opinion later in life concerning some of the judgments expressed in these paragraphs. In his sermon "On Faith" he describes the difference between the faith of a *servant* and the faith of a *son*. Both are saving faith though the former lacks full assurance. On

"Are they read in philosophy? So was I. In ancient or modern tongues? So was I also. Are they versed in the science of divinity? I too had studied it many years. Can they talk fluently upon spiritual things? The very same could I do. Are they plenteous in alms? Behold, I gave all my goods to feed the poor. Do they give of their labor as well as of their substance? I had labored more abundantly than they all. Are they willing to suffer for their brethren? I had thrown up my friends, reputation, ease, country; I had put my life in my hand, wandering into strange lands; I had given my body to be devoured by the deep, parched up with heat, consumed by toil and weariness, or whatsoever God should have pleased to bring upon me. But did all this—be it more or less, it matters not—make me acceptable to God? Does all I ever did or can know, say, give, do, or suffer, justify me in His sight? Yea, or the constant use of all means of grace? (which, nevertheless, is meet, right and our bounden duty). Or that I knew nothing of myself; that I was, as touching outward, moral righteousness, blameless? Or (to come closer yet) to having a rational conviction of all the truths of Christianity? Did all this give me a claim to the holy, heavenly, divine character of a Christian? By no means. If the oracles of God are true; if we are still to abide by the Scriptures, all these things, though, when ennobled by faith in Christ,[14] they are holy and just and good, yet without it, 'dung and dross,' meet only to be purged away by 'the fire that shall never be quenched.'"[15]

Today I would temper these words with some years of wisdom, realizing that I had more faith than I was aware. This is what I believed at the time: "that I 'was fallen short of the glory of God;' that my whole heart was 'altogether corrupt and abominable'; and consequently my whole life

---

board ship, however, and for some years following Aldersgate (cf. his sermon "The Almost Christian") Wesley believed that he lacked saving faith. Then, some years later, he interprets servant faith (his experience between 1725 and 1738) as saving faith. Cf. *Sermons*, Vol. I, pp. 60f, n. 13.

[14]Wesley's own footnote inserted here reads: "I had even then the faith of a *servant*, though not of a son.

[15]*Works*, Vol. I, p. 76.

(seeing it cannot be that an 'evil tree' should 'bring forth good fruit'): that, 'alienated' as I was from the life of God, I was 'a child of wrath,'[16] an heir of hell: that my own works, my own sufferings, my own righteousness, were so far from reconciling me to an offended God, so far from making an atonement for the least of those sins, which 'were more in number than the hairs of my head,' that the most specious of them needed an atonement: that 'having the sentence of death' in my heart, and having nothing in or of myself to plead, I had no hope, but that of being justified freely, 'through the redemption that is in Jesus'; I had no hope, but that if I sought I would find Christ, and 'be found in Him, not having my own righteousness, but that which is through the faith of Christ, the righteousness which is of God by faith.'

"If it be said that I had faith (for many such things I heard, from many miserable comforters), I answer, so have the devils—a sort of faith; but still they are strangers to the covenant of promise. So the apostles had even at Cana in Galilee, when Jesus first 'manifested forth his glory'; even then they, in a sort, 'believed on him'; but they had not then 'the faith that overcometh the world.' The faith I wanted was 'a sure trust and confidence in God, that, through the merits of Christ, my sins were forgiven, and I reconciled to the favor of God.' I needed that faith which St. Paul recommends to all the world, especially in his Epistle to the Romans: that faith which enables everyone that hath it to cry out, 'I live not; but Christ liveth in me; and the life which I now live, I live by faith in the son of God, who loved me, and gave himself for me.' I needed that faith which none can have without knowing that he hath it (though many imagine they have it, who have it not); for whosoever hath it, is 'freed from sin, the' whole 'body of sin is destroyed' in him; he is freed from fear, 'having peace with God through Christ, and rejoicing in hope of the glory of God.' And he is freed from doubt, 'having the love of God shed abroad in his heart, through

---

[16]Again, Wesley's own footnote reads: "I believe not."

the Holy Ghost which is given unto him'; which 'Spirit itself beareth witness with his spirit, that he is a child of God.'"[17]

Now I can see the choice more clearly (such is our wisdom for things past). Perhaps the fear and uncertainty was best. Perhaps I "should look upon it as my cross; when it comes, to let it humble me, and quicken all my good resolutions, especially that of praying without ceasing; and at other times, to take no thought about it, but quietly go on 'in the work of the Lord.'"[18] On the other hand, perhaps I needed to start afresh, to count all that I had done before as "dung and dross" (there being no middle ground in the days of our youth), and seek a new foundation.

I was soon to believe (though I retract it now, this being far too strong)[19] that the mystics were the most dangerous enemies of Christianity (all others being but triflers). I wrote: "They stab it in the vitals; and its most serious professors are most likely to fall by them. May I praise Him who hath snatched me out of this fire."[20] If I had the faith of a servant, I still lacked the faith of a son. I had no power, no heart, no expectation to see God at work among His people. Perhaps the mystics also had the faith of a servant; but their "dark night" could never produce that of a son. My objections at this point, however, were still on the fringe of the issue. As in my letter to Samuel some months earlier, I objected only to their neglect of the means of grace. As long as I did not have the witness of the Spirit, I would be vulnerable to mysticism.

Yet, I still feared the alternative. Both Luther and Calvin seemed to magnify faith to such an amazing degree that it hid all the rest of the commandments. I did not then see that this was the natural effect of their overgrown fear of

---

[17]*Works*, Vol. I, pp. 76f.

[18]*Journal*, Vol. I, p. 418.

[19]*Works*, Vol. X, p. 395; cf. *Letters*, Vol. VI, p. 43, where Wesley commends the mystics for "many excellent things."

[20]*Journal*, Vol. I, p. 420. These comments, from the *Standard Journal*, were omitted in the journal portion of his published works.

Popery.[21] The mystic writers in their "noble" descriptions of union with God and internal religion made everything else appear "mean, flat, and insipid, . . . even good works appear so too; yea, and faith itself."[22]

If faith in the evangelical sense was to win out and lead to that of a son, it would take a person of considerable reason and candor to show me the way.

---

[21]Ibid., p. 419.
[22]Ibid., p. 420.

13

Peter Böhler

Oh, thou Saviour of men, save me from trusting in anything but Thee! Draw me after Thee! Let me be emptied of myself, and then fill me with all peace and joy in believing; and let nothing separate me from Thy love in time or in eternity.

John Wesley

Once again the Oxford spires made me feel at home. As we (a new friend and I) walked through the quads, I must admit that I felt some pride until a few undergraduates laughed at my friend who was bearded and rather oddly dressed. I was more than a little embarrassed and apologized (or rather made excuses), but my friend dismissed the affront by simply replying: "My brother, it does not even stick to my clothes."

This friend was a young Moravian, recently from Germany en route to Georgia. His name was Böhler, Peter Böhler. I had met Mr. Böhler and several of his companions nearly two weeks earlier (February 7, 1738) at the London house of a Dutch merchant, Mr. Weinantz.[1]

After landing at Deal on February 1, I immediately preached to a large company in the inn, and then journeyed to London by way of Feversham (where I again preached) and Blendon Hall (where I received a surprisingly warm welcome from the parents of Charles Delamotte who journeyed with us to America, against their advice). Once in London (arriving February 3), I lodged with my friend, John Hutton, greeted my brother Charles, met with Mr. Oglethorpe, and reported to the colony Trus-

---

[1]Wesley writes that this was "a day much to be remembered." *Journal*, Vol. I, p. 436.

tees, who had some question concerning the circumstances of my departure.[2]

Upon meeting the Moravians at Mr. Weinantz's I quickly obtained rooms for them near my own lodgings. After several days which were filled with visiting friends and with preaching, I journeyed with Mr. Böhler to Oxford. We traveled by coach, so we had considerable opportunity for conversing closely. I spoke at some length concerning my opinion of the Moravian brethren in Georgia and of my intent to return to that colony if the Trustees (no small obstacle) agreed. I also discussed my plans to visit Herrnhut in July or August. I wanted to see for myself if this be "the place where the Christians live."[3]

While at Oxford (in spite of the incident in the University quad) we were well received by some, especially by my friend, John Sarney. Then from Oxford, Mr. Böhler and I journeyed on to the rectory at Stanton-Harcourt to visit John Gambold. My sister Kezzy was a guest there as well. At first I thought that Mr. Gambold had recovered fully from his mystic delusion (such a lingering virus), but Mr. Böhler soon convinced me otherwise, stating that he even "looked like a mystic."[4]

Furthermore, I had the strange feeling that Böhler was also passing some kind of judgment upon me. The more we talked, the less I understood, at least at first. He spoke of faith almost constantly and in such a manner as I had never before heard. He kept repeating: "My brother, my brother, that philosophy of yours must be purged away." I was still seeking access to God by my own righteousness, either by outward works (I was once again at the prison upon our return to Oxford) or, more subtly, by inward works (the

[2]John Hutton lived on Great College Street near Westminster Abbey. He was later offended by the preaching of the Methodists and the Wesleys moved to the home of his son James in Little Wild Street.

[3]In contrast to the impiety around her, Antoinette Bourignon, as a small child (after reading an account of the early apostles), kept searching for the place where the Christians lived. This story impressed Wesley and he refers to it on a number of occasions. Cf. *Journal*, Vol. II, pp. 15, 16, with Bourignon's *The Light of the World*, p. xvi, "Introduction," English translation, 1696.

[4]Böhler's *Diary*, March 6, 1738.

spiritual exercises of the mystics). So, what did I do? More resolutions!

From Stanton-Harcourt Mr. Böhler and I returned to Oxford, where he remained for some weeks (working six hours a day in the library and forming bands among the students), while I returned to London, arriving February 21.[5] After giving yet another account to the Trustees, visiting with friends, and preaching three times on Sunday, I journeyed to Salisbury in order to visit my mother who was then a guest of my sister Martha and her husband (a former student of mine), Westley Hall. En route, I had several opportunities on the coach to converse seriously with my fellow travelers, but trying to mend the wisdom of God by the worldly wisdom which teaches that we must begin serious conversation with light and then (after the mystics) leave them to themselves, all that I had said was written on the sand. I could only pray that God would not lay this sin to my charge. I quickly determined not to make the same mistake again, and I renewed my former resolution "to use absolute openness and unreserve with all that I should converse with."[6]

On February 28 I saw my mother once more, but my scheduled trip to visit my brother Samuel at Tiverton was delayed by the news that Charles was dying from pleurisy at Oxford.

Back in Oxford by March 4, I found my brother much improved and Peter Böhler at his side. Mr. Böhler and I again talked at length. It was then (after thirteen years of wandering) that I began to see holiness as the *fruit* of faith, not the *cause*. For many years I had sought to travel a route different (in effect putting sanctification before justification) from that of faith in Jesus Christ. I remember asking Mr. Böhler, as I was ready to believe that I should stop

---

[5]The "bands" referred to here were religious societies. Schmidt writes: "the 'bands' were based upon the closest personal unity of their members, a unity derived from an awareness of the life of God hidden in them. Since this was expressed in mutual conversation, a band consisted originally of only two or three persons." Schmidt, *John Wesley*, Vol. I, p. 231.

[6]*Journal*, Vol. I, pp. 440f.

preaching, whether or not I should continue. How could I preach to others and not have faith myself? He answered: "By no means neglect the talent which God has given to you." To which I replied: "But what can I preach?" His response: "Preach faith *till* you have it; and then, *because* you have it, you *will* preach faith."[7]

The next day (March 6), I determined to preach this new doctrine "though my soul started back from the work."[8] The first person to whom I offered salvation by faith alone was a prisoner under the sentence of death. His name was Clifford. Though I had previously refused to speak to him (since for many years I had been a zealous asserter of the impossibility of a deathbed repentance), he seemed to respond. Less than three weeks later "he kneeled down in much heaviness and confusion, having 'no rest in' his 'bones, by reason of' his 'sins.' After a space he rose up, and eagerly said, 'I am now ready to die. I know Christ has taken away my sins; and there is no more condemnation for me.' This same composed cheerfulness he showed when he was carried to execution; and in his last moments he was the same, enjoying a perfect peace, in confidence that he was 'accepted in the Beloved.'"[9]

Thus, my first convert to salvation by faith alone was delivered from the very fear that had plagued me for so many years. Perhaps the enemy was about to yield to me as well. I wanted a faith of my own. The words of Böhler, "Preach faith till you have it," became motivation enough. I would do it!

After taking a few days in order to write the account entitled, "An affair with Miss Sophy Hopkey," Charles Kinchin and I journeyed north preaching (as best we could) faith in Christ alone.[10]

By March 23 I was back at Oxford where my brother and I met Mr. Böhler again (he had been in London for nearly

---

[7]*Journal*, Vol. I, p. 442.
[8]Ibid.
[9]Ibid., p. 448.
[10]This account concerning Sophy Hopkey was written for the Trustees and the manuscript is in the possession of the W. M. Conference Office.

two weeks). I began the conversation by asking: "Faith alone is perhaps well enough for salvation, but how shall we become victors over sin and death?" He amazed me even more by the accounts he gave of the fruits of living faith—the holiness and happiness which he affirmed attended it. Yet, I objected (à Kempis and the mystics still hung on): "But what of the Christian ethic? What of asceticism?" Böhler (Bless God), refused to give way. He explained further that *everything* depended upon our coming to know the Savior, and only *in this way* could we help others. Using the main tenet of Pietism he described the difference between "living externally to the Savior" (Christ as our ideal or the faith of a servant) and "living in the Savior" (Christ as our Savior and Lord or the faith of a son.)[11] The next morning I searched the Scriptures. The confirmation was there. This doctrine was of God. I surrendered. I needed faith as a "sure trust" in God and I knew it. Emotionally I was still involved with the mystics (I read them extensively until the end of April), but intellectually I had chosen a different route to travel.[12]

Some men are content to live with their doubts, but I was too vulnerable. First drawn to the illusion of mystical "knowing" (most mystics *after* years of struggle enjoyed a fellowship with God which I interpreted as a kind of assurance, but I had waited long enough) and then to the Moravians, I wanted to *feel* accepted by God.[13] The mystics exhorted me to practice a *blind* trust in God. Böhler promised me a *sure* trust in God. Admittedly, some of this now seems more a question of terms: the mystic called the

---

[11]Böhler's *Diary*, April 3, 10, 12, 13; May 13, 1738.

[12]The fact that Wesley was still reading the mystics can be judged from his *Diary*. When the *Diary* resumes, the mystics reappear almost immediately. For April 6 he notes: "Began M. de Renty's *Life*." Haliburton appears on April 9, and on April 11 Wesley read de Renty to Miss Molly (who was ill) and to those who attended her. On April 13 Wesley read de Renty once again. Haliburton follows on April 15 and on April 17 he began the *Life of A. M. Schurmann*. On April 20 Wesley talked of the mystics with James Hutton.

[13]*Journal*, Vol. I, pp. 415, 471. At Aldersgate "inward feeling" was interpreted as the "most infallible proof." Wesley writes: "I well saw no one could, in the nature of things, have such a sense of forgiveness, and not feel it."

process of acceptance with God, faith; whereas the Moravian called the *awareness* of acceptance with God, faith. Nonetheless, the issue seemed large. It is important to remember that the mystical concept of faith (although using the same word) is not faith in the evangelical sense, but a process of "mystical matters" directed toward union with God. This mystical union involved holiness and perfection (with a degree of assurance) while the Moravian faith involved assurance (with a degree of holiness and perfection).

Even more to the point, I finally understood that the mystics not only denied the means of grace, but endangered the very foundation upon which our acceptance with God is built—faith in the blood of Christ. According to Böhler I had falsely imagined faith to be a form of imagination or self-persuasion. At best, I had assumed that saving faith was only that of a servant (devoid of assurance) and I quickly refrained from speaking about it in order to move on to that of a son, which I had assumed came only by the process of sanctification (including rigid acetism). Böhler again and again sought to make clear that the faith of a son (including assurance), in its essential nature, was also a part of justification (the "coming to know Jesus"). I needed to wait no longer. All that I had ever wanted from religion was no farther away than the simple act of trusting Christ alone.

This, on the one hand, was more simple; but on the other, it was infinitely more difficult. John Gambold, in a letter to my brother Charles, states the case of "religious" men (so-called) profoundly: "The doctrine of faith is a downright robber. It takes away all this wealth (self-denial and mental refinement), and only tells us it is deposited for us with somebody else, upon whose bounty we must live like mere beggars. Indeed, they that are truly beggars, vile and filthy sinners till very lately, may stoop to live in this dependent condition—it suits them well enough. But they who have long distinguished themselves from the herd of vicious wretches, or have even gone beyond *moral* men— for them to be told that they are either not so well, or but the same needy, impotent, insignificant vessels of mercy with others, this is more shocking to reason than trans-substantiation."[14]

I spent the next few weeks continuing to preach a doctrine still foreign to my heart. I did all the good I could (just in case) until April 22, when, after still another conversation with Peter Böhler (we both had returned to London), I concluded: "I have no more objection to what he said of the nature of faith." I was fully convinced that faith was (to use the words of our Church of England) "a sure trust and confidence which a man hath in God, that through the merits of Christ his sins are forgiven and he reconciled to the favor of God." That is to say, "the Spirit itself beareth witness with our spirit that we are the children of God," and "He that believeth hath the witness in himself." Neither could I deny either the happiness or holiness which he described as fruits of this living faith: "Whatsoever is born of God doth not commit sin," and "Whosoever believeth is born of God."[15]

Yet, I still could not comprehend how this faith could be given in a moment: "How a man could *at once* be thus turned from darkness to light, from sin and misery to righteousness and joy in the Holy Ghost. I searched the Scriptures again touching this very thing, particularly the Acts of the Apostles: but, to my utter astonishment, found scarce any instances thereof other than *instantaneous* conversion; scarce any so slow as that of St. Paul, who was three days in the pangs of the new birth. I had but one retreat left; namely, 'Thus, I grant, God wrought in the first ages of Christianity; but the times are changed. What reason have I to believe He works in the same manner now?'"[16]

The next morning (April 23), Mr. Böhler was kind enough to hear me preach at St. Ann's. He was not satisfied. I had not been able to promise a sudden beginning of faith to those who put their trust in Christ. There-

---

[14]*Journal*, Vol. I, p. 463.
[15]Ibid., p. 454.
[16]Ibid., pp. 454ff.

fore, he brought with him that evening four of his English brethren who openly testified that "God had thus wrought in themselves, giving them in a moment such a faith in the blood of His Son as translated them out of darkness into light, out of sin and fear into holiness and happiness. Here ended my disputing. I could now only cry out, 'Lord, help Thou my unbelief!'"[17] Here faith indicated a completely new beginning, a new creation by God, not merely a restoration of a divine image, as the more naturalistic theology of à Kempis and the mystics suggested. Now, with both the Scriptures and experience at Böhler's back, I had no more retreat for the mind, but my heart still was not in it. I again asked as to whether I ought not refrain from preaching this way, and again he replied: "No; do not hide in the earth the talent God hath given you."[18]

On April 25 I journeyed to Blendon where I confessed my unbelief as a poor sinner who hungered after a better righteousness through faith in the blood of Jesus Christ. Several (including my brother) were offended that I, "who had done and suffered such things," should not admit to such faith.

Two days later I returned to Oxford. Mr. Böhler accompanied me as far as Kensington. He now attempted to rescue me from self-despair and urged me not to place the grace of the Savior so far from me and to believe that it was near.

By May 1, the reoccurance of my brother's illness forced me to return to London. I found my brother better than I had expected, but still "strongly averse from what he called 'the new faith.'" That evening our little Society (which later moved to Fetter Lane) met for the first time at the house of James Hutton, and under the direction of Böhler drew up its fundamental rules.

On May 3 Charles, after some convincing, was persuaded by Mr. Böhler to accept "the nature of that one true living faith, whereby alone, 'through grace, we are

---

[17]Ibid., p. 455.
[18]Ibid.

saved."'[19] The following day Böhler left London in order to embark for Carolina, where he was to minister among the Negroes before going on to Georgia. I wrote in my *Journal*: "O what a work hath God begun, since his coming into England! Such an one as shall never come to an end till heaven and earth pass away."[20]

I spent the next few weeks preaching, but I was still thorougly convinced of my lack of faith and resolved to seek it to the end. In spite of all I continued with strange indifference, dullness, coolness, and unusual relapses into sin, until Wednesday, May 24. Before the events of that day can be described, however, the final chapter in the struggle against trusting my own righteousness must be told.[21]

I was going to have faith as "the assurance of things hoped for, the evidence of things not seen" or perish in the pursuit. I determined to cut the knot which I believed to be preventing it. On April 30 I laid my *Diary* aside and ceased many of the spiritual exercises (apart from the normal means of grace), lest I should count these for righteousness; but one more thing had to be done.[22] I had to deliver my soul to the one who had influenced me most (for good or for ill) during these torturous years. On May 14, and again on May 20, I wrote to William Law. A brief review of this correspondence with him will serve as a summary for much of what has gone before. If I were to rewrite these letters today, some of the phrases would be stated differently. Much of the language is unguarded and some of the logic suffers from overstatement, but you must remember that I was desperate! Although my preaching of faith alone had on occasion (remember the prisoner) produced results

---

[19]Ibid., p. 459.

[20]Ibid., Vol. I, pp. 459f. Schmidt writes that "in the succeeding period Böhler became Zinzendorf's special commissioner for England and in America he met Heinrich Melchior Muhlenberg. He became a bishop and died on April 27, 1775 at Fulneck in England, following a paralysis which affected his mind" (*John Wesley*, Vol. I, p. 225).

[21]Cf. *Journal*, Vol. I. p. 472.

[22]An unexplained break in the *Diary* occurs on April 30, 1738. The next entry, on the same page, is "Wed. May 23, 1739." Though the explanation provided here is conjecture, it may well provide a clue.

that I would not have thought possible, I was still a stranger to the experience myself. Law epitomized my fruitless struggle. The major thrust of this correspondence was a condemnation of his substitution of "mystical matters" for what I then believed to be justifying faith (perhaps more accurately stated, the faith of a son which I still believe to be the *common privilege* of all those who trust Christ alone for "justification, and redemption").

The teacher and his pupil had finally parted. Although the man "I greatly reverenced and loved, the doctrine I utterly abhor"; it is "totally subversive to the very essence of Christianity."[23] Law had unashamedly declared himself for the mystic writers, especially the Germans. I had sided with the Moravians. Law was to become the chief representative of the Jakob Boehme type of "piety" in England. I (at least for the moment) was a follower of Peter Böhler.[24]

To renounce Law at this point was to renounce mysticism at its core. My earlier rejection of the mystic denial of the means of grace (the letter to Samuel, November, 1736, and the comments on board ship a few months previous) had not begun to fathom the subtle depths exposed in these two letters. Here the atonement itself was in question. In the first letter I asked: "Why did I scarce ever hear you name the name of Christ? Never, so as to ground anything upon 'faith in His blood?'"[25] Law's "Pearl of Eternity" (the favorite metaphor in his *Spirit of Prayer*), the "touch of the Divine loadstone" was to be sought, not by faith in Christ, but by looking within; One must "search and dig in thine own field." This mystical substitution of an internal subjective "ascent" emanating from within the nature of man for faith in the objective atoning work of Christ was the crowning issue.

In my second letter I again objected to the fact that Mr.

---

[23] *Letters*, Vol. III, p. 345.

[24] Böhler had visited Law the previous year. Wesley records a part of that interview between Böhler and Law in his letter to Law on the 14th of May: "I (Böhler) began speaking to him of faith in Christ: he was silent. Then he began to speak of mystical matters again. I saw his state at once; and a very dangerous one in his judgement, whom I know to have the Spirit of God" (*Letters*, Vol. I, p. 240).

[25] Ibid.

Law had never advised me "to seek first a living faith in the blood of Christ."[26] In his reply to my first letter, he sought to defend this point by reminding me that he had recommended the treatise *Theologia Germanica* commenting that "if that book does not plainly lead you to Jesus Christ, I am content to know as little of Christianity as you are pleased to believe." I replied here "In *Theologia Germanica* I remember something of Christ, our pattern, but nothing expressed of *Christ our atonement.*"[27]

To summarize, I felt there were at least five reasons why Mr. Law should be held accountable (at least in part) for my not having had faith. They were: He did not tell me plainly that I lacked it. He did not advise me once to seek or pray for it. He assumed that I had it. His advice led me from it; and finally, he recommended books to me which had no tendency to plant this faith in me, but a direct tendency to *destroy good works.*[28] In this lay the impasse. I noted in Law a malicious lightheartedness so inconsistent with the example of other mystics like de Renty and Lopez. I would later understand that the mysticism of the Roman Catholics was significantly different from that of the Germans. The practical pietistic mysticism of the former would eventually overrule some of the dark, speculative, passive, and unsocial mysticism of the latter, and I would once again enjoy the influence of these great and good men; but for now the break with the mystics was complete. I had condemned them in a lump and it would be several years before I could begin to sort the gold from the dross.

During these crisis days before Aldersgate I continued to preach faith. In each place that I preached, however, I was quickly informed that I should preach there no more.[29] On

---

[26]Ibid., p. 241.

[27]Ibid.

[28]Ibid., cf. Wesley, *Poetical Works*, Vol. I, pp. xix-xx.

[29]The principal theological objection to Wesley's preaching here and throughout the Revival had to do with the sacramentalism within the Church of England which insisted that one is saved at the time of baptism (infant or otherwise) and a subsequent experience of faith is simply redundant.

May 19 my brother contracted pleurisy again, but two days later I received the surprising news that he had found both strength for his body and rest for his soul.[30] I felt like the dead sent to raise the dead, a Judas sent to cast out devils, a lion in a den of Daniels. I could only pray in my despair: "Oh, thou Saviour of men, save me from trusting in any thing but Thee! Draw me after Thee! Let me be emptied of myself, and then fill me with all peace and joy in believing; and let nothing separate me from Thy love in time or in eternity."[31]

---

[30]For a full account of Charles' evangelical conversion, see his *Journal*, p. 146.

[31]*Journal*, Vol. I, p. 465.

AN

EXTRACT

OF THE

Rev. Mr. JOHN WESLEY's

JOURNAL

From his Embarking for GEORGIA

To his Return to LONDON.

What fhall we fay then?——That Ifrael *which follow'd after the Law of Righteoufnefs, hath not attained to the Law of Righteoufnefs.—— Wherefore? Becaufe they fought it not by Faith, but as it were by the Works of the Law.* Rom. ix. 30, 31.

BRISTOL:

Printed by S. and F. FARLEY.

And fold at the New School-Houfe in the Horfe-Fair: and by the Bookfellers in Town and Country.

Title page of the first edition of John Wesley's Journal

The PREFACE.

1. IT was in Purfuance of an Advice given by Bp. *Taylor*, in his *Rules for Holy Living and Dying*, that about fifteen Years ago, I began to take a more exact Account than I had done before, of the manner wherein I fpent my Time, writing down how I had employed every Hour. This I continued to de, wherever I was, till the Time of my leaving *England*. The Variety of Scenes which I then paft thro', induced me to tranfcribe from time to time, the more material Parts of my Diary, adding here and there fuch little Reflections as occurr'd to my Mind. Of this Journal thus occafionally compiled, the following is a fhort Extract: It not being my Defign to relate all thofe Particulars, which I wrote for my own Ufe only; and which would anfwer no valuable End to others, however important they were to me.

2. Indeed I had no Defign or Defire to trouble the World with any of my little Affairs: As can't but appear to every impartial Mind, from my having been fo long *as one that heareth not*, notwithftanding the loud and frequent Calls I have had, to anfwer for myfelf. Neither fhou'd I have

Preface to the first edition of John Wesley's Journal

George Whitefield (1714-70).

The Foundry, Moorfields, London

The First Methodist Conference, 1744.

"JOHN WESLEY PREACHING
FROM A MARKET CROSS"

The First Methodist Class Meeting, Bristol, 1742

Christ Church College at Oxford

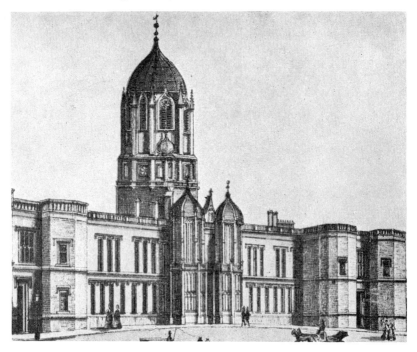

HYMNS
AND
Sacred Poems.

Published by
JOHN WESLEY, M.A.
Fellow of Lincoln College, Oxford;
AND
CHARLES WESLEY, M.A.
Student of Christ-Church, Oxford.

BRISTOL: Printed and sold by Felix Farley,
in Castle-Green; J. Wilson in Wine-street; and
at the School-Room in the Horse-Fair; In Bath,
by W. Frederick, Bookseller: And in London,
by T. Harris on the Bridge; also, at the Foundry in Upper-Moor-Fields, MDCCXLII.

HYMNS
AND
SACRED
POEMS.
IN
TWO VOLUMES.

BY
CHARLES WESLEY, M.A.
Student of Christ-Church, Oxford.

VOL. I.

BRISTOL:
Printed and Sold by FELIX FARLEY.
MDCCXLIX.

Title pages of some of Wesley's publications.

Susanna Wesley and the Epworth parishioners

Charles Wesley

General James Oglethorpe (1696-1785)

John Wesley preaching on his father's tomb at Epworth after having been barred from the church

The statue of John Wesley, City Road, London

14

May 24, 1738

Faith is a divine work in us, which changes us and makes us newly born of God, and kills the old Adam, makes us completely different men in heart, disposition, mind and every power, and brings the Holy Spirit with it. Martin Luther

In little more than two months I will celebrate the fiftieth anniversary of the experience at Aldersgate, May 24, 1738. Whether I had, until that moment, been accepted by God (perhaps through the faith of a servant) is a question worthy of some consideration. This should not cloud the issue, however. Even more important is the fact that it was here where I first began to understand experientially what I had been preaching for some weeks and what I have continued to preach (though hopefully with a bit more light) these many years since. As I think back over the space of half a century, let me first describe the events as I remember them, and then give you a brief analysis as I now understand what was actually taking place.

I had been preaching "faith alone" since March 6, yet with little fruit (though there must have been some fruit since the Word of God will not return void). My heart was not in it, although this was about to change.

I think it was about 5:00 in the morning when I opened my Testament on these words: "Whereby are given unto us exceeding great and precious promises: that by these ye might be partakers of the divine nature" (2 Peter 1:4). I claimed those promises with all the faith I could muster. However, even though I believed, I had not been renewed in the image of God. I had no communion with God so that I could dwell in Him and He in me.[1]

As I prepared to leave my lodgings, I opened my Testament once again, this time to the words: "Thou art not far from the kingdom of God" (Mark 12:34). I remember thinking (to use the words that follow), I "durst question Him any more." In the afternoon I was asked to go to St. Paul's. I listened to the words of the anthem closely: "Out of the deep have I called unto thee, O, Lord: Lord, hear my voice. O, let thine ears consider well the voice of my complaint. If Thou, Lord, wilt be extreme to mark what is done amiss, O, Lord, who may abide it? For there is mercy with Thee; therefore, shalt Thou be feared. O, Lord, *trust in the Lord:* for with the Lord there is mercy, and with Him is plenteous redemption. And He shall redeem Israel from all his sins."[2] The phrase, "trust in the Lord" (repeated constantly throughout) seized me.[3] Trust, trust, trust; I would; I must; I could think of nothing else.

Again, wanting to retire alone that God might find *me,* I went very unwillingly that evening to a Society in Aldersgate Street.[4] Someone was reading these words from Luther's Preface to his commentary on the *Epistle to the Romans:* "Faith is a divine work in us, which changes us and makes us newly born of God, and kills the old Adam, makes us completely different men in heart, disposition, mind and every power, and brings the Holy Spirit with it. O faith is a lively, creative, active, powerful thing, so that it is impossible that it should not continually do good works. It does not even ask if good works are to be done, but before anyone asks, it has done them, and is always acting."[5] Before I could raise *my* usual question (concerning

---

[1]Cf. *Notes on the New Testament,* 2 Peter 1:4, p. 890.

[2]*Journal,* Vol. I, p. 472.

[3]Schmidt, *John Wesley,* Vol. I, p. 262 notes that this anthem (taken from Psalm 130) probably was sung to the setting of W. Croft which frequently repeats the words: "Trust in the Lord."

[4]This was probably a Herrnhut "band." Curnock suggests that the reader was a William Holland, a member of the Church of England in union with the German brethren (*Journal,* Vol. I, p. 475, n. 2).

[5]W. A., *German Bible,* pp. 7, 9-10: quoted in Schmidt, *John Wesley,* Vol. I, p. 263.

this change that God works in the heart through faith in Christ) the Holy Spirit performed *His* miracle, and "I felt my heart strangely warmed. I felt I did trust in Christ, Christ alone for salvation; and an assurance was given me that He had taken away *my* sins, even *mine* and saved *me* from the law of sin and death."[6]

I began immediately to act upon this new faith and prayed "with all my might for those who had in a more especial manner despitefully used and persecuted me. I then testified openly to all there what I now first felt in my heart. But it was not long before the enemy suggested, 'this cannot be faith; for where is thy joy?' Then was I taught that peace and victory over sin are essential to faith and the Captain of our salvation; but that, as to the transports of joy that usually attend the beginning of it, especially in those who have mourned deeply God sometimes giveth, sometimes withholdeth them, according to the counsels of His own will.

"After my return home, I was much buffeted with temptation; but cried out, and they fled away. They returned again and again. I as often lifted up my eyes, and He 'sent me help from His holy place.' And herein I found the difference between this and my former state chiefly consisted. I was striving, yea, fighting with all my might under the law, as well as under grace. But then I was sometimes, if not often, conquered; *now, I was always conqueror.*"[7] The worm that would not die had been dealt a fatal blow. The fire that would not be quenched was now under control. I remember thinking:"enemy beware." Though there would be struggle to follow, I had experienced faith. If for only a moment, I had felt peace with God. The "new doctrine" had been written upon my heart. Expectation had become fulfillment. Hope had become assurance. Faith had become "the evidence of things not seen." I remember thinking, enemy beware! If I could find thirty men totally committed to Jesus Christ, who

---

[6]*Journal*, Vol. I, pp. 476f.

[7]*Works*, Vol. I, pp. 103f.

knew such faith in Him, I would give England back to God.

You might well ask: How would you interpret this experience now?[8] First, let me review the case as I understood it then. I believed that I was *not* (though almost) a Christian before Aldersgate.[9] I did not have saving faith. In my sermon "Salvation by Faith," first preached at St. Mary's, Oxford, on June 18, 1738, I described clearly the kind of faith through which we are saved.

It was not that of a heathen, of a devil, nor even of the apostles while Christ remained upon the earth. It was faith in Christ, and in Christ alone! The heathen believes that God is and that He is faithful to reward those who diligently seek Him. The devil believes (to go much farther) that God is wise and powerful; that He is gracious to reward and just to punish; but also that Jesus is the Son of God, the Christ, the Savior of the world. While Christ was still with the apostles, they had faith and power even to work miracles, yet none of them had saving faith in Christ.

Saving faith is more than that of a heathen or a devil; it is more than a speculative, rational thing; a cold, lifeless ascent, a train of ideas in the head. Saving faith is a disposition of the heart which acknowledges the necessity and merit of His death, and the power of His resurrection; "a recumbency upon him as our atonement and our life, *as given for us,* and *living in us;* and, in consequence hereof, a closing with him, and cleaving to him, as our 'wisdom,

---

[8]What follows is how I think Wesley would have interpreted Aldersgate in 1788 (nearly fifty years later). My own analysis follows (chapter 17).

[9]In fact, there were times when Wesley doubted if he was a Christian *after* Aldersgate. Cf. *Works,* Vol. I, pp. 170f.: "My friends affirm I am mad, because I said I was not a Christian a year ago. I affirm, I am not a Christian now. Indeed, what I might have been I know not, had I been faithful to the grace then given, when, expecting nothing less, I received such a sense of the forgiveness of my sins, as till then I never knew. But that I am not a Christian at this day, I as assuredly know, as that Jesus is the Christ." This (the *Journal* entry for January 4, 1739), in my opinion, is indicative of a rather irresponsible Arminian doctrine held during the first few years following Aldersgate which convinced Wesley that if he did not at that moment *feel* love for and acceptance by God as the all-consuming fire, he was not a Christian. This interesting development will be described in detail later.

righteousness, sanctification, and redemption,' or, in one word, our salvation."[10]

Furthermore, this saving faith is salvation from sin, for there is now no condemnation to them who believe in Christ Jesus. It is salvation from guilt and fear, for "they have not received again the spirit of bondage, but the Spirit of adoption, whereby they cry, Abba, Father: The Spirit itself also bearing witness with their spirits, that they are the children of God."[11]

I truly believed that I did not have this faith. I believed that I had heathen honesty, a form of godliness, and sincerity; yet, I was (so I believed) not a Christian. I wrote: "Brethren, great is 'my boldness towards you in this behalf.' And 'forgive me this wrong,' if I declare my own folly upon the house-top, for yours and the gospel's sake."

"I did go thus far for many years, as many of this place can testify; using diligence to eschew all evil, and to have a conscience void of offence; redeeming the time; buying up every opportunity of doing all good to all men; constantly and carefully using all the public and all the private means of grace; endeavouring after a steady seriousness of behaviour, at all times, and in all places; and, God is my record, before whom I stand, doing all this in sincerity; having a real design to serve God; a hearty desire to do his will in all things; to please him who had called me to 'fight the good fight,' and to 'lay hold of eternal life.' Yet my own conscience beareth me witness in the Holy Ghost, that all this time I was but *almost a Christian*."[12]

I then (and still do) wanted to be altogether a Christian. I had faith as to fear God and to work righteousness, but I wanted that faith that sends the Spirit of God into my heart crying, Abba, Father. I had a measure of love for God and neighbor, but I wanted that love that engrosses the whole heart.[13] I wanted to be stripped of all self-righteousness, to

---

[10]*Works*, Vol. V, p. 9.

[11]Ibid., pp. 10f.

[12]*Works*, Vol. V, p. 21. This quotation is from the sermon "The Almost Christian" which was preached at St. Mary's before the University on July 25, 1741.

[13]Wesley's view of the nature of saving faith here actually goes

become naked before the naked Jesus, that God in His providence might apply His word and fulfill His promise (as He will surely do in you). Aldersgate was the answer. My opinion now regarding saving faith remains much the same. The understanding of my relationship to this faith prior to Aldersgate has changed, however. I now believe that there are degrees or levels of saving faith (even among altogether Christians) that can be gathered generally into two categories—the faith of a servant and the faith of a son.[14] I now believe that the faith of a servant (admittedly somewhat analagous to that of the "almost Christian," but subsequent to it), though young and immature, is acceptable to God for salvation.[15]

I now see clearly that even prior to Aldersgate I had the faith of a servant.[16] Again, I had heathen honesty, the form of godliness, the sincerity of a real desire to serve God (to use the description of an "almost Christian") but slightly more than that, I had, even then, a divine conviction which enables one to "fear God and work righteousness" (the faith of a servant).

Unfortunately, when all the preachers (including myself) "commonly called Methodists, began to preach that grand scriptural doctrine, salvation by faith, they were not sufficiently apprized of the difference between a servant and a child of God. They did not clearly understand, that even one 'who feareth God, and worketh righteousness, is accepted of him.' In consequence of this, they were apt to make sad the hearts of those whom God had not made sad. For they frequently asked those who feared God: 'Do you know that your sins are forgiven?' And upon their answer-

---

beyond that of Böhler's. Wesley was still a product of Böhler's influence but, still within the shadow of Aldersgate, quickly returned (if he in fact ever left it) to a more theocentristic view of God focusing upon love as the all in all. We will develop this further.

[14]*Works*, Vol. VII, pp. 195ff. A sermon, "On Faith": cf. pp. 231ff; a sermon, "On Discoveries of Faith," where the faith of the servant and that of the son are contrasted clearly.

[15]Ibid., p. 199.

[16]Wesley's mind changes during a period of "theological readjustment" between the years 1763-1767. See next page.

ing, 'No,' immediately replied, 'Then you are a child of the devil.' No; that does not follow. It might have been said, (and it is all that can be said with propriety,) 'Hitherto you are only a *servant*, you are not a *child* of God.' You have already great reason to praise God that he has called you to his honourable service. Fear not. Continue crying unto him, 'and you shall see greater things than these.'"[17]

Assurance was the issue. As a servant I had no assurance. As a son I had a measure of assurance so as to testify a childlike confidence and love. I was an altogether Christian (though young and immature indeed) who not only feared God and worked righteousness, but whose faith, as the ground of all, knew (though not without some relapse into sin and fear) myself to be saved from damnation, the bondage of sin, and to possess forgiveness and reconciliation with God.[18]

Aldersgate was an evangelical conversation (in the Reform sense) of faith as assurance. It was not the full assurance of some (namely the Moravians as you will soon discover) but assurance nevertheless. I had then the faith of a son. The faith of a servant trusts Christ, loves God, and is accepted by God, but after Aldersgate I *knew*, and believed that others should know as well. I then believed that the almost Christian was not a Christian because he had no assurance. I should have focused more upon the issue of faith, not as assurance, but as the ability to fear God and work righteousness. I had this, even prior to Aldersgate. This, however, does not diminish the significance of Aldersgate. Although I no longer believe that assurance is essential for salvation (it still remains the "common

---

[17]*Works*, Vol. VII, p. 199. An interesting quotation from a letter to Mr. Melville Horne is even more to the point: "When fifty years ago my brother Charles and I, in the simplicity of our hearts, told the good people of England that unless they *knew* their sins were forgiven, they were under the wrath and curse of God, I marvel, Melville, they did not stone us!" (Southey, *Life of Wesley*, Vol. II, pp. 180f.). Cf. *Sermons*, Vol. I, p. 61n; cf. also, "The Conference Minutes," 1774, where assurance is not faith, but a common privilege available to the faithful.

[18]Less than three months later (June 11, 1788) Wesley wrote the sermon mentioned earlier, "On the Discoveries of Faith," where the same comparison (fresh upon his mind) between servant and son is made. Ibid. pp. 231ff., especially p. 236.

privilege" of every Christian), Aldersgate became the impetus for the evangelical revival.

To summarize, Aldersgate was indeed a watershed between law and grace. The experience of faith, love, and power, as well as assurance, is no small thing, but the sum total of my agonizing search for the life of God in the soul of man must be considered. Struggle alone never justifies a man; but man is rarely justified without it. Man can never be saved by works; but he can never be saved without them either. I was determined not to substitute one extreme for the other. A measure of faith had left me blind to my own dependence upon self-righteousness. I was not to be saved *by* works but *for* works. The Aldersgate experience taught me that faith alone was the source of power. The experience of these last fifty years has proven this to be true without doubt.

Following Aldersgate I then had to pursue God as wholeheartedly by grace through faith as I had previously done by the law. I was a "brand plucked from the burning" and the intensity of my desire to serve God (since 1725) perhaps made Aldersgate inevitable: "Unless the servants of God halt by the way, they will receive the adoption of sons. They will receive the *faith* of the children of God, by His *revealing* His only begotten Son in their hearts." Yet, I had to keep moving. Faith is a process. Had I stopped there the experience of Aldersgate would not have lasted through the night.

So, the Aldersgate experience was the difference not between saving faith and condemnation, the almost and the altogether Christian, but between servant and son. Assurance would become not the infallible evidence, but the common privilege. That servant faith could and must move toward that of a son was a great truth I first began to understand during my stay in Germany, but before that can be told, let me pick up briefly where I left off.

On Thursday morning, May 25, "the moment I awaked, 'Jesus, Master,' was in my heart and in my mouth; and I found all my strength lay in keeping my eyes fixed upon him, and my soul waiting on him continually. Being again at St. Paul's in the afternoon, I could taste the good word of God in the anthem, which began, 'My song shall be always of the loving kindness of the Lord: with my mouth will I ever be showing forth thy truth from one generation to another.' Yet the enemy injected a fear, 'If thou dost believe, why is there not a more sensible change?' I answered (Yet not I), 'That I know not. But this I know, I have now peace with God.' And I sin not today, and Jesus my master has forbid me to take thought for the morrow.

"'But is not any sort of fear,' continued the tempter, 'a proof that thou dost not believe?' I desired my master to answer for me, and opened his book upon those words of St. Paul, 'Without were fightings, within were fears.' Then, inferred I, well may fears be within me; but I must go on, and tread them under my feet."[19]

This I did, experiencing alternately peace and heaviness, joy and temptation, but more peace and joy than I had ever known before. Truly the tide had turned! Preaching came easier. People responded as if by the power of God.

Yet, there was a kind of soreness in my heart not fully healed. On June 13 I decided to retire a short time into Germany to visit with my Moravian friends where God might complete His work in a more tender climate.

---

[19]*Works*, Vol. I, p. 104.

15

Germany

*I plainly perceived, this full assurance was a distinct gift from
justifying faith, and often not given until long afterward; and
that justification does not imply that sin should not stir in us,
but only that it should not conquer.*   Christian David

On Wednesday, June 14, 1738, we lost sight of England.
The time aboard ship was brief, so my old enemy had no
chance to bare his teeth; but I was nonetheless grateful for a
new-found faith that kept the bit in his mouth.

Thursday morning we landed safely at Rotterdam. We
were eight in all. The Englishmen, along with myself, were
Mr. Ingham (who had journeyed with us to Georgia), Mr.
Viney (Peter Böhler's interpreter in London), and Mr.
Holmes and Mr. Brown (both tailors making the pilgrimage partly for business).[1] Only the latter traveled with me
as far as Herrnhut. One of the three Germans was Mr.
Töltschig (who, as a result of my new experience, seemed
far better disposed toward me than in Georgia). From
Rotterdam we walked on to Goudart along a smooth road
lined with walnut trees, accompanied for an hour or so by a
kind physician, Dr. Koker. After an evening at an inhos-
pitable inn, sleeping on bad beds, we arrived at Ysselstein
shortly after 2:00 in the afternoon on June 16.

This was my first opportunity to observe the Brethren in
Europe. Here we were warmly received. It was a small
settlement with only three or four houses. The Community
House was still under construction (I found it completed

---

[1]The identity of John Brown is the only one in question. Cf. Schmidt,
John Wesley, Vol. I, p. 273.

ENGLAND TO HERRNHUT

on my return trip). Saturday, June 17, was their intercession (or community) day, monthly occasions important to
the Moravian people. Everyone was expected to be in
attendance and the event lasted a full day. The celebration
consisted of three great gatherings (morning, afternoon,
and evening). The first, after the custom of Herrnhut, was
spent in singing. The second (though interspersed with
prayer and singing) focused upon their mission abroad
with the reading of letters and journals from the Brethren
in other parts of the world. The third consisted of a word of
exhortation, the reception of new members, and concluded with prayer, for which everyone knelt. Although I
excused myself from the morning gathering in order to
administer the Lord's Supper to our English brethren, I
willingly participated in the afternoon and evening sessions. I was impressed by the pace and timing (one event
after the other while no one seemed to tire), a distinct
historical and ecclesiastical consciousness, and the display
of genuine primitive Christianity.

The next morning at 6:00 we took a boat down the river
to Amsterdam. Here we were entertained with true Christian hospitality by a Mennonite minister, Dr. Decknatel,
who had translated part of the Herrnhut hymnbook into
Dutch. We remained in Amsterdam for five days, during
which time I attended a Society on two occasions. The
grace of our Lord Jesus was at work among us. I left
Amsterdam on June 22, much encouraged and refreshed.

We journeyed directly to Cölen. The cathedral there
(then still unfinished and consisting of two misshapen
heaps) is conducive neither to worship nor community:
"One prays at one shrine or altar, and another at another,
without any regard to, or communication with, one
another."[2] As we came out of the church, we saw that a
crowd had gathered. Since one of our company had pulled
off his hat the crowd could see that we were Protestants.
One of the zealous Catholics then cried out, "Knock down
the Lutheran dog." We prevented any trouble simply by
returning to the church.

---

[2]*Works*, Vol. I, p. 109.

I was happy to begin our journey up the River Rhine to Mentz, arriving July 2, and the next day at Frankfurt. Since we had no pass, I could only think to send word to Johann Böhler (a brewer and the father of Peter Böhler). He received us kindly, and after a pleasant evening we set out for Marienborn the next morning.

At Marienborn I was pleased (if not a bit overwhelmed) to meet Count Zinzendorf, though our first conversation was cut short since I was so ill I had to lie down. For some months I had longed to visit this man face to face (though we had corresponded at some length). The Moravians seemed to reverence him as the all in all. Since his banishment from Saxony two years earlier, he had taken refuge, first in an old castle nearby, and then in another at Marienborn. We remained among the brethren there for two weeks (ten days longer than I had intended).

I remember one exchange that was especially significant. Someone from Frankfurt posed a question to the Count: "Can a man be justified and not know it?" I summarized the reply in my *Journal:* " 1. Justification is the forgiveness of sins. 2. The moment a man flies to Christ he is justified; 3. And has peace with God; but not always joy: 4. Nor perhaps may he know he is justified, till long after. 5. For the assurance of it is distinct from justification itself. 6. But others may know he is justified by his power over sin, by his seriousness, his love of the brethren, and his 'hunger and thirst after righteousness,' which alone prove the spiritual life to be begun. 7. To be justified is the same thing as to be born of God. 8. When a man is awakened, he is begotten of God, and his fear and sorrow, and sense of the wrath of God, are the pangs of the new birth."[3]

As I now consider the Count's response, at least two reactions come to mind immediately. First of all, he insisted that one may *not* know that he is justified until long after. This contradicted the teaching of Böhler (and Spangenberg) that one cannot be justified without knowing it. My own experience seemed to bear out the word of the Count, since I still had not "that joy in the Holy Ghost;

---

[3]Ibid., pp. 110f.

no settled, lasting joy. Nor had I such a peace as excludes the possibility either of fear or doubt. When holy men told me I had no faith, I had often doubted whether I had or no. And those doubts made me very uneasy, till I was relieved by prayer and the Holy Scriptures."⁴ True, the faith that I had since Aldersgate kept the enemy at bay, but I wanted him dead. I wanted the complete victory I had seen in many others. I could not bear the threat of the enemy's sting. I remember thinking: What more must I do? I dare not stop short!

Second (and not unrelated to the first), the Count insisted that "to be justified is the same thing as to be born of God."⁵ I take issue with this.⁶ Let me explain.

To be justified is the act of God *for* us. To be born of God has to do with the witness of our own spirit that follows, that is the work of God *in* us. Faith precedes feeling.⁷ To be justified (the sovereign act of God appropriated by an *utter*

---

⁴Ibid., p. 162.

⁵It is possible that Wesley misunderstood Zinzendorf here as this seems inconsistent with the rest of his teaching and was certainly not the opinion of the Moravians as a whole (see the discussion at Herrnhut on pp. 209-11).

⁶Wesley adds in parenthesis following number 7 above: "Not so." Cf. Wesley's sermons, "The Marks of the New Birth" (*Works*, Vol. V, pp. 212ff.); "The Great Privilege of Those That Are Born of God" (Ibid., pp. 223ff.); and "The New Birth" (Ibid., Vol. VI, pp. 65ff.) where his own doctrine is laid out in some detail. The following paragraph is typical: "But though it be allowed, that justification and the new birth are, in point of time, inseparable from each other, yet are they easily distinguished, as being not the same, but things of a widely different nature. Justification implies only a relative change, the new birth a real, change. God in justifying us does something *for* us; in begetting us again, he does the work *in* us. The former changes our outward relation to God, so that of enemies we become children; by the latter our inmost souls are changed, so that of sinners we become saints. The one restores us to the favour, the other to the image of God. The one is the taking away the guilt, the other the taking away the power, of sin: So that, although they are joined together in point of time, yet are they wholly distinct natures" (Ibid., Vol. V, pp. 223f.)

⁷Wesley writes in his sermon, "The Witness of the Spirit," Discourse 1: "The testimony of the Spirit of God must, in the very nature of things, be antecedent to the testimony of our own spirit. . . . Since, therefore, the testimony of his Spirit must precede the love of God, and all holiness, of consequence it must precede our consciousness thereof" (Ibid., p. 127). Perhaps more to the point (concerning justification and the new birth), Wesley in his sermon, "The New Birth," further explains: "In

dependence upon Christ alone for salvation) is to be an heir of the promise; but to be born of God (the Holy Spirit dwelling constantly in the heart) is regeneration brought to completion in love (though perhaps still not perceptible at every moment).

The failure to distinguish between justification and the new birth is, in effect (the Count being inconsistent with himself), to insist that saving faith necessarily implies *full* assurance. One cannot be saved without knowing it, in fact, while any doubt remains. Though I preached this doctrine (may God forgive me) for nearly ten years, I now believe that one can be genuinely converted either in a "lower" sense (where some doubt remains) or in a "higher" sense (where no doubt remains).[8] This will be developed further in a moment.[9]

Before leaving Marienborn, I had opportunity to observe another intercession day. The ninety Brethren from the next community (though gathered out of many nåtions), together with many strangers (from different parts), met for prayer and fellowship. I remember writing: "O how pleasant a thing it is for brethren to dwell together in unity!"[10]

I set out for Herrnhut on July 19 with Mr. Brown and Mr. Hauptman (a native of Dresden). We journeyed by way of Jena (to see the University) and Halle. At Halle I proposed to see Professor Francke (the son of August Hermann Francke whose name is indeed as precious ointment); but he was away.[11] By the providence of God I managed to see

---

order of *time,* neither of these is before the other; in the moment we are justified by the grace of God, through the redemption that is in Jesus, we are also 'born of the Spirit;' but in order of *thinking,* as it is termed, justification precedes the new birth. We first conceive his wrath to be turned away, and then his Spirit to work in our hearts" (Ibid., Vol. VI, pp. 65f.)

[8]Ibid., Vol. I, p. 172. Cf. Wesley's sermons "Justification by Faith" (Ibid., Vol. V, p. 61) where full assurance is the *condition* of justification and "The Witness of the Spirit," Discourse I (a later sermon), where full assurance is the *privilege* of justification (Ibid., p. 134).

[9]See the Herrnhut account on pp. 209-11.

[10]Ibid., Vol. I, p. 110.

[11]Wesley had read Francke's description of the Orphanage at Halle on his voyage to Georgia.

the Orphan House, an amazing structure large enough to house 650 children. The professor had done his work well. O may I follow him, as he did Christ!

We reached Herrnhut (after a few difficult days and nights due to the German senseless, inhuman usage of strangers) on August 1, and remained there (as at Marienborn) for two weeks. I now had "abundant opportunity of observing whether what I had heard was enlarged by the relators, or was neither more nor less than the naked truth."[12] Mr. Hermsdorf, an old acquaintance from Georgia, did all in his power to make our stay there useful and agreeable. As a result, little time was wasted, our days being nearly filled with services and conversation. As at Marienborn, the testimonies of the power of faith amazed me—"persons saved from inward as well as outward sin, by 'the love of God shed abroad in their hearts;' and from all doubt and fear, by the abiding witness of the 'Holy Ghost given unto them.'"[13] I interviewed eleven of the community members.[14] Several questions concerning justification were resolved.

Again the question of faith by degrees was confirmed, but here I found a contradiction, not only of Böhler, but of Zinzendorf as well. The Herrnhut Brethren (especially Christian David, a carpenter by trade but a most experienced spokesman) not only insisted that a man could be justified without knowing it, but they (and consistent with it) also distinguish between justification and the new birth. I recall the words of Martin Döber (one of their elders): "It is very common for persons· to receive remission of sins, or justification through faith in the blood of Christ, before they receive the full assurance of faith; which God many times withholds, till he has tried whether they will work together with Him in the use of the first gift.

---

[12]Ibid., p. 115.
[13]Ibid., p. 110.
[14]These being Christian David, Michael Linner, David Nitschmann, Alvin Theodor Feder, Augustin Neisser, Wenzel Neisser, Hans Neisser, Zacharias Neisser, David Schneider, Christoph Demuth, and Arvid Gradin. These testimonies were important to Wesley. Much of the material appears almost verbatim in several of his sermons.

Nor is there any need to incite anyone to seek that assurance by telling him the faith he has is nothing. This will be more likely to drive him to despair, than to encourage him to press forward. His single business, who has received the first gift, is, *credo credere, et in credendo perseverare:* (To believe on, to hold fast that whereunto he hath attained:) To go on, doing his Lord's will, according to the ability God hath already given; cheerfully and faithfully to use what he has received, without solicitude for the rest."[15]

To go farther, Christian David described an "intermediate state" where one (though weak in faith) has received forgiveness through the blood of Christ and a measure of assurance so as to *suppose* these things are so; yet, without, in the full sense, "new hearts," without the "full glorious liberty of the children of God."[16] Although their initial experiences were much like my own (some nearly identical) they had all gone beyond me describing to the man their own *full* assurance. Their testimonies were unmistakable. I was a Christian, yet I dare not affirm it without the constant witness of God's Spirit. I could only admit my ungodliness. That I might lay the right foundation, I pinned my hope on God's Word: "to him that believeth on God that justifieth the ungodly, his faith is counted for righteousness." Clearly the foundation is nothing in us! This kind of *utter* dependence upon Christ

---

[15]*Works*, Vol. I, p. 131. These are almost the exact words used in Wesley's sermon: "On Faith" (Ibid., Vol. VII, pp. 195ff.). Cf. the testimonies by Michael Linner (Ibid., Vol. I, p. 128) and David Nitschmann (Ibid., Vol. I, pp. 129ff.) to the same effect.

[16]Ibid., pp. 117f. Christian David states: "Here I found the peace I had long sought in vain; for I was assured *my* sins were forgiven. Not indeed all at once, but by degrees; not in one moment, nor in one hour." Cf. Ibid., p. 121, where he states farther: "I now clearly saw, we ought not to insist on anything we *feel* any more than any thing we do, as if it were necessary previous to justification, or the remission of sins. I saw that least of all ought we so to insist on the full assurance of faith, or the destruction of the body of sin, and the extinction of all its motions, as to exclude those who had not attained this from the Lord's table, or to deny that they had any faith at all. I plainly perceived, this full assurance was a distinct gift from justifying faith, and often not given until long afterward; and that justification does not imply that sin should not *stir* in us, but only that it should not *conquer* " (Ibid., pp. 126f.).

had brought Christian David the assurance that I wanted for myself. In a similar situation, Peter Böhler had advised: "Preach faith till you get it!" I had faith (so as to believe for a moment), but not the joy, the constant peace. My decision was made. Though I was grateful for their teaching concerning my own acceptance (and can testify to it at times), I decided to preach full assurance till I received it. The result was that for nearly ten years, in an effort to experience this myself, I taught (in effect) full assurance as the *condition* (not just the privilege) of all believers who were justified. Some years later I came to realize that I was preaching a doctrine not only foreign to the heart, but to the Scriptures as well. [17]

If I may bare my soul, I now see that my doctrine of justifying faith as full assurance was due to an overgrown fear of faith as some "dark night." My attachment to Böhler caused me to go (as he had done) beyond his masters. I could testify to faith in Christ and even to a degree of knowing, but when I no longer *felt* it, I no longer *claimed* it. If I wanted to claim it constantly I needed (or so I believed) to feel it constantly. This was the dilemma that lay at the root of my problem.

In spite of all, I left Herrnhut greatly encouraged, fully expecting this full assurance at any moment. I determined to trust Christ completely for all that was mine. Let me say to you that now, nearly fifty years later, the experience (as I then understood it) has never really come. Something else, however, has made the long pilgrimage of faith worthwhile. God began using my ministry to convert others (many with experiences beyond my own), but before that

---

[17]This realization came to Wesley during his correspondence with "John Smith." Wesley, between 1738 and 1747, virtually taught salvation by assurance: "Every believer hath a direct perceptible testimony" (December 30, 1745). Following correspondence with "John Smith," however, as expressed in a letter to Charles (July 31, 1747), assurance is only the *common privilege* as justification by faith does *not nesessarily* imply a sense of pardon. There is a good possibility that "John Smith" was responsible for changing Wesley's mind on assurance. The reference to assurance as an *ordinary privilege* (to my knowledge) first appears in a letter to John Smith, dated March 25, 1747 (*Letters*, Vol. II, p. 91), in answer to his charge against "perceptible inspiration" (cf. Ibid., pp. 97ff.).

story can be told, I need to relate the rest of the Herrnhut episode, my own journey home, and the beginning of a "wider parish."

During my remaining days at Herrnhut, I studied carefully the offices of the church and how the people were divided (especially their classes and bands). I examined their conferences, lectures, services (though I objected to their frequent use of *mental* prayer as I had with the mystics before them), and the government of their children. I remember observing the funeral of a child and was surprised that the father should (upon my query as to how he was) reply: "Praise be the Lord, never better. He has taken the soul of my child to himself. I have seen, according to my desire, his body committed to holy ground. And I know that when it is raised again, both he and I shall ever be with the Lord."[18] How I longed to stay in a place where my old enemy had such little success among the people of God. I noted in my *Journal* that "I would gladly have spent my life here; but my Master calling me to labor in another part of His vineyard, on *Monday,* [August 14], I was constrained to take my leave of this happy place; Martin Döber, and a few others of the Brethren, walking with us about an hour. O when shall this Christianity cover the earth, as the 'waters cover the sea.'"[19]

Our return trip was much as our journey out. At Hauswalde I was surprised to find that the Lutherans as well as the papists were irreconcilable enemies to the Brethren at Herrnhut. At Halle I had the pleasure of an audience with Professor Francke (who received us in a most friendly

---

[18]*Works,* Vol. I, p. 117. For the broader picture, see Ibid., p. 147, where a part of *The Constitution of the Church of the Moravian Brethren* reads: "Most of our brethren and sisters have, in some part of their life, experienced holy mourning and sorrow of heart; and have afterwards been assured, that there was no more 'condemnation for them, being passed from death unto life.' They are, therefore, far from fearing to die, or desiring to live on earth; knowing that to them 'to die is gain,' and being confident that they are the care of him whose are the 'issues of life and death.' Wherefore they depart as out of one chamber into another. And after the soul has left its habitation, their remains are deposited in the earth, appointed for that purpose. And the survivors are greatly comforted and rejoice over them with a 'joy the world knoweth not of.'"

[19]Ibid., p. 120.

manner) and I could not help but relay the opinions I had
recently heard against the Moravians. Again, to my surprise, he seemed to suggest that not all of their charges
were groundless.[20] From that moment on I began to have a
more critical eye and recorded some concerns of my own
upon my return to England, which I expressed in a letter
(though never sent).[21]

On our way back through Jena I visited the Pietist
schools. I thought of my old friend, Spangenberg. After
only two days at Marienborn (the Count being away), we
continued on, reaching London on September 16. Little
did I realize that upon my return the whole of England
would be open to me. "A brand plucked from the burning"
would then be ready to make its mark on the soul of
a nation not long forgotten by a gracious and merciful
God.

On Sunday, September 17, "I began again to declare in
my own county the glad tidings of salvation, preaching
three times, and afterwards expounding the Holy Scriptures to a large company in the minories. On *Monday*, I
rejoiced to meet with our little Society, which now consisted of thirty-two persons. The next day I went to the
condemned felons, in Newgate, and offered them free salvation. In the evening I went to a Society in Bear-Yard, and
preached repentance and remission of sins. The next evening I spoke the truth in love at a Society in Aldersgate-

[20]Curnock (*Journals*, Vol. II, p. 58n) informs us that James Hutton and
the Moravians believed that Francke prejudiced Wesley against the
Moravians and especially against Zinzendorf. The relations between
Zinzendorf and the Pietists at Halle were probably not good. Although
Wesley's contacts with the Moravians no doubt increased his appreciation for the more mystical tradition of German Pietism, Professor
Francke might well have criticized Zinzendorf and the Moravians for
their likeness to mysticism. Zinzendorf was strongly influenced by
Madame Guyon through Wolf von Metternich and, as a result, appealed
to many of the followers of Count Marsay and Bourignonism. At any
rate Wesley, from this point on, seemingly changed his opinion of
Moravianism. This, therefore, is perhaps where Wesley first began to
understand the true nature of the Moravian synthesis, their marriage of
the simple gospel with the mystical philosophy of man (*Letters*, Vol. I, p.
258. Cf. *Journal*, Vol. V, p. 46).

[21]*Letters*, Vol. I, pp. 257f. Wesley published this letter in September,
1741, after his breach with the Moravians (*Journal*, Vol. II, pp. 496f.).

Street: Some contradicted at first, but not long; so that nothing but love appeared at our parting."[22]

Less than a month after my return, I journeyed to Oxford. In walking I read the "Truly Surprising Narrative of the Conversions Lately Wrought in and About the Town of Northampton, in New England." I remember thinking to myself: "A revival in North America? If God is one God then surely He will bless this people as well." I began that moment to expect it. Jonathan Edwards was one against many, but God had prevailed. England could supply such a man as well. Little did I know that I was that man.

---

[22]*Works*, Vol. I, pp. 158f.

The Analysis, Part III

Until his heart was 'strangely warmed' in Aldersgate Street, Wesley neither knew, as a normal experience, the meaning of saving faith, nor had he the power to fulfill his Lord's mission.

Nehemiah Curnock

Some will no doubt insist that I justify an entire section on Aldersgate.[1] Although it is important not to exaggerate or misrepresent Aldersgate as a single experience, an isolated moment, the proverbial "bolt out of the blue," the effects of the total experience were significant indeed. Although the assurance of faith, known for the first time on May 24, was not as constant (as we have already observed) as some would apparently like to believe, Wesley's life had been changed. There was virtually nothing left untouched by the events occurring between December, 1737 and September, 1738. Wesley was a different man. His works (especially his sermons) demonstrate this beyond doubt.[2] Consequently with Wesley, as with

---

[1] Here "Aldersgate" refers not just to the "heart strangely warmed," but to the larger experience, including many of the events both preceding and following May 24. It would be good to remember that the whole of Part III is entitled "Aldersgate."

[2] Prior to Aldersgate, Wesley's primary concern was with imitating the suffering Christ. He stressed the Incarnation, not the cross, as the central fact in Christianity. He emphasized man's reconciliation to God, not God's reconciliation to man. After Aldersgate, however, he emphasized the triumphant Christ and the cross as an atonement for sin; victory was assured over the power of Satan. The basic differences here can be observed clearly in a comparison between Wesley's sermons before and after Aldersgate. Compare *The Almost Christian, The Lord Our Righteousness*, or even the expositions on the *Sermon on the Mount* with any of the earlier sermons. The first of Wesley's sermons in the series on the Sermon on the Mount argues that Christianity begins where other religions leave off. Most religions maintain a degree of morality, most emphasize the poverty of spirit, conviction of sin, and renouncing ourselves: but the "first point in the religion of Christ is the *not having our own righteousness*" (*Sermons*, Vol. I, pp. 315ff., italics mine).

anyone who "wipes the slate clean," the historian must begin his task anew. Wesley wrote to his brother Samuel: *"nihil est quod hactenus feci"* (What I have hitherto done is nothing).[3] Perhaps this phrase demonstrates Wesley's use of the hyperbole, but the fact remains that Aldersgate marks a point of redeparture when dealing with an ultimate influence on John Wesley. The need for complete spiritual reconstruction expressed in this Latin phrase (it was also stated in January, 1738, when Wesley was struggling with his heaviness on board ship) reveals the magnitude of the Aldersgate experience. It is significant that Wesley, from this point on, uses two systems of chronology: one *anno domini,* and the other *anno meae conversionis.*[4] By the twenty-fourth of May, Wesley had overcome the objections to faith.[5] Faith had triumphed, exchanging its wealth of imputed righteousness for the poverty of self-righteousness.

Having said this, however, I am personally convinced that the nature of Wesley's religious conversion in 1725 and the relentless consistency of his religious pursuits beyond, made an Aldersgate (in one form or another) inevitable. Wesley, between 1725 and 1738, was more than the pharisee with a facade of religious duty disguising a deceitful heart. He was a determined seeker, through and through. God would not have denied grace to a man in dead earnest about being altogether a Christian. To be sure, the strength of Wesley's ability to reason and the passion of his pilgrimage through the various stages of development made it difficult for him to trust Christ *utterly* by faith alone (a doctrine thought robbery by most men of "religious" worth), but it had to happen.[6] God would not allow Wesley to bury his talent only to become bankrupt by his own self-sufficiency. A lesser man might have failed in his attempt at self-saving acceptance much sooner and would have recog-

---

[3]*Letters,* Vol. I, p. 263. This quotation is from à Kempis, *Imitation,* I.xix.I.

[4]Cf. Ibid., p. 262; Vol. IV, p. 298; Vol. V, p. 358, etc.

[5]Cf. the letter from John Gambold to Charles recorded in the *Journal* for May 14, 1738.

[6]The "stages of development" here include Wesley's high appreciation for several dominant influences, including reason, the means of grace, Puritanism, mysticism, etc. Sorting out the extremely complex nature of these influences (and others) combined, defines our primary goal throughout.

nized the need for faith much more easily, but in spite of all, Wesley was never far from the truth. He was always in process. He never let up. He was never satisfied with less than all that God could offer. So, interpreting the larger experience (especially the months since his leaving America) is our present task. It is an important one indeed.

Although Aldersgate (in my opinion) was inevitable, it also was absolutely necessary for Wesley, both as a Christian and an evangelist. Aldersgate did not so much make him great, for the ingredients for greatness were already there; *it made him useful*. Aldersgate made Wesley a Christian in the full sense of the word and directed his greatness to the needs of the people. Aldersgate was necessary for revival. Without it, Wesley would not have known an effect upon men beyond his own special gifts. Revival is the work of God through men, not of men alone, no matter how great. Wesley would now trust God for the change he had so diligently sought to create himself. Again, Aldersgate was not only necessary for him personally, but for his ministry among others as well.

Let us take a moment to review the larger picture before focusing upon Aldersgate. Wesley, for thirteen years, had sought Platonic ends by Aristotelian means. He sought an experience (full assurance) by works (in whatever form) that only faith could produce.[7] The influences of childhood and early ministry had been honed and sharpened by a tremendous desire to make "religion the business of his life," but he had no peace with God, and no joy in the Holy Spirit.

In achieving his final goal, the Deists were little help. Reason alone (though important) would not lead to an assurance of faith. His High Church tradition was little help. The means of grace alone (though important) would not lead to an assurance of faith.[8] Even the Puritans were little help. Although they

---

[7]In the Analysis, Part IV, we will see Wesley come to grips with those (especially the Roman Catholic mystics) who manifested the fruits of faith (assurance and a degree of holiness) without clearly defining (or even understanding) the evangelical means. Influenced by John Fletcher's "Evangelical Mysticism" Wesley concludes that such have faith because their lives exhibit fruits that only faith could produce. Wesley would become just as concerned with the *fruits* of faith, as with the *roots* of faith.

[8]Evangelical faith for the High Church Anglicans was thought redundant since they assumed that one had it from the moment of baptism.

spoke of evangelical faith, Wesley was so predisposed to their ascetism that he could not hear it, and ascetism alone (though important) would not lead to an assurance of faith. Solitude was little help, for time apart with God (though important), being the result of faith but not the cause, would not lead to an assurance of faith. Finally, the mystics were little help. Internal works-righteousness alone (though important) would not lead to an assurance of faith. Only after Wesley had experimented with all of these influences, to one degree or another, would he look elsewhere. Now he was ready for a change. On the journey back from America he decided to look to the Moravians. Before that door can be opened, however, another (and perhaps the strongest of all) has to be closed.

Although many Wesley scholars believe that he broke with mysticism before his journey home from America, such was not the case. The letter to Samuel in November, 1736, denounced mysticism as "the rock upon which I nearly made shipwreck," but John does not begin to fathom the depths of his attachment to the mystic way as we have already noted. The issue is still very much alive. So much so, that early in January he seriously contemplates sinking wholly into mysticism. As he reads de Renty he remembers the advice of William Law: "Be still and go on."[9]

When Wesley was either troubled or afraid, his first reaction had been to turn to the mystics where his spiritual dryness could be attributed to *in orco* (the mystical dark night). He then read St. Cyprian who made him realize that the real source of his fear and doubt lay within, the result of sin. This is an interesting reversal. Previously he believed that his lack of faith had been God-imposed, forcing him to find assurance by

---

[9]*Journal,* Vol. I, p. 418. It would be good to remember that Wesley, at this point in time, read all the mystics as one and did not realize that the mysticism of de Renty (being both practical and pietistic) was far different from that of Law (being speculative and passive). Though both were mystics (emphasizing the various steps to union with God) de Renty's mysticism (like many of the Roman Catholics) was that of service (including works of charity), whereas Law's was that of the contemplatives (being dark and unsocial). Later on Wesley understood this difference, and although the mystics at this time were soon to seem a part of an unwanted and distant dream, Wesley would again begin to see the value of their exemplary lives for convicting sinners and for challenging Christians to go on in perfection.

contemplating the divine spark within. Now he understood his lack of faith to be self-imposed, forcing him to find assurance by trusting Christ alone without, that is in God. Stated briefly, *assurance comes from on high as a gift found by faith, not from within, as a wage earned by works.* In the quiet after a storm, Wesley lashed out at what nearly consumed him, realizing that *in orco* stifled spiritual growth, making one content to remain still. Old habits are not easily broken, however. At the time of writing his *Journal* review for January 24, 1738, he paused once again to consider the advice of his mystical mentors. Wesley, now beginning to realize his inconsistency, was baffled. He was still a desperate man "grasping at the edge of a precipice."[10]

At this point let us return to his review which continues from a "private paper" quoted by Moore.[11]

John admits to being "tossed by various winds of doctrine." At first he was warned against too much stress on outward works. At the other extreme, however, the Lutherans and Calvinists "magnified faith to such an amazing size that it quite hid all the rest of the commandments." Wesley "did not then see that this was the natural effect of their overgrown fear of Popery."[12] As he became acquainted with the mystic writers, their "noble descriptions of union with God and internal religion made everything else appear mean, flat, and insipid . . . even good works appear so too; yea, and faith itself."[13] At this point Wesley more or less repeats an abbreviated form of the mystical scheme presented to Samuel earlier. He cites their exaltation of love at the expense of the means of grace. John states that he "had no heart, no vigour, no zeal in obeying; continually doubting whether I was right or wrong, and never out of perplexities and entanglements."[14] Again we are reminded that Wesley (because of his background) was unhappy in his mysticism. This review, then, concludes with the statement that the mystics are the most dangerous enemies of Christianity (all others being but triflers). "They stab it in the

---

[10]Wilson, "The Influence of Mysticism," pp. 89ff.
[11]Moore, *Life* Vol. I, p. 342.
[12]*Journal,* Vol. I, p. 419.
[13]Ibid., p. 420.
[14]Ibid.

vitals; and its most serious professors are most likely to fall by them. May I praise Him who hath snatched me out of this fire."[15] Many who do not interpret John's statement to Samuel in November of 1736 as the ultimate break with mysticism find it here. Dunn Wilson writes that by the time Wesley landed in England he was a man freed from mysticism's fatal snare. This conclusion, however, is still premature. Although the mystical door was closed, the enemy's foot was still in it. As long as Wesley did not have the witness of the Spirit, he would be vulnerable to mysticism. Even after Aldersgate, his moments of despair almost inevitably led him to cast a longing look back to the way of the mystics. Until his fits of darkness left him reasonably free to grow in faith, mysticism hung just on the fringe, waiting to move in at the slightest sign of weakness. Nonetheless, Wesley was now prepared to try another route.

The next part of the Analysis involves what I refer to as "the Moravian Synthesis."[16] After the year 1735 (the height of Wesley's mystical experiment), the Moravians became associated with many of the critical phases in his spiritual development.

---

[15]Ibid.

[16]We should examine briefly the history of the Moravians which reveals the origin of this synthesis. Toward the latter part of the seventeenth century, Philip Spener rallied the devotional circles within Lutheranism in order to recall personal piety (thus he is known as the founder of Pietism). Spener, partially through the influence of Jean de la Badie (the Labadists, like the Quietists, emphasized "immediate inspiration" and they rarely celebrated the Eucharist) and, according to Ronald Knox, partially through the influence of the Roman Catholic devotional authors like Gregory Lopez, gave a mystical turn to Spener's evangelical fervor (R. Knox, *Enthusiasm*, pp. 398ff.). The personal interior religion of Spener and his *collegia pietatis* (devotional meetings which met twice weekly in his house) greatly impressed A. H. Francke who extended the influence of the Pietists at Halle where, in 1696, he founded his *Paedagogium* and his Orphanage. In turn, Francke (whose mystical bias we have already mentioned) passed this synthesis of mysticism and reform theology on to Nikolas Zinzendorf, the founder of the "Herrnhuter Brudergemeine," who was educated at his Orphanage in Halle. Ronald Knox writes that the Moravians owed their existence, as a system of thought, to Spener and the Pietists (Ibid.). Yet, the Moravians had no creed as such; their particular brand of spirituality simply emphasized a high degree of spiritual discipline. In many ways Moravianism (like Jansenism and even Methodism) involved in a reaction against the deistic thought which offered Christianity without Christ. The Moravians, therefore, while appealing to Wesley's inbred fear of external works, also struck a blow at the root of his mystical philosophy of internal works-righteousness.

Their impression of peace during the Atlantic storms, Spangenberg's questions concerning Wesley's "inner witness" (Vulliamy describes this encounter as a "momentous experience"), and finally the introduction to Peter Böhler, are all important to Wesley's evangelical conversion and have a direct bearing on his ultimate break with mysticism as well. The Moravians were to serve as a kind of "decompression chamber" for Wesley, in that they had a strong Lutheran doctrine of justification by faith tied to a rich mystical heritage. According to Alexander Knox, the Moravians "weaned" Wesley from mysticism.[17] The Moravian synthesis of mystical piety and reform theology appealed to Wesley's greatest weakness and fulfilled his greatest need. Both Spangenberg and Böhler combined a strong sense of mystical piety with the internal witness of the Holy Spirit appropriated through faith in Jesus Christ. Their experience in both of these areas impressed Wesley and the resulting synthesis was appealing to him, especially now. Earlier, in Georgia, Wesley had ears only for the mystical Quietism of the Moravians. We mentioned that they "dotted all the 'i's'" in Lutheran theology and consequently taught that there could be no salvation by any action or work.[18] They recommended a completely passive attitude extremely close to the mystical writers that he had been reading at the time (Madame Bourignon, for example). Deeply involved in yet another mystical experiment, Wesley had found it relatively easy to seize upon Spangenberg's Quietism and then substitute his own "internal" works-righteousness for the Moravian faith in Christ. By February, 1738, however, Wesley was ready to listen to the other side of the Moravian synthesis, but it would take someone who understood Wesley's mystical mind to lead him from it. In Georgia he had continued in his mystical exercises in hopes of raising himself to a "coveted pitch of Christian rectitude."[19] The bankruptcy of his mystical self-discipline during that season of trial, "humbled him almost to despondency, and predisposed him for listening to the lessons of Peter Böhler."[20]

---

[17]Southey, *Life of Wesley,* Vol. II, p. 322.
[18]Ronald Knox, *Enthusiasm,* p. 410.
[19]Southey, *Life of Wesley,* Vol. II, pp. 300f.
[20]Ibid.

When the two men first met (February 7, 1738), Böhler (like Spangenberg before him) immediately sensed Wesley's need. Although the mystical common denominator in both Böhler and Wesley recognized in religion much the same end, the means were vastly different. Böhler, like Wesley and the mystics, emphasized holiness, but as the *fruit* of faith, not the *cause*. He stressed the means of justification more than the end result of sanctification. Yet, Wesley was drawn to Böhler because he could build upon a "new" foundation—justification by faith, and still retain holiness and perfection as the end of religion.

By the time Böhler left for Carolina (May 4, 1738), Wesley was intellectually prepared for Aldersgate.[21] Whereas previously he had understood faith only in the mystical sense of a blind trust in God (an inferior state eventually to be "swallowed up in love"), he now understood faith in the evangelical reform sense, or perhaps it is more accurate to say in the sense of the sixteenth-century Anglican reformers.[22] Consequently, his statement in the *Journal* (January, 1738) that "he had from the very beginning valued faith," carried little weight since it was written at a time when he did not really understand faith. Wesley insists in a letter to his brother Charles, dated July 31, 1747, that before this time (1738) he had heard nothing about either justification by faith or a sense of pardon.

At this point it should be mentioned that Wesley was prone to overreact at times. When he exaggerated or overreacted to the doctrine of justification by faith, most would agree that it was in the area of *assurance*.

It has been suggested that Wesley struggled in mysticism for as long as he did because he was seeking in mysticism an experience of assurance which did not exist, at least in the initial stages. For the mystic (in spite of the deluge of phrases concerning an immediate communion with God) there was *no*

---

[21]After April 30, 1738, the unexplained break in the *Diary* occurs. The next entry, on the same page, is "Wednesday, May 23, 1739."

[22]Although various modern books (Cannon, Cell, Deschner, Williams, Schmidt, etc.) portray Wesley heir to the continental reformers (Outler adds: "a notion which would have shocked Wesley") Wesley's concept of faith at this time is taken largely from the sixteenth-century Anglican reformers. Neither Luther nor Calvin appear in the *Christian Library*.

assurance and *no* sensible comfort from God for those who could not master the dark night of the soul. Since Wesley was incapable of reaching even this inferior stage of mysticism, assurance was perhaps the one thing he wanted most. One can imagine the impact of a Moravian synthesis on Wesley which offered (within the context of a quasi-mysticism) the promise of assurance, involving not the dark night of the soul, but faith in Jesus Christ.

Ronald Knox, in fact, sees this period between November, 1736, and May, 1738, as a watershed between Quietism (with its emphasis on perfection) and Jansenism (with its emphasis on assurance).[23] By the first of May, however, Wesley had left this fence in favor of the promise of assurance. This assurance was perhaps the one thing most responsible for Wesley's leaving the mystics for the Moravians. Pope's *Compendium of Christian Theology* states that the mystic teaching is opposed to the doctrine of assurance, or at best is indifferent to assurance.[24] Although the Moravians nurtured the Quietistic approach to grace (both were against the formalization of worship and both minimized eternal works-righteousness) the major difference between the Moravian and the Quietist (apart from the question of the atonement) lay in the area of assurance. The Moravian enjoyed a peace of mind through the conviction that he stood in God's favor while the Quietist mystic preferred to remain ignorant of his acceptance with God.[25] The mystic wished to love God regardless of the prospect of assurance. Faith which led to "pure love" coveted no sense of divine protection. The mystics in general, and William Law in particular, exhorted Wesley to accept his heaviness as the discipline of God.[26] Ronald Knox states correctly that Wesley hated Law's "darkness."[27] His formula of trust without assurance made a melancholy thing of religion. Spangenberg and Böhler, on the other hand, reinterpreted this mystical *in*

---

[23]Knox, *Enthusiasm,* p. 435.

[24]Ibid., pp. 410ff.

[25]Pope, *Compendium,* Vol. III, pp. 123f. quoted in A. S. Yates, *Doctrine of Assurance.*

[26]Cf. Law on the "dark night of the soul," Law's *Works,* Vol. IV, pp. 135-136.

[27]Knox, *Enthusiasm,* pp. 480ff.

orco, exhorting Wesley not to be content, but "to *believe* in *your* Jesus Christ."[28] It is significant that Wesley now turns to the personal application of Bohler's doctrine and away from the broad generalities of Law's.

Wesley, in the final analysis, although *drawn* to the Moravians through their mysticism, was eventually *driven* to the Moravians because their synthesis emphasized the one thing that he wanted most and that mysticism alone could not promise: assurance.

Before moving on to the crisis days from May 14 to May 24, we should ask the question whether or not Wesley himself was aware of the significance of the Moravian synthesis for his partial break with mysticism. The evidence seems to suggest that he did not fully understand the nature of the significance of this synthesis. There is a good possibility that just as Wesley's preoccupation with mysticism in early 1736 blinded him to the theological strengths in Moravianism (faith and assurance), so his preoccupation with faith and assurance in 1738 blinded him to the theological weaknesses in Moravianism (mystic Quietism). Yet, the effectiveness of the Moravian influence resulted from its synthesis. The mystical flavor in Moravianism made their doctrine of faith palatable.

Consciously or unconsciously, the Moravian appeal for Wesley was as strong as it was because they couched a "new" doctrine within a familiar setting. If, however, the Moravian affinity for mysticism in 1738 was an asset for Wesley (which it undoubtedly was, as it served to wean him from his mystical "depths"), it later revealed itself as a liability. Perhaps Wesley did not fully appreciate the nature of the Moravian synthesis until the events of Fetter Lane.[29] Once free himself from the subtlety of the mystical trap he was able to react against what he had earlier failed to understand. In a letter to the Moravian brethren, dated August 8, 1740, he writes that the mystics "mix religion with man's wisdom and accommodate it to the mystic theory." Again on April 2, 1741, he criticizes their scheme for

---

[28]A letter from Böhler to Wesley (May 8, 1738) quoted in the *Journal,* Vol. I, p. 461.

[29]The controversy at Fetter Lane over Moravian "stillness" dates roughly from November 1, 1739 to July 20, 1740. See pages 273-275.

being "mystical and not Scriptural." A more complete explanation of these and other similar accusations will be presented in the Analysis, Part IV. Suffice it for now to say that Wesley's partial break with mysticism was now near completion. The fruit of the Moravian synthesis reveals itself clearly during the crisis period leading up to Aldersgate.

The crisis broke during the eleven-day period, May 14 to May 24 (which includes the time of Charles Wesley's "evangelical" conversion on May 21). We have established that the Moravian inner tranquility and assurance (seasoned with just enough of the mystical spirit to make it palatable) appealed to John Wesley's troubled mind and melancholy spirit: yet the Moravians also unmasked the true depths of the mystical error. The problem with mysticism went deeper than Wesley's previous objections (registered in November, 1736, and in January, 1738) indicated. There he criticized their denial of the means of grace while the most dangerous mystical heresy extended even to Pelagianism.[30] All of this is clearly demonstrated in Wesley's correspondence (dated May 14 and 20) with William Law.[31]

Since Wesley (at this point) was aware of the issue himself, these letters have been described in some detail in the biographical chapter.[32] We need only to be reminded that Law, by way of Boehme, in 1737, *chose* a route deeper into mysticism. Wesley, by way of Bohler, in 1738, incapable of the mystical alternative, *was driven* deeper into the tradition of the English and continental reformers. In spite of their parting sentiments concerning the means of religion, however, their concept of perfection as the end of religion remained much the same.

Any eventual similarities should not cause us to underestimate their differences. Tyerman states (somewhat naively) that the difference between Wesley and Law led to "an estrangement between two great and good men which ought never have existed."[33] The differences between Wesley and the Mys-

---

[30]Pelagianism (to state it simply) seeks access to God by works, not by faith. Cf., Orcibal, p. 91f.

[31]*Letters,* Vol. I, pp. 238-244.

[32]See chapter 15.

[33]Tyerman, *Life and Times,* Vol. I, p. 188.

tics (as represented by Law) at this point, however, were perhaps even greater than Tyerman imagined. Law, placing sanctification before justification, proclaimed the *duty* of holiness, but lacked the *power*. Again Wesley's earlier reaction against the mystic denial of the means of grace had not even begun to fathom the subtle depths of mysticism revealed in these two letters. Here the whole of the atonement is in question. Intellectually, Wesley was now committed to salvation by faith alone.

Wesley's theology was changing at its core. Perhaps this can be observed best by his attitude toward the mystic exaltation of love.[34] His strongest criticism of this imbalance appears in the 1756 letter to Law. According to mysticism, God's love "postulated an ultimate unity and singleness of being and will behind all manifestation."[35] Boehme (who influenced Law) had one bias—"God is love"—and consequently the phrase, the "wrath of God," was for Law a contradiction in terms.[36] This, of course, affected the mystical concepts of original sin. Law's *Spirit of Prayer*, for example, denies the imputation of sin: contrarily, the volume of Wesley's *Works* in the Jackson edition entitled "Original Sin" strongly emphasizes this doctrine within the context of God's justice and righteous indignation. Consequently, another key to Wesley's rejection of mysticism can be seen in the fact that Wesley emphasized sin and repentance leading to faith in Christ while the mystic emphasized *love* and *self-discipline*. The mystical "imitation" was concerned primarily with sanctification, not justification. Wesley, on the other hand, exalted faith as the condition of "pardon and justification." Salvation and faith presumed God's initiative. The only condition of faith was yielding to prevenient grace which led to repentance as one turned grief-stricken with sin, fleeing the wrath to come, to the love of God revealed in His crucified, but risen Son.[37] For the mystic,

---

[34]This is not to overstate our case and lose perspective, however. Perfect love as the fruit of faith becomes the most telling characteristic of one going on to perfection. See chapter 19.

[35]Brazier Green, *John Wesley and William Law*, p. 102.

[36]Cf. Law's *Works*, Vol. V, p. 156. Even "hell" is a creation of God's love; cf. Law's *Spirit of Prayer* (Part I, p. 27), "no wrath (anger, vindictive justice) ever was or ever will be in God"; and *Letters*, Vol. III, p. 246.

[37]Green, *Wesley and Law*, pp. 84ff.

however, there was no need for divine reconciliation, since there was no wrath between God and man, except man's.[38] Man must, therefore, allow the example of Christ to turn his wrath to love. Wesley replaced the mystical reproach for the historical incarnation and the objective atonement with a strong doctrine of original sin.[39] Justification had to precede sanctification.

Although Aldersgate was more than a moment ("the heart strangely warmed"), we dare not underestimate the significance of the Society meeting on May 24. Signs of Aldersgate appear as early as 1725 (Wesley received a foretaste of "sensible comforts" from à Kempis) and Wesley was convinced of his *need* for faith as early as March 1, 1738; yet, the influence of this experience is far-reaching.

The 1725 awakening created in Wesley a desire for holiness which would find fulfillment only through faith in Christ. Perhaps in order to purify his motives, to intensify his desire, or even to increase his ultimate joy, God tarried; but eventually Aldersgate was God's answer to Wesley's prayer first recorded in 1725.

Having said this, we must realize that although Wesley was never really far from the kingdom of God for the duration of his spiritual quest, to refer to the accelerated religious fervor of 1725 as *the* conversion is to detach it arbitrarily from his experience as a whole. To disregard the full significance of the fact that Wesley continued to fight his own personal battle until Aldersgate when he was virtually "beaten into submission" is to substitute one exaggeration (1725) for another (1738). John, in 1725, had yet to learn by experience that internal and external righteousness are the effect, not the cause, of saving faith. Wesley's venture into mysticism blinded him from recognizing the need for faith in Christ and delayed his experience of the heart until 1738.[40] Although he recognized his need for power and correctly identified its source in the Holy Spirit, in his romance with mysticism he failed to understand that the power of the Holy Spirit was appropriated through a personal faith in Christ. Most of the classical works on Wesley (written

[38]Ibid., p. 117.
[39]Ibid., p. 119.
[40]*Letters*, Vol. II, p. 65

or edited by men like Curnock, Telford, Sugden, Tyerman, Jackson, and Simon) emphasize the fact "that until his heart was 'strangely warmed' in Aldersgate Street, he neither knew, as a normal experience, the meaning of saving faith, nor had he the power to fulfill his Lord's mission."[41] Alderstage linked his understanding of the work of the Holy Spirit to God through justification by faith.

The concluding events of Part III to be analyzed have to do with the journey into Germany. It is interesting that though the Moravians in Marienborn and Herrnhut described degrees of faith following their conversions (suggesting that full assurance usually came sometime *after* justification), they all testified to full assurance as a present reality. Wesley wanted this full assurance, the constant witness of the Spirit with his spirit that he was a child of God. For the next nine years (in a letter to Charles, dated July 31, 1747, he seems to have altered his opinion) saving faith, for Wesley (as with Böhler and Spangenberg), was nearly synonymous with full assurance. Later, full assurance would become the "common privilege" for Christians: but for now at least, it was an indispensable quality of faith. One does not have to agree with Wesley here to understand how the doctrine evolved. Aldersgate was the turning point (there can be no question about it), but it still did not provide the *abiding* witness described by Böhler. Surprisingly, he decides once again to preach what he did not have himself.[42] He would preach "full assurance till he had it," even if it meant that he was not himself a Christian when doubts were upon him. One needs to realize that when Wesley, during the months to follow, claimed that he was not a Christian, this did not mean that he had not *been* a Christian. It simply meant that he did not know it *then* and a Christian, in order to claim the promises of God, had to know it as a present reality. As described above (and in the last chapter), Wesley later altered this opinion and even later altered other more fundamental opinions as well. Not only would full assurance become the "common privilege," but any assurance at all. One did not

---

[41]*Journal,* Vol. I, p. 33.

[42]Wesley, for the whole of his life, had no qualms about "wanting the world to know what he knew not himself" (*Letters,* Vol. V, pp. 15ff.)

have to know he had faith; he simply had to have it.[43] After 1767, Aldersgate would no longer be interpreted as a conversion from condemnation to saving faith, but as a "conversion" from the faith of a servant (clearly acceptable to God) to the faith of a son. One should not, however, allow this amended interpretation (which will be described more fully) to detract from the importance of Aldersgate. Again, Wesley, prior to Aldersgate, had no power, no peace, no joy, no heart, no expectation to see God at work among his people.[44] He did not preach faith (as he did consistently for the rest of his life) and there was no revival. Now, all this was to change!

---

[43]This will be developed further in chapter 20.

[44]At the risk of repeating myself, it should be reiterated that prior to Aldersgate the word faith is *never* used in the personal sense in any of his extant pre-1738 sermons. He never uses the phrase "justification by faith." He speaks of faith less than a dozen times total and only in terms of *the* faith of the church or *the* Christian faith. After Aldersgate, however, his sermons are literally permeated with this important doctrine and personal faith becomes the all in all.

Bibliography, Part III[1]

Primary Sources

John Wesley, *A Christian Library Consisting of Extracts From and Abridgments of the Choicest Pieces of Practical Divinity, Which Have Been Published in the English Tongue.* Bristol (1749-55), 50 vols.

_____, *A Collection of Hymns for the Use of the People Called Methodists* (1780).

_____, *Explanatory Notes Upon the New Testament* (1755).

_____, *An Extract of the . . . Journal from His Embarking for Georgia to His Return to London.* Bristol (1739).

_____, *Journal.* Curnock, ed.

_____, *Letters.* Telford, ed.

_____, *Poetical Works of John and Charles Wesley.* Collected and arranged by G. Osborn (1868-72), 13 vols.

_____, *Sermons on Several Occasions,* 1st ed., in 4 vols. (1746-60); 4th ed., in 8 vols. (1787-88); Vol IX (1800).

_____, *Standard Sermons,* 4th annotated ed., Edward H. Sugden, ed. (1955-56), 2 vols.

_____, *Works,* Pine.

_____, *Works,* Jackson, ed.

Green, Richard, *Bibliography.*

Union Catalogue of Publications.

Secondary Sources

Abbey, C. J., *The English Church and Its Bishops.*

Baker, E. W., *Herald of the Evangelical Revival.*

Baker, Frank, *Charles Wesley.*

_____, "Study of Wesley's Readings," LQHR.

Cannon, William R., *The Theology of Wesley.*

Cell, George C., *The Rediscovery of John Wesley.* New York (1935).

Coke, Thomas, and Moore, H., *Life.*

Davies, Rupert E., *The Church in Bristol.* Bristol (1960).

Francke, August Hermann, *Pietas Hauensis.*

Green, Brazier, *Wesley and Law.*

_____

[1]For details on abbreviated sources see Bibliographies, Parts I and II.

Green, Richard, *John Wesley*.

Green, V. H. H., *The Young Mr. Wesley*.

———, *John Wesley*.

Jackson, Thomas, *Life of Charles Wesley*.

Knox, Ronald A., *Enthusiasm; a Chapter in the History of Religion With Special Reference to the XVII and XVIII Centuries*. Oxford (1950).

Law, William, *Weeks*.

Léger, A., *La Jeunesse de Wesley*.

Moore, Henry, *Life*.

Orcibal, Jean, "Les Spirituels Francois."

Outler, Albert C., ed., *John Wesley*. New York (1964).

Overton, J. H., *John Wesley*.

———, *William Law*.

Piette, Maximin, *John Wesley in the Evolution of Protestantism*. New York (1937).

Rattenbury, J. E., *The Conversion of the Wesleys*. London (1938).

Schmidt, Martin, *John Wesley*, Vol. I.

Simon, John S., *John Wesley and the Methodist Societies*. London (1923).

Southey, Robert, *Life*. 2 vols.

Telford, John, *Life*.

Tuttle, Robert G., Jr., "Influence of the Roman Catholic Mystics on Wesley."

Tyerman, Luke, *Life of John Wesley*.

———, *Life of George Whitefield*.

Vulliamy, C. E., *John Wesley*.

Wesley, Charles, *Journal*, Telford, ed.

Wesley Historical Society, *Publications* and *Proceedings*.

Whitefield, George, *The Works*. J. Gillies, ed. London (1771-72), 6 vols.

———, *Journals*. I. Murray, ed. London (1960).

Whitehead, John, *Life*.

Williams, Colin, *John Wesley's Theology Today*. New York (1960).

Wilson, D. Dunn, "The Influence of Mysticism on Wesley."

Woodward, Josiah, *The Religious Societies in Canaan*.

Part IV
The Revival

16

Setting the Stage

The work of God still prospers exceedingly. Sinners—men, women, and children—are still convinced and converted to God every day; and there are exceeding few who draw back, as they are much united in affection, and watch over each other in love.
John Wesley

Today is Friday, April 4, 1788. I just received a letter from Samuel Bradburn, one of our preachers in London, informing me that my brother died last Saturday and will be buried tomorrow.[1] I can only give thanks to God who will raise up His saints at that general resurrection when earth and sea shall give up their dead and He "shall wipe away all tears from their eyes; and there shall be no more death, neither sorrow, nor crying, neither shall there be any more pain: for the former things are passed away. And he that sat upon the throne said, Behold, I make all things new."[2]

Mr. Bradburn wrote: "He had no disorder but old age (being in his 80th year). He had very little pain. His mind was as calm as a summer evening. He fell asleep so quietly that they who set by him did not know when he died."[3] Bless God! If a Methodist cannot drop into dust rejoicing, at least he can die in peace. "What a comfort it is to think the Lord liveth! Nay, and that our union with our human friends will be more perfect hereafter than it can be while we are encumbered with the house of clay."[4]

---

[1]Charles Wesley died on March 29, 1788, and was buried in Marylebone parish churchyard.
[2]Revelation 21:3.
[3]*Journal*, Vol. VII, p. 367n.
[4]*Letters*, Vol. VIII, p. 56.

I spoke with you last in Birmingham (nearly two weeks ago) where I remained four days during which I preached no less than eight times and always to a crowded congregation.[5] While in Birmingham, when I was not preparing or preaching sermons, I managed to redeem the time by writing letters, conversing, reading, and praying. I also served communion, baptized, and met with the Society and bands.

At 11:00 on Wednesday, March 26, I arrived at Wednesbury. Our Society there is the mother society of Staffordshire. After dinner with Mr. Turner I prayed and conversed, pausing only for tea before preaching at 6:00 a sermon preached the Sunday before from Luke 24:34: "The Lord is risen indeed." After the sermon, I met with the Society, had supper, and conversed before praying myself to bed at 9:30.

Although the Methodists at Wednesbury (as in Birmingham) have recovered from the threat of Antinomianism, I think an even greater victory (though perhaps not more dangerous) was won against all manner of persecution.[6] Although a small tract entitled "Modern Christianity exemplified at Wednesbury" gives a full account of these "surprising transactions," let me describe some of them to you now.

Less than five years into the Revival (1743) the mob of Wednesbury "hired for that purpose by their betters, broke open their poor neighbors' houses at their pleasure by night and day; exploited money from the few that had it; took away or destroyed their victuals and goods; beat and wounded their bodies; threatened their lives; abused their women, (some in a manner too horrible to name,) and openly declared they would destroy every Methodist in the country: the Christian country, where His Majesty's innocent and loyal subjects have been so treated; and are now,

---

[5]The texts for those sermons were:Philippians 3:13; Luke 24:34; Romans 8:33; Luke 24:26; 1 Peter 1:3; Colossians 3:1; James 2:22; and 2 Corinthians 5:15.

[6]The "threat of Antinomianism" here was the tendency among some to exact God's grace almost to the complete exclusion of the necessary fruits or works to follow.

by their wanton persecutors, publicly branded for rioters and incendiaries!'"[7]

Rather than defend our cause by argument (a cause already defended by the verdict of time) let me give you a few paragraphs, taken chiefly from my *Journal,* describing the most memorable events without embellishment. You who are candid and reasonable can judge for yourselves.

Thursday, October 20, 1743—"After preaching to a small, attentive congregation (at Birmingham), I rode to Wednesbury. . . . I was writing at Francis Ward's, in the afternoon when the cry arose, that the mob had beset the house. . . . The cry of one and all was, 'Bring out the Minister; we will have the Minister.' I desired one to take their captain by the hand and bring him into the house. After a few sentences interchanged between us, the lion was become a lamb. I desired him to go and bring one or two more of the most angry of his companions. He brought in two, who were ready to swallow the ground with rage; but in two minutes they were as calm as he. I then bade them make way, that I might go out among the people. As soon as I was in the midst of them, I called for a chair; and standing up, asked, 'What do any of you want with me?' Some said, 'We want you to go with us to the Justice.' I replied, 'That I will, with all my heart.'. . .

"The night came on before we had walked a mile, together with heavy rain. However, on we went to Bentley-Hall, two miles from Wednesbury. One or two ran before, to tell Mr. Lane they had brought Mr. Wesley before his Worship. Mr. Lane replied, 'What have I to do with Mr. Wesley? Go and carry him back again.' By this time the main body came up, and began knocking at the door. A servant told them Mr. Lane was in bed. His son followed, and asked what was the matter. One replied, 'Why, they sing psalms all day; nay, and make folks rise at five in the morning. And what would your Worship advise us to do?' 'To go home,' said Mr. Lane, 'and be quiet.'

"Here they were at a full stop, till one advised, to go to

Justice Persehouse, at Walsal. All agreed to this; so we hastened on, and about seven came to his house. But Mr. Persehouse likewise sent word, that he was in bed. Now they were at a stand again; but at last they all thought it the wisest course, to make the best of their way home."[8] About fifty of them undertook to escort me, and their rage seemed abated, but they were quickly reinforced (or rather *attacked* by another mob) and I was delivered from one pit to another.

To attempt now to speak was vain, "for the noise on every side was like the roaring of the sea. So they dragged me along till we came to the town; where seeing the door of a large house open, I attempted to go in; but a man, catching me by the hair, pulled me back into the middle of the mob. They made no more stop till they had carried me through the main street, from one end of the town to the other. I continued speaking all the time to those within hearing, feeling no pain or weariness. At the west end of the town, seeing a door half open, I made toward it, and would have gone in; but a gentleman in the shop would not suffer me, saying, they would pull the house down to the ground. However, I stood at the door, and asked, 'Are you willing to hear me speak?;' Many cried out, 'No, no! knock his brains out; down with him; kill him at once.' Others said, 'Nay, but we will hear him first.' I began asking, 'What evil have I done? Which of you all have I wronged in word or deed?' And continued speaking for above a quarter of an hour, till my voice suddenly failed: Then the floods began to lift up their voice again; many crying out, 'Bring him away! Bring him away.'

"In the mean time my strength and my voice returned, and I broke out aloud into prayer. And now the man who just before headed the mob, turned, and said, 'Sire, I will spend my life for you: Follow me, and not one soul here shall touch a hair of your head.' Two or three of his fellows confirmed his words, and got close to me immediately. At the same time, the gentleman in the shop cried out, 'For shame, for shame! Let him go.' An honest butcher, who

---

[8]Ibid., pp. 436f.

was a little farther off, said, it was a shame they should do thus; and pulled back four or five, one after another, who were running on the most fiercely. The people then, as if it had been by common consent, fell back to the right and left; while those three or four men took me between them, and carried me through them all. But on the bridge the mob rallied again: We therefore went on one side, over the milldam, and thence through the meadows; till, a little before ten, God brought me safe to Wednesbury; having lost only one flap of my waistcoat, and a little skin from one of my hands.

"I never saw such a chain of providences before; so many convincing proofs, that the hand of God is on every person and thing, overruling all as it seemeth him good.

"The poor woman of Darlaston, who had headed that mob, and sworn, that none should touch me, when she saw her followers give way, ran into the thickest of the throng, and knocked down three or four men, one after another. But many assaulting her at once, she was soon overpowered, and had probably been killed in a few minutes, (three men keeping her down and beating her with all their might,) had not a man called to one of them, 'Hold, Tom, hold!' 'Who is there?' said Tom: 'What, honest Munchin? Nay, then, let her go.' So they held their hand, and let her get up and crawl home as well as she could.

"From the beginning to the end I found the same presence of mind, as if I had been sitting in my own study. But I took no thought for one moment before another; only once it came into my mind, that if they should throw me into the river, it would spoil the papers that were in my pocket. For myself, I did not doubt but I should swim across, having but a thin coat, and a light pair of boots.

"The circumstances that follow, I thought, were particularly remarkable: 1. That many endeavoured to throw me down while we were going down-hill on a slippery path to the town; as well judging, that if I was once on the ground, I should hardly rise any more. But I made no stumble at all, nor the least slip till I was entirely out of their hands. 2. That although many strove to lay hold on my collar or clothes, to pull me down, they could not fasten at all: Only one got fast hold of the flap of my waistcoat, which was soon left in his hand; the other flap, in the pocket of which was a bank note, was torn but half off. 3. That a lusty man just behind, struck at me several times, with a large oaken stick; with which if he had struck me once on the back part of my head, it would have saved him all farther trouble. But every time the blow was turned aside, I know not how; for I could not move to the right hand or left. 4. That another came rushing through the press, raising his arm to strike, on a sudden let it drop, and only stroked my head, saying, 'What soft hair he has!' 5. That I stopped exactly at the Mayor's door, as if I had known it, (which the mob doubtless thought I did,) and found him standing in the shop, which gave the first check to the madness of the people. 6. That the very first men whose hearts were turned were the heroes of the town, the captains of the rabble on all occasions, one of them having been a prize-fighter at the bear-garden. 7. That, from first to last, I heard none give a reviling word, or call me by any opprobrious name whatever; but the cry of one and all was, 'The Preacher! The Preacher! The Parson! The Minister.' 8. That no creature, at least within my hearing, laid any thing to my charge, either true or false; having in the hurry quite forgot to provide themselves with an accusation of any kind. And, Lastly, That they were as utterly at a loss, what they should do with me; none proposing any determinate thing; only, 'Away with him! Kill him at once!'

"By how gentle degrees does God prepare us for his will! Two years previous a piece of brick grazed my shoulders. It was a year after that a stone struck me between the eyes. The month before this incident I received one blow, and that evening two; one before we came into the town, and one after we were gone out; but both were as nothing: For though one man struck me on the breast with all his might, and the other on the mouth with such force that the blood gushed out immediately, I felt no more pain from the blows, than if they had touched me with a straw."[9]

---

[9]Ibid., pp. 437-440.

"I cannot close this head without inserting as great a curiosity in its kind as, I believe, was ever yet seen in England; which had its birth within a very few days of this remarkable occurance at Walsal.

> *Staffordshire.*
> To all High-Constables, Petty-Constables, and other of His Majesty's Peace Officers, within the said County, and particularly to the Constable of Tipton: (near Walsal:)
> WHEREAS, we, His Majesty's Justices of the Peace for the said County of Stafford, having received information that several disorderly persons, styling themselves Methodist Preachers, go about raising routs and riots, to the great damage of His Majesty's liege people, and against the peace of our Sovereign Lord the King:
> These are, in His Majesty's name, to command you and every one of you, within your respective districts, to make diligent search after the said Methodist Preachers, and to bring him or them before some of us His said Majesty's Justices of the Peace, to be examined concerning their unlawful doings.
> Given under our hands and seals, this day of
> October, 1743.   J. Lane.
>   W. Persehouse.[10]

From Wednesbury I continued north on Thursday, March 27 (Mr. Turner traveling with me), passing through Dudley, where I preached at noon on 2 Corinthians 5:19: "God was in Christ, reconciling the world unto himself." Dudley, too, was formerly a den of lions, but the steady behavior of the Society has made an impression on most of the town. I had much liberty of spirit to explain the "taking away that enmity (between God and man), which could no otherwise be removed than by the blood of the Son of God."[11] Such a change! My, how does "a praying congregation strengthen the Preacher."[12]

---

[10]These were the justices to whose houses Wesley was carried, and who refused to see him. Ibid., p. 441.

[11]Wesley, *Notes on the New Testament*, p. 657.

[12]*Works*, Vol. II, p. 165.

At 6:00 in the evening I preached at Wolverhampton on Luke 13:23: "Are there few that be saved?" Nearly thirty years ago, since no one had yet preached in the open air in this furious town, "I was resolved, with God's help, to make a trial, and ordered a table to be set in the inn-yard. Such a number of wild men I have seldom seen; but they gave me no disturbance (their intent being but to stare), either while I preached, or when I afterwards walked through the midst of them."[13] I was not always so fortunate, however. I remember, during those unruly days, being struck with a stone flung by a Mr. Moseley whose vicious act pursued him, bless God, until he was soundly converted in Noah's Ark Chapel. Now, it seems, the last will be first.

Last Friday morning I was up at 4:00, prayed, had tea, and conversed with Mr. Turner before leaving town by carriage. I arrived at Madeley at 12:30 (a pleasant village, surrounded by trees and hills) where I immediately visited with my dear friends there, especially Mrs. Fletcher, whose health had surprisingly improved. What an impression was left upon those good people by her late husband who some affectionately called (and I think correctly), the "Shropshire saint."

John Fletcher, Swiss by birth and education, came to England in 1752. Although I knew and admired him almost from the time of his arrival, we did not become close friends until he came to Madeley in 1760.

I soon became so impressed by his total devotion that I once believed that he would be the one to succeed me in sustaining the Revival, but God has taken him from us. Perhaps God will continue His work by the example of this exceptional man as related in my *Life of Fletcher*. In this *Life* Mr. Fletcher is portrayed as a man constantly pleading with God to take fuller possession. Once while prostrate in prayer, he received a vision of Christ bleeding on the cross. He sat up two whole nights a week in order to enter more deeply into communion with God through reading, meditation, and prayer. He would not even move from his chair

---

[13]Ibid., Vol. III, pp. 47f.

without first looking to God. I must admit that for many years I despaired of finding any inhabitant of Great Britain that could compare in any degree with Gregory Lopez, or Monsieur de Renty. But no person can ever say that Mr. Fletcher was at all inferior to them. Did he not experience as deep communion with God, and as high a measure of inward holiness, as was experienced by either one or the other of those burning and shining lights?

At 1:30 I had dinner and continued to converse and pray with my Shropshire friends until tea. At 6:00 I preached on Colossians 3:1: "If ye then be risen with Christ, seek those things which are above, where Christ sitteth on the right hand of God." The congregation was surprisingly large, and they listened with joy while I applied that happy verse. After preaching I ate and again conversed before praying myself to bed at 10:00.

On the day that my brother died I was up at 4:15, praying, writing, and preaching before 8:00 on Hebrews 12:1: "Wherefore seeing we also are compassed about with so great a cloud of witnesses, let us lay aside every weight, and the sin which doth so easily beset us, and let us run with patience the race that is set before us." Little did I realize that my brother was at that moment among those witnesses. As best as I can ascertain, the very moment my brother fell asleep, our congregation was singing the words from his hymn: "Come, come, let us join our friends above that have obtained the prize." To be sure, I feel the loss of my brother deep within my heart. I do not despair, however. Being cut off from any worldly hope, I can simply and nakedly hang upon the living God; bless His name.

That same day I went over to Salop where two poor wretches were executed in the afternoon. This had a sobering effect upon the people so that our preaching house was more crowded than I have ever seen it before. "It was given me to speak strong words, such as made the stout-hearted tremble. Surely there is now, if there never was before, a day of salvation to this town also."[14]

---

[14]Ibid., Vol. IV, p. 411.

The next day (being Sunday) I returned to Madeley and preached to crowded congregations both morning and afternoon. How long will these good Methodists be an example for all those yet to follow?

From Madeley I continued north, leaving last Monday morning, traveling through Stafford, Lane-End, Burslem, Newcastle-Under-Lyne, Leek, and Congleton, arriving here at Macclesfield this afternoon at 4:00 during a violent storm. At Stafford I preached at noon; at Lane-End (a village two or three miles from Newcastle-Under-Lyne) at 6:00, but the chapel could not contain one third the congregation.

On Tuesday (April 1), we made our way to Burslem. There "the work of God still prospers exceedingly. Sinners—men, women, and children—are still convinced and converted to God every day; and there are exceeding few who draw back, as they are much united in affection, and watch over each other in love."[15] There have been at least two great revivals at Burselm. One, twenty-five years ago, when the power of God and the fire of His love was kindled among the people. Then again, just last year (1787), an account of which is recorded in my *Journal:* "Observing the people flocking together, I began half an hour before the appointed time. But, notwithstanding this, the House would not contain one half of the congregation: So, while I was preaching in the House to all that could get in, John Broadbent preached in a yard to the rest. The love-feast followed; but such a one as I have not known for many years. While the two or three first spoke, the power of God so fell upon all that were present, some praying, and others giving thanks, that their voices could scarce be heard: And two or three were speaking at a time, till I gently advised them to speak one at a time; and they did so, with amazing energy. Some of them had found peace a year ago, some within a month or a week, some within a day or two; and one of them, a potter's boy, told us, 'At the prayer-meeting I found myself dropping into hell; and I cried to the Lord, and he showed me he loved me. But Satan came immediately, and offered me a bag of money, as long as my arm; but I said, "Get thee behind me, Satan."' Several also testified that the blood of Christ had cleansed them from all sin. Two declared, after bitter cries, that they knew their sins were just then blotted out by the blood of the Lamb; and I doubt not but it will be found, upon inquiry, that several more were either justified or sanctified. Indeed there has been, for some time, such an outpouring of the Spirit here, as has not been in any other part of the kingdom; particularly in the meetings for prayer. Fifteen or twenty have been justified in a day. Some of them had been the most notorious, abandoned sinners, in all the country; and people flock into the society on every side; six, eight, or ten, in an evening."[16]

Wednesday I was at Newcastle-Under-Lyne. Yesterday, after crossing over to Leek in the afternoon where we no longer plow upon the sand before the fruit appears, I arrived at Congleton in time to preach in the evening. I have here part of a letter written by a Methodist, dated August 1, 1962, which describes the beginning of our revival there: "The work of God for sometime stood still here; but at the love-feast, on the 21st of March last, (glory for ever be to God!) there was an out-pouring of his Spirit among us. Five persons were assured of their acceptance with God, of whom, by his free grace, I was one; four believed he had not only forgiven their sins, but likewise cleansed them from all unrighteousness. Many more have since found him gracious and merciful: Nor is his hand as yet stayed at all."[17] Yet, I fear so now. Though the congregation yesterday included the minister, the mayor, and several aldermen, "they seemed astonished while I opened and strongly applied, 'Thou shalt have no other gods before me.'"[18]

Here at Macclesfield the work of God goes steadily on. I recall a description of the beginning of the revival here as well. I received the following account: "In March last

[16]Ibid., pp. 365f.
[17]Ibid., Vol. III, p. 108.
[18]Ibid., Vol. IV, p. 412.

(1762), after a long season of dryness and barrenness, one Monday night John Oldham preached. When he had done, and was going away, a man fell down and cried aloud for mercy. In a short time, so did several others. He came back, and wrestled with God in prayer for them. About twelve he retired, leaving some of the brethren, who resolved to wrestle on till they had an answer of peace. They continued in prayer till six in the morning; and nine prisoners were set at liberty. They met again the next night; and six or seven more were filled with peace and joy in believing: So were one or two more every night until the Monday following, when there was another general shower of grace; and many believed that the blood of Christ had cleansed them from all sin."[19]

What a blessing to see so many continuing to rejoice in the Lord. Just this evening I preached again on John 9:4: "I must work the works of him that sent me, while it is day: the night cometh, when no man can work." Just now I stand convicted by my own preaching. Perhaps the news of Charles' death has sobered me. Though my old enemy is now as bleary-eyed as I, the thought of dying still has its effect. Since my brother's death is still fresh upon my mind, and so many memories are impressed upon me, I thought it might be a good time to share with you the story of our Revival, which God has accomplished these fifty years.

---

[19]Ibid., Vol. III, pp. 109f.

17

The Call to Bristol

If the brethren, after prayerful direction, think proper, I wish you would be here [Bristol] the latter end of next week. . . . I go away, God willing, next Monday Se'enight. If you were here before my departure, it might be best. Many are ripe for bands. I leave that entirely to you. George Whitefield

Bristol, May 21, 1739, while I was enforcing the words from Psalm 46:10—"Be still, and know that I am God"— our Lord "began to make bare his arm, not in a close room, neither in private, but in the open air, and before more than 2,000 witnesses. One, and another, and another was struck to the earth; exceedingly trembling at the presence of His power. Others cried, with a loud and bitter cry, 'What must we do to be saved?' and in less than an hour seven persons, wholly unknown to me till that time, were rejoicing and singing, and with all their might giving thanks to the God of their salvation."[1] For seven weeks, at an appointed time, I had been preaching at various places in and around Bristol.[2] Monday afternoons at 4:00 I went to a brickyard, a convenient place near Bristol. That was the present setting.[3] This was the first time (as a result of *my* preaching) that such outward manifestations had affected people standing in the open air (putting to rest the earlier

[1] *Works*, Vol. I, p. 196.

[2] Wesley, in these early months of the revival, regularly conducted fourteen meetings indoors and eight to ten meetings outdoors each week.

[3] Wesley first preached in the open air on April 2 at another brickyard not far from the one mentioned here. On April 23 the location for the Monday afternoon preaching changed as the owner of the previous location withdrew his permission. For the exact identification, see "Proceedings of the Wesley Historical Society," vol. 6, pp. 106f.

objection that these were purely *natural* effects; that these people fainted away only because of the heat and closeness of the rooms).

In the evening of that same day I was interrupted at the Nicholas-Street Society. "Almost as soon as I had begun to speak, one who was 'pricked at the heart,' cried out and strongly groaned for pardon and peace. Yet I went on to declare what God had already done, in proof of that important truth, that he is 'not willing *any* should perish, but that *all* should come to repentance.' Another person dropped down, close to one who was a strong assertor of the contrary doctrine. While he stood astonished at the sight, a little boy near him was seized in the same manner. A young man who stood up behind fixed his eyes on him, and sunk down himself as one dead; but soon began to roar out, and beat himself against the ground, so that six men could scarcely hold him. His name was Thomas Maxfield."[4] With but one exception, "I never saw one so torn of the evil one. Meanwhile, many others began to cry out to the 'Saviour of all' that He would come and help them, insomuch that all the house (and indeed all the street for some space) was in an uproar. But we continued in prayer; and before ten the greater part found rest to their souls.

"I was called from supper to one who, feeling in herself such a conviction as she never had known before, had run out of the Society in all haste that she might not expose herself. But the hand of God followed her still; so that, after going a few steps, she was forced to be carried home; and, when she was there, grew worse and worse. She was in a violent agony when we came. We called upon God, and her soul found rest.

"About twelve I was greatly importuned to go and visit one person more. She had only one struggle after I came, and was then filled with peace and joy. I think twenty-nine in all had their heaviness turned into joy this day."[5]

---

[4]*Works*, Vol. I, p. 196. Maxfield would become one of Wesley's strongest preachers.

[5]Ibid., pp. 196f.

These are fact. Let any judge them as they please. That "such changes were then wrought appears (not from their shedding tears only, or falling into fits, or crying out: these are not the fruits whereby I judge; but) from the whole tenor of their life, till then, many wicked; from that time, holy, just, and good."[6]

For those who would still object, I will show them more: one who "was a lion till then, and now is a lamb; him that was a drunkard, and is now exemplarily sober; the whoremonger that was, who now abhors the very 'garment spotted by the flesh.' These are my living arguments for what I assert, viz., 'That God does now, as aforetime, give remission of sin, and the gift of the Holy Ghost, even to us and to our children; yea, and that always suddenly, as far as I have known, and often in dreams or in the visions of God.' If it be not so, I am found a false witness before God. These things I *do*, and by his grace *will*, testify."[7]

The revival had begun! For nearly two months I had been preaching to congregations totaling nearly 50,000 a week. Though the crowds attracted by Mr. Whitefield were even greater, our results were far more lasting.[8] By this time our first preaching house (the New Room) was under construction. New converts were being organized into Societies which were multiplying daily. Books had been ordered for the bands demonstrating the need for perfection.[9] Our first hymnbook was on the press and another was being prepared.[10] God was accomplishing a mighty work. Let me describe its beginning.

---

[6]Ibid., p. 195.

[7]Ibid., pp. 195f.

[8]See *Works*, Vol. VII, p. 411, for a word concerning the lack of discipline among some of Whitefield's converts.

[9]By June, 1739, Wesley had already published an extract from the life of Haliburton. He prepared the preface and corrected the text in January and February, and by June 7, 1739, Wesley writes that twelve Haliburtons are already overdue in Bristol. On June 11, 1739, the words "Christian Perfection" appear in the *Diary* for 6:00 and 9:00 in the morning. This was one of the earliest appearances of the phrase apart from the references to the treatise by Mr. Law.

[10]*Hymns and Sacred Poems*, published in 1739 and the second published in 1740.

Our last narrative left off as I was in route to Oxford, October 9, 1738. While at Oxford I soon saw miracles performed in our midst. Within days, fourteen were added to our Society so that we increased to eight bands (again, small groups within the Society intending effectually to build one another up in love) consisting of fifty-six persons, all of whom sought salvation only in the blood of Christ.[11]

I returned to London on October 18. Although more and more churches were closed to me, I continued to preach where I could (as best I could while nagging doubt still plagued me) and minister among the societies. Then, on November 30, Mr. Whitefield, after some months in Georgia (our ships, the *Samuel* bringing me in from America and the *Whitaker* taking him out, passed each other in the port of Deal), returned to England after an absence of just eleven months. As I was in the west country I did not learn of his arrival until December 11. Since I had not seen him for three-and-a-half years, I hastened to London where we enjoyed sweet fellowship the next day. We talked of Georgia until well past midnight (he was much too kind in his evaluation of my ministry there), Aldersgate, and Herrnhut.[12] It was his specific intent to raise money for an orphanage in America. His popularity, however (prior to his leaving for America he had enjoyed great success), had won him not only friends, but enemies as well. Though he received the approval of the Archbishop of Canterbury to

---

[11]The interrelationship of society to class to bands, etc., will be described in some detail later.

[12]Relevant to Georgia, Whitefield writes (Whitefield's *Journal*, p. 157): "What the good Mr. Wesley had done under God, in America, is inexpressible. His name is very precious among the people." While Wesley no doubt needed this word of affirmation, Whitefield's comment was such an exaggeration that he omitted it from the later edition. Regarding Aldersgate, although Whitefield dates his conversion from 1735, he writes in his journal for 1736 (while Wesley was still in Georgia): "About this time God was pleased to enlighten my soul, and bring me into the knowledge of His free grace and the necessity of being justified in His sight by *faith only*. This was more extraordinary, because my friends at Oxford had rather inclined to the mystic divinity . . ." (Whitefield's *Journal*, p. 62). The two men obviously had a great deal in common to talk about.

plead his cause in any parish available to him, five churches were immediately denied, while four remained open (with a few more to follow, though frequently he was preaching a "strange doctrine to polite audiences"). For the next two months, Mr. Whitefield and I preached at every opportunity and continued our work among the Societies.[13] Most of the remaining time was spent writing letters, the abridgment of Haliburton and its preface, and correcting the *Hymns and Sacred Poems*.

New Year's Eve found "Mr. Hall, Kinchin, Ingham, Whitefield, Hutchings, and my brother Charles, present at our love-feast in Fetter Lane, with about sixty of our brethren. About three in the morning, as we were continuing instant in prayer, the power of God came mightily upon us, insomuch that many cried out for exceeding joy, and many fell to the ground. As soon as we were recovered a little from that awe and amazement at the present of his Majesty, we broke out with one voice, 'We praise thee, O lord; we acknowledge thee to be the Lord.'"[14]

On New Year's Day, 1739, I was at peace; yet, three days later I was deep in despair insisting (as has already been mentioned) that I was not a Christian since I did not at that moment feel it. True, the enemy had been mortally wounded, but his hideous threat still lingered. He held on tenaciously. I fought back thoughts of death. I began to experience the most unworthy desires. As I watched and listened to Mr. Whitefield, for example, I found myself somewhat envious. This caused me to reflect upon my own state of mind and heart, concluding that I not only lacked his gifts, but his love for God as well. Whitefield had a full assurance of faith. I admired (and loved) him

---

[13]Wesley preached more than thirty sermons during this period and Whitefield is said to have preached fifty-seven times in fifty-six days.

[14]*Works*, Vol. I, p. 170. We are reminded that the Fetter Lane Society (like the others) was neither Methodist nor Moravian (as some suppose), but a new religious society with bands and love feasts attached to the Church of England, using the Book of Common Prayer, and taking the Sacrament of Holy Communion in the parish churches. Neither the Methodists nor the Moravians, as such, were organized in London at this time.

more than anyone I had known or seen, even in Germany. I could pay him no greater tribute. Yet, our talents were different. I lacked his eloquence and polish; whereas he could slay thousands simply by the way he pronounced Mesopotamia. I was reminded of Apollos and Paul. I remember thinking (God forgive the unlikely comparison) I would be Paul. I would organize Methodist societies. I had a vision, a dream. Even as I considered these thoughts I felt a surge of purpose. I would not only preach for conversion, but go beyond and gather those affected into the kind of body that would both nurture and sustain, insuring their perfection.

Much to my surprise, on January 21 I began to see openly the fruits of my own preaching. "While I was expounding in the Minories a well-dressed, middle-aged woman suddenly cried out as in the agonies of death. She continued so to do for some time, with all the signs of the sharpest anguish of spirit. When she had somewhat recovered, I requested her to call on me the next day. She then told me that about three years before, she was under strong convictions of sin and in such terror of mind, that she had comfort in nothing, nor had she any rest, day or night. She sent for the minister of her parish, and told him the distress she was in, upon which he told her husband that she was stark mad, and advised him to send for a physician immediately. A physician was sent for accordingly, who ordered her to be blooded, blistered, and so on. But this did not heal her wounded spirit, so she continued much as she was before. But the night before, He whose word she at first found to be 'sharper than any two-edged sword,' gave her a faint hope, that He would undertake her cause, and heal the soul which had sinned against Him."[15]

I saw it again on March 6 (one of the most surprising instances of His power I ever remember to have seen), when I visited a Mrs. Compton, who was "above measure enraged at this *new way*, and zealous in opposing it. Finding argument to be of no other effect, than to inflame her more and more, I broke off the dispute, and desired we

---

[15]Ibid., p. 172.

might join in prayer, which she so far consented to as to kneel down. In a few minutes she fell into an extreme agony, both of body and soul; and soon after cried out with the utmost earnestness, 'Now I know I am forgiven for Christ's sake.' Many other words she uttered to the same effect, witnessing a hope full of immortality. And from that hour, God hath set her face as a flint to declare the faith which before she persecuted."[16]

These experiences had a strange effect upon me. The depression caused by my lack of full assurance subsided. I do not recall another season of deep despair for better than a quarter of a century.[17] I could even allow myself to think freely upon death without any great consequence. My ministry had been confirmed, authenticated. It was working! By God's grace, England would have its apostle Paul!

Mr. Whitefield had left for Bristol (again, collecting monies for his Georgia orphan house) on February 7.[18] A week later he arrived, and with boundless energy (he was but twenty-five at the time, ten years my junior) began preaching, first in the prison and religious societies, but then (as the churches were closed to him) in the fields.[19] I remember an article from the *Gentlemen's Magazine* (1739)

---

[16]Ibid., p. 175.

[17]According to the *Works*, Wesley does not again express deep despair until June 27, 1766 (*Letters*, Vol. V, pp. 15ff.).

[18]In route, Whitefield visited Wesley's mother in Salisbury. She wrote to Samuel, Jr.: "Mr. Whitefield has been making a progress through these parts, to make a collection for a house in Georgia for orphans. . . . He came thither to see me, and we talked about your brothers. I told him I did not like their way of living, and wished them in some place of their own, wherein they might regularly preach, etc. He replied, 'I could not conceive the good they did in London; that the greatest part of our clergy were asleep, and that there never was a greater need for itinerant preachers than now.' . . . I then asked Mr. Whitefield if my sons were not for making some innovations in the church, which I much feared. He assured me that they were so far from it, that they endeavored all they could to reconcile Dissenters to our communion. . . . His stay was short, so I could not talk with him as much as I desired. He seemed to be a very good man, and one who truly desires the salvation of mankind. God grant that the wisdom of the serpent may be joined with the innocence of the dove!" (George J. Stevenson, *Memorials of the Wesley Family*, London, 1876, p. 216).

[19]Howell Harris, a Welshman, had established a strong precedent for field preaching which Whitefield greatly admired.

describing his ministry at this time: "On Saturday, 18th inst., he [Mr. Whitefield] preached at Hannam Mount to five or six thousand persons, and in the evening removed to the Common, about half a mile farther, where Three Mounts and the plains around were crowded with so great a multitude of coaches, foot and horsemen, that they covered three acres and were computed at 20,000 people; and, at both places, he collected fourteen pounds, ten shillings for the Orphan House in Georgia."[20]

While Mr. Whitefield had begun the work in Bristol I labored on, mostly in London, strengthening the Societies. Then, toward the end of March, I received the following letter from Mr. Whitefield: "If the brethren, after prayerful direction, think proper, I wish you would be here the latter end of next week. Brother Hutchins [John Hutchings] sets out to-morrow for Dummer. Mr. Chapman brings a horse to London, which you may ride. I go away, God willing, next Monday Se'enight. If you were here before my departure, it might be best. Many are ripe for bands. I leave that entirely to you." In a postscript, dated March 23, he adds: "I beseech you, come next week; it is advertised in this day's journal . . . the people expect you much . . . our brethren advise you should go through Basingstoke and call at Dummer, and there take the horse Brother Hutchins rides thither. Whosoever you may appoint shall ride Brother Chapman's. The Lord direct us in all things!"[21] It would appear that Mr. Whitefield had left little to chance. Yet, I was not convinced! Since it was a rule of the Society first to consult the bands, I sought their counsel (more especially the Fetter Lane Society, since this was the one to which I was particularly accountable.)[22] Many in the Soci-

---

[20]*Gentlemen's Magazine* for 1739, p. 162.

[21]*Journal*, Vol. II, p. 156n. The mention of bands is significant. The letter is addressed: "The Reverend Mr. John Wesley, at Mr. John Bray's (the location of Charles Wesley's conversion, May 21, 1738), a brazier, in Little Britain in Aldersgate Street, London."

[22]Wesley's ties with the Society at Fetter Lane remained close until it was infested by a strange form of Moravian stillness (where one was asked to remain perfectly quiet or still, daring not to use even the means of grace lest they relied too much upon their own righteousness) so that he was forced to take a part of that society to the Foundery a year or so later.

ety, and especially my brother Charles, were opposed.[23] Furthermore, each time we consulted the Scriptures, they seemed to suggest that such a move would result in my martyrdom, so that once again (though without the despair that usually accompanied it) I became nearly obsessed with thoughts of dying.[24] I was certain that I was about to finish my course (I felt that the burden of ministry had finally taken its toll upon my entire constitution), but I was determined to do so with joy. So, all other things being equal, we resorted to casting the "lot" with the result that on Thursday, March 29, 1739, I left London for Bristol.

I arrived in Bristol on Saturday evening and immediately met with Mr. Whitefield. It seemed that someone had said to him upon his return from Georgia: "If you would preach to the heathen, then go to the colliers of Kingswood (a short distance from Bristol)." In all of England these Kingswood colliers, or miners, were notorious for their godlessness and evil tempers. In the bitter winter weeks of February, 1739 (the coldest I remember for these fifty years), Mr. Whitefield gathered out of doors a congregation of colliers on Kingswood Hill. Although the influence of his powerful sermons opened for a brief interval certain churches in Bristol, before the month of February closed he was once again excluded from every church. He then preached in the upper room of the Baldwin Street Society, in the meeting place of the Nicholas Street Society, and in the room of the Society outside Lawford's Gate (which was connected with the parish poorhouse), and at various villages around Bristol. He extended his labors to Wales, where he was associated with Howell Harris. Perhaps his most striking

[23]Charles Wesley writes: "We dissuaded my brother from going to Bristol, from an unaccountable fear that it would prove fatal to him. A great power was among us. He offered himself willingly to whatsoever the Lord should appoint. The next day he set out, commended by us to the grace of God. He left a blessing behind. I desired to die with him."

[24]The Scriptures referred to were (as they occurred): "Get thee up unto this mountain . . . and die in the mount whither thou goest up, and be gathered unto thy people" (Deuteronomy 32:49,50). "And the children of Israel wept for Moses in the plains of Moab thirty days" (Deuteronomy 34:8). "I will shew him how great things he must suffer for my name's sake" (Acts 9:16). "And devout men carried Stephen to his burial, and made great lamentation over him" (Acts 8:2).

successes, however, were won in the open air at Kingswood, including Hannam Mount, Rose Green, and the Fishponds. By the time of my arrival, therefore, a proper revival had begun, especially among these miners. As Mr. Whitefield was about to leave for Wales I was determined to sustain this great work and follow the example of his *remarkable* ministry. I say remarkable mostly because of his strange way of preaching in the open fields, "having been all my life so tenacious of every point relating to decency and order, that I should have thought the saving of souls almost a sin if it had not been done in a church."

The following morning at 8:00, he set me a proper example for such field preaching at the Bowling Green, then again at Hannam Mount at 12:30, and again at Rose Green at 4:00, to crowds so large that I would have thought it impossible for one quarter of them to hear. However, all were as quiet as the grave and none, bless God, left without food enough on which to feast.

That evening, I expounded our Lord's Sermon on the Mount (one pretty remarkable precedent of field preaching, though there were houses of worship at that time also) to a little society which was accustomed to meeting once or twice a week in Nicholas Street.

The next afternoon at 4:00, speaking from a little hill in a parcel of ground adjoining the city, to about 3,000 people, I became more forceful than I ever thought possible and proclaimed in the highways the glad tidings of salvation. The Scripture on which I preached was this: "The Spirit of the Lord is upon me, because he hath anointed me to preach the gospel to the poor; he hath sent me to heal the brokenhearted, to preach deliverance to the captives, and recovering of sight to the blind, to set at liberty them that are bruised, to preach the acceptable year of the Lord" (Luke 4:18,19). Surely this should be true of every sincere minister of Christ.

Then at 7:00 I followed the natural sequence (which is the genius of our Revival) and met with our society in Baldwin Street in order to gather the seed which fell upon good soil for confession and prayer. Without this we become little more than a rope of sand.

Even as I speak it occurs to me that I should not give you the impression that those within the Societies were without blemish. In December, 1738, I noticed that the perennial problem of backsliding, even among the bands, had again returned. With the outbreak of revival and the formation of new Societies the problem increased. My only solution was the introduction of a doctrine of perfection which implicitly required a doctrine of perseverance. This brings us to a subject I hold dear—the absolute necessity of a doctrine which should be the distinguishing mark among the people called Methodist. It arose out of a practical need. It was not enough to emphasize only the Moravian concept of imputed righteousness. In order to survive spiritually the Christian needed to live his life in such a way that imputed righteousness might give rise to imparted righteousness. Involving both the *teleiosis* of Marcarius and Syrus and the holiness of Taylor, *going on* to perfection meant that the goal of life was holiness, fullness of faith, and the consecration of the whole self to God and neighbor in love. If one was not delivering one's whole life to God continually, backsliding was the inevitable result. I remember a letter I wrote on July 2, 1739: "It was incredible what advantage Satan hath gained here by my absence of only eight days. Disputes had crept in, and the love of many was waxed cold; so that all our society was falling in pieces." Again on July 23, I wrote: "To guard young converts from fancying that they had already attained, or were already perfect, I preached on those words: 'So is the kingdom of God, and when a man casteth seed into the ground, . . . first the blade, then the ear, then the full corn'" (Mark 4:26-28).[25] As I endeavored to guard those who were in their first love from falling into inordinate affection, the preaching of perfection was the only answer.

As I conclude this part of the narrative, it must be said that the organization of the Societies (and the doctrines which sustained them) was not the only thing important to the beginning of the Revival. There was another sig-

[25] *Works,* Vol. I, p. 212.

nificant influence as well—the building of our preaching houses. These gave both a stability and a high degree of visibility throughout. On May 9, 1739, just a month and ten days after my arrival in Bristol, we took possession of a piece of ground, near St. James' churchyard in the Horsefair, where we could build a room large enough to contain both the Societies of Nicholas and Baldwin Streets, and such of their friends who might desire to be present with them whenever the Scripture was expounded. On Saturday, May 12, the first stone was laid, with the voice of praise and thanksgiving.

I remember paying the workmen out of my own pocket. This was the first of our Methodist chapels.[26] Now there is not a county, and hardly a sizable town, without a similar room built specifically for expounding the Scripture and housing our Societies and bands. Shortly after our Societies in Bristol were strong enough to carry on the work of the Revival independently of me, and had, in fact, raised up other shepherds to tend the flock, our ministry began to spread rapidly.

---

[26]The Foundery, you might recall, was not taken over in London until 1740, after the Moravian split.

18

The Wider Parish

I look upon all the world as my parish; thus far I mean, that, in whatever part of it I am, I judge it meet, right, and my bounden duty, to declare unto all that are willing to hear, the glad tidings of salvation. This is the work which I know God has called me to do; and sure I am, that His blessing attends it.

John Wesley

For some weeks I had been entertaining thoughts concerning the manner of this new work. Before leaving Bristol (having received a pressing letter from London to come there, our brethren in Fetter Lane being in great confusion for want of my presence and advice), I wrote to Mr. Hervey weighing whatever objections I had heard against the direction that my ministry had taken![1] An extract from that letter is as follows:[2]

---

[1]The Reverend James Hervey was a former student of Wesley's.
[2]These objections and answers are taken from a letter in *Works*, Vol. I, pp. 200-202.

Objection:	"That I should settle in college."
I answered:	"I have no business there, no office, and no pupils."
Objection:	"That I should accept a cure of souls" (that is, a local parish).
I answered:	"It will be time enough to consider, when one is offered to me."
Objection:	"That in the meantime I ought to sit still; because otherwise I should invade another's office, if I interfered with other people's business and intermeddled with souls that did not belong to me."

Allow me now to tell you my principles in this manner. "I look upon all the world as my parish; thus far I mean, that, in whatever part of it I am, I judge it meet, right, and my bounden duty, to declare unto all that are willing to hear, the glad tidings of salvation. This is the work which I know God has called me to do; and sure I am, that his blessing attends it. Great encouragement have I, therefore, to be faithful in fulfilling the work he hath given me to do. His servant I am, and, as such, am employed according to the plain direction of his Word, 'As I have opportunity, doing good to all men:' And his providence clearly concurs

I answered:	"God in Scripture commands me, according to my power, to instruct the ignorant, reform the wicked, confirm the virtuous. Man forbids me to do this in another's parish; that is, in effect, to do it at all; seeing I had now no parish of my own, nor probably ever shall. Whom then shall I hear, God or man? 'If it be just to obey man rather than God, judge you. A dispensation of the Gospel is committed to me; and woe is me, if I preach not the Gospel.' But where shall I preach it, upon the principles you mentioned? Why, not in Europe, Asia, Africa or America; not in any of the Christian parts, at least, of the habitable earth. For all these are, after a sort, divided into parishes. If it be said, 'Go back, then, to the Heathens from whence you came:' Nay, but neither could I now (on your principles) preach to them; for all the Heathens in Georgia belong to the parish either of Savannah or Frederica."
Objection:	"'How is it that I assemble Christians who are none of my charge, to sing psalms, and pray, and hear the Scriptures expounded?' Is it not hard to justify doing this in other men's parishes, upon catholic principles?"
I answered:	"If by catholic principles you mean any other than Scriptural, they weigh nothing with me: I allow no other rule, whether of faith or practice, than the Holy Scriptures: But on Scriptural principles, I do not think it hard to justify whatever I do."

with his word; which has disengaged me from all things else, that I might singly attend on this very thing, 'and go about doing good.'"[3]

Thus, by the time I left Bristol (June 12), the Revival (which some people call Methodist) was begun. For the next fifty years I would travel some quarter of a million miles and preach, so I am told, some 40,000 sermons.[4] Before we change the scene, however, I must describe some events which help to capture the mood of these opening months in Bristol.[5]

I have always thought it interesting that early in the Revival someone unsympathetically described me when I preached as resembling a standing statue, claiming that the only thing that moved was my mouth and that I read my sermons so rapidly that it was all you could do to follow my logic; yet hundreds were slain as if by God Himself. Although I later used more of an extemporaneous style of preaching, God honored those earlier sermons. People cried out as if in the throes of death, begging God for mercy and forgiveness.

I remember a physician who was greatly offended at the cries of those on whom the power of God came. He was afraid there might be fraud or deception. He attended a service at Newgate and one whom he had known for many years was the first who cried out. "He could hardly believe his own eyes and ears. He went and stood close to her, and observed every symptom, till great drops of sweat ran down her face and all her bones shook. He then knew not

---

[3]Ibid., pp. 201f.

[4]Wesley preached an average of 800 sermons a year for 50 years.

[5]Wesley describes his routine for this period in his *Journal:* "My ordinary employment, in public, was now as follows:—Every morning I read prayers and preached at Newgate. Every evening I expounded a portion of Scripture at one or more of the Societies. On Monday, in the afternoon, I preached abroad, near Bristol; on Tuesday, at Bath and Two-Mile-Hill alternately; on Wednesday, at Baptist-Mills; every other Thursday, near Pensford; every other Friday, in another part of Kingswood; on Saturday, in the afternoon, and Sunday morning, in the Bowling-Green; (which lies near the middle of the city;) on Sunday, at eleven, near Hannam-Mount; at two, Clifton; and at five on Rose Green; and hitherto, as my days, so my strength hath been" (*Works*, Vol. I, p. 193).

what to think, being clearly convinced, it was not fraud, nor yet any natural disorder. But when both her soul and body were healed in a moment, he acknowledged the finger of God."[6]

Soon afterward, a weaver named John Haydon had an even more striking experience. I must tell you the story. God forgive me if I enjoy the telling too much! Mr. Haydon "was (I understood) a man of a regular life and conversation, one that constantly attended the public prayers and sacrament, and was zealous for the Church. . . . Being informed that people fell into strange fits at the societies, he came to see and judge for himself. But, he was less satisfied than before; insomuch that he went about to his acquaintance, one after another, till one in the morning, and labored above measure to convince them it was a delusion of the devil. We were going home, when one met us in the street, and informed us, that John Haydon was fallen raving mad. It seems he had sat down to dinner, but had a mind first to end a sermon he had borrowed on 'Salvation by Faith.' In reading the last page, he changed color, fell off his chair, and began screaming terribly, and beating himself against the ground. The neighbors were alarmed, and flocked together to the house. Between one and two I came in, and found him on the floor, the room being full of people whom his wife would have kept without; but he cried aloud, 'No; let them all come; let all the world see the just judgment of God.' Two or three men were holding him as well as they could. He immediately fixed his eyes upon *me* and, stretching out his hand, cried, "Ay, this is he, who I said was a deceiver of the people. But God has overtaken me. I said it was all a delusion; but this is no delusion.' He then roared out, 'O thou devil! Thou cursed devil! Yea, thou legion of devils! Thou canst not stay. Christ will cast thee out. I know his work is begun. Tear me to pieces, if thou wilt; but thou canst not hurt me.' He then beat himself against the ground again; his breast heaving at the same time, as in the pangs of death, and great drops of sweat trickling down his face. We all betook

[6]Ibid., p. 189.

ourselves to prayer. His pangs ceased, and both his body and soul were set at liberty.''[7]

From Bristol we went first to the surrounding cities, such as Bath. During the early months of the Revival "there was great expectation there of what a noted man was to do to me; and I was much entreated not to preach, because no one knew what might happen. By this report I also gained a much larger audience, among whom were many of the rich and the great. I told them plainly the Scripture had concluded them all under sin—high and low, rich and poor, one with another. Many of them seemed to be a little surprised, and were sinking apace into seriousness, when their champion appeared, and coming close to me, asked by what authority I did these things. I replied, 'By the authority of Jesus Christ, conveyed to me by the (now) Archbishop of Canterbury, when he laid hands upon me, and said, Take thou authority to preach the Gospel.' He said, 'This is contrary to Act of Parliament.' I answered, 'Sir, the conventicles mentioned in that Act (as the preamble shows) are seditious meetings; But this is not such; here is no shadow of sedition; therefore it is not contrary to that Act.' He replied, 'I say it is; And besides, your preaching frightens people out of their wits.' 'Sir, did you ever hear me preach?' 'No.' 'How, then, can you judge of what you never heard?' 'Sir, by common report.' 'Common report, is not enough. Give me leave, sir, to ask, is not your name Nash?' 'My name is Nash.' 'Sir, I dare not judge of you by common report: I think it is not enough to judge by.' Here he paused awhile, and, having recovered himself, said, 'I desire to know what this people comes here for:' On which one replied, 'Sir, leave him to me: Let an old woman answer him. You, Mr. Nash, take care of your body [Beau Nash was a frivolous gamester expelled from Oxford for his intrigues and wild adventures]; we take care of our souls; and for the food of our souls we come here.' He replied not a word, but walked away.

"As I returned, the street was full of people, hurrying to and fro, and speaking great words. But when any of them

[7]Ibid., pp. 190f.

asked, 'Which is he?' and I replied 'I am he,' they were immediately silent not really wishing to encounter me. Several ladies followed me into Mr. Merchant's house, the servant told me there were some wanted to speak to me. I went to them, and said, 'I believe, ladies, the maid mistook; you only wanted to look at me.' I added, 'I do not expect that the rich and the great should want either to speak with me or to hear me; for I speak the plain truth,—a thing you hear little of, and do not desire to hear.' A few more words passed between us, and I retired."[8]

Immediately upon my return to London (June 13) I went to the Society at Fetter Lane.[9] I was quite concerned with the many misunderstandings and offenses that had crept in among them. I warned them (especially the women): "'Believe not every spirit, but try the spirits, whether they be of God.' I told them, they were not to judge of the spirit whereby any one spoke, either by appearances, or by common report, or by their own inward feelings: No, nor by any dreams, visions, or revelations, supposed to be made to their souls; any more than by their tears, or any involuntary effects wrought upon their bodies. I warned them, all these were, in themselves, of a doubtful, disputable, nature; they might be from God, and they might not; and were therefore, not simply to be relied on, (any more than simply to be condemned,) but to be tried by a farther rule, to be brought to the only certain test, the Law and the Testimony."[10] In just a few days, determined that we should not rest in those little beginnings of sanctification, "the spirit of love and of a sound mind" was restored.[11] By Tuesday, June 19, I was back in Bristol but could hardly believe the way God had justly withdrawn His Spirit from

---

[8]Ibid., pp. 198f.

[9]In route to London, Wesley visited his mother in Salisbury. He seems to have put to rest any fears she might have had regarding his new-found faith (cf. *Works*, Vol. I, pp. 202f.). Wesley had not been in London since March 29.

[10]Ibid., p. 206; cf. Vol. II, p. 48 and Vol. VIII, pp. 253f. for an additional word on "Testing Spirits."

[11]During his five days in London, Wesley spent considerable time with George Whitefield. They ministered together both by preaching and working with the Societies.

us. In spite of our great unfaithfulness, however, the next day our hearts were sweetly drawn together and united as at first.

Although this present advantage over Satan (however tentative) was an encouragement, I found a few days later I "had no life or spirit in me; and was much in doubt, whether God would not lay me aside, and send other laborers into his harvest."[12] Then, once again my ministry was confirmed. While I was speaking at the Society, "one before me dropped down as dead, and presently a second and a third. Five others sunk down in half an hour, most of whom were in violent agonies. 'The pains' as 'of hell came about them; the snares of God overtook them.' In their trouble we called upon the Lord, and he gave us an answer of peace. One indeed continued an hour in strong pain; and one or two more for three days. But the rest were greatly comforted in that hour, and went away rejoicing and praising God."[13]

Thus, my spirit revived as the doctrine I preached was used of God in effecting real change in the hearts and lives of others. Let me describe to you briefly that doctrine as I *then* understood it. At its heart was justification by faith alone. Furthermore, my motive for preaching thus was because thousands for whom Christ died were allowed to perish for lack of that knowledge. "They perish for want of knowing that *we*, as well as the Heathens, 'are alienated from the life of God;' that 'every one of us,' by the corruption of our inmost nature, 'is very far gone from original righteousness;' so far, that 'every person born into the world deserveth God's wrath and damnation;' that we have by nature no power either to help ourselves, or even to call upon God to help us: All our tempers and works, in our natural state, being only evil continually. So that *our* coming to Christ, as well as *theirs*, must infer a great and mighty change. It must infer not only an *outward change*, from stealing, lying, and all corrupt communication; but a thorough *change of heart*, an *inward* renewal in the spirit of

---

[12]*Works*, Vol. I, p. 205.
[13]Ibid., p. 206.

our mind. Accordingly, 'the old man' implies infinitely more than outward evil conversation, even 'an evil heart of unbelief,' corrupted by pride and a thousand deceitful lusts. Of consequence, the 'new man' must imply infinitely more than outward good conversation, even 'a good heart, which after God is created in righteousness and true holiness;' a heart full of that faith which, working by love, produces all holiness of conversation.

"The change from the former of these states to the latter, is what I call *The New Birth:* 'a sure trust and confidence in God, that by the merits of Christ our sins are forgiven, and we are reconciled to the favor of God.' And from this will spring many other things, which till then we experienced not; as, the love of God shed abroad in our hearts, the peace of God which passeth all understanding, and joy in the Holy Ghost; joy, though not *unfelt*, yet '*unspeakable*, and full of glory.'"[14]

This is basically the doctrine I preached until 1747: that is justifying faith is a divine assurance that Christ loved *me* and gave Himself for *me*, which, by the nature of it, includes a sense of pardon.[15] In 1747, however, my opinion of justifying faith as necessarily including a sense of pardon, changed. Two years previously I had engaged in a rather lengthly debate with Thomas Secker, the Bishop of Bristol, and I had refused to give ground.[16] Then, I noticed that much of the testimony of those justified bore him out. Since the issue had been raised once again at our recent Conference, I realized the necessity of examining the question again. The result of this reappraisal can best be related by a letter to Charles dated July 31, 1747:

"Beercrocomb, July 31, 1747.

DEAR BROTHER,—Yesterday I was thinking on a de-

---

[14]Ibid., pp. 214f.

[15]The question: "Is justifying faith a divine assurance that Christ loved *me* and gave Himself for *me*?" was posed at the Conference for 1747 and the answer was: "We believe it is." This same opinion is expressed clearly in his "Earnest Appeal to Men of Reason and Religion" (*Works*, Vol. VIII, pp. 4ff.).

[16]This debate took place in the correspondence with "John Smith" a nom de plume of Secker (so it is believed, see *Letters*, Vol. II, p. 42n.).

sideratum among us, a *genesis problematica* on Justifying
Faith. A skeleton of it, which you may fill up, or any one
that has leisure, I have roughly set down.

Is justifying faith a sense of pardon? *Negatur.*

I. Every one is deeply concerned to understand this
question well: but preachers most of all; lest they should
either make them sad whom God hath not made sad, or
encourage them to say peace where there is no peace.

Some years ago we heard nothing about either justifying
faith or a sense of pardon: so that, when we did hear of
them, the theme was quite new to us; and we might easily,
especially in the heat and hurry of controversy, lean too
much either to the one hand or to the other.

II. By justifying faith I mean that faith which whosoever
hath not is under the wrath and curse of God. By a sense of
pardon I mean a distinct, explicit assurance that my sins are
forgiven.

I allow (1) that there is such an explicit assurance; (2)
that it is the *common* privilege of *real* Christians; (3) that it
is *the proper Christian faith,* which purifieth the heart and
overcometh the world.

But I cannot allow that justifying faith is such an assurance, or necessarily connected therewith.

III. Because, if justifying faith *necessarily* implies such
an explicit sense of pardon, then every one who has it not,
and every one so long as he has it not, is under the wrath
and under the curse of God. But this is a supposition
contrary to Scripture (Isaiah I.10; Acts x.34). Contrary to
experience: for Jonathan Reeves, &c. &c., had peace with
God, no fear, no doubt, before they had *that sense of pardon;*
and so have I frequently had.

Again, the assertion that justifying faith is a sense of
pardon is contrary to *reason;* it is flatly *absurd.* For how can
a sense of our having received pardon be the *condition* of our
receiving it?

IV. If you object, (1) 'Job, Thomas, St. Paul, &c., had
this sense,' I grant they had; but they were justified before
they had it. (2) 'We know fifteen hundred persons who
have this assurance.' Perhaps so; but this does not prove
that they were not justified till they received it. (3) 'We
have been exceedingly blessed in preaching this doctrine.'
We have been blessed in preaching the great truths of the

gospel; although we tacked to them, in the simplicity of our hearts, a proposition which was not true. (4) 'But does not our Church give this account of justifying faith?' I am sure she does of *saving* or *Christian* faith; I think she does of justifying faith too. But to the law and testimony. All men may err; but the word of the Lord shall stand for ever.''[17]

Before moving on, let me make an additional note. It has always remained a mystery to me that in spite of my preaching justification by faith alone (let the issue of assurance, which little affects the basic doctrine, rest) there have been numerous reports throughout the Revival ''that I was a Papist, if not a Jesuit. Some added, that I was born and bred in Rome; which many cordially believed. O ye fools, when will ye understand that the preaching of justification by faith alone; the allowing no meritorious cause of justification, but the death and righteousness of Christ; and no condition or instrumental cause but faith; is overturning Popery from the foundation? When will ye understand, that the most destructive of all those eras which Rome, the mother of abominations, hath brought forth, (compared to which transubstantiation, and a hundred more) are 'trifles light as air,' is, 'That we are justified by works;' or (to express the same thing a little more decently,) by faith and works? Now, do I preach this? I did for ten years: I was (fundamentally) a Papist, and knew it not. But I do now testify to all, (and it is the very point for asserting which I have, to this day, been called in question,) that 'no good works can be done before justification; none which have not in them the nature of sin.''[18]

This reminds me that some years later, while I was preaching in Dublin, one of the congregation, after listening for some time, cried out, shaking his head, ''Ay, he is a Jesuit; that's plain.'' To which a popish priest, who happened to be near, replied loudly, ''No, he is not; I would to God he was.''[19]

---

[17]*Letters*, Vol. II, pp. 108f. This important letter describes a significant change which will bear even greater fruit.

[18]*Works*, Vol. I, pp. 218f. Cf. his basic objections to Roman Catholic doctrine (*Works*, Vol. I, p. 221).

[19]Ibid., Vol. II, p. 99.

So, in the summer of 1739, using Bristol and London as our base, our ministry expanded rapidly. Sometimes traveling with Mr. Whitefield (at least for a season), my brother Charles, or other friends, we extended our preaching to other places. Since much of our activity during the next fifty years reads repetitiously (and the details can be gleaned from my *Journal*), allow me to describe the events and issues which come to mind.

Early in September (1739) I talked at length with my mother. Much to my surprise, she told me that until recently, she had scarcely heard of the experience of the forgiveness of sins now, or of God's Spirit bearing witness with our spirit: much less did she imagine that this was the testimony of all true believers (even though her father, Dr. Annesley, experienced this himself shortly before his death). "Therefore," she said, "I never durst ask for it myself. But two or three weeks ago, while my son Hall [Westley Hall] was pronouncing those words, in delivering the cup to me, 'the blood of our Lord Jesus Christ, which was given for thee;' the words struck through my heart, and I knew God for Christ's sake had forgiven *me* all *my* sins."[20] Less than a week later she went with us to Kennington, where there must have been 20,000 people. There may well have been more (as in later years), but I caution against that hateful custom of painting things beyond life. "Let us make a conscience of magnifying or exaggerating any thing. Let us rather speak under, than above, the truth. We, of all men, should be punctual in all we say; that none of our words may fall to the ground."[21] Yet, in spite of the great crowds, "I wonder at those who still talk so loud of the indecency of field-preaching. The highest indecency is in St. Paul's Church, when a considerable part of the congregation are asleep, or talking, or looking about, not minding a word the Preacher says. On the other hand, there is the highest decency in a churchyard or field, when the whole congregation behave

---

[20]Ibid., Vol. I, p. 222.
[21]Ibid., Vol. II, p. 88.

and look as if they saw the Judge of all, and heard him speaking from heaven."[22]

Perhaps I should reiterate that, to the best of my knowledge, the doctrines we preach are the same doctrines preached by those clergymen faithful to the Church of England. Indeed we agree with the fundamental doctrines of the churches as clearly laid down, both in her Prayers, Articles, and Homilies. "But from that part of the Clergy who dissent from the Church, (though they own it not,) I differ in the following points:

"First, They speak of justification, either as the same thing with sanctification, or as something consequent upon it. I believe justification to be wholly distinct from sanctification, and necessarily antecedent to it.

"Secondly, They speak of our own holiness, or good works, as the cause of our justification; or, that for the sake of which, on account of which, we are justified before God. I believe, neither our own holiness, nor good works, are any part of the cause of our justification; but that the death and righteousness of Christ are the whole and sole cause of it; or, that for the sake of which, on account of which, we are justified before God.

"Thirdly, They speak of good works as condition of justification, necessarily previous to it. I believe no good work can be previous to justification, nor, consequently, a condition of it; but that we are justified (being till that hour ungodly, and, therefore, incapable of doing any good work) by faith alone, faith without works, faith (though producing all, yet) including no good work.

"Fourthly, They speak of sanctification (or holiness) as if it were an outward thing; as if it consisted chiefly, if not wholly, in those two points, 1. The doing no harm; 2. The doing good, (as it is called,) that is, the using the means of grace, and helping our neighbour.

"I believe it to be an inward thing, namely, the life of God in the soul of man; a participation of the divine nature; the mind that was in Christ; or, the renewal of our heart, after the image of Him that created us.

"Lastly, They speak of the new birth as an outward

---

[22]Ibid., p. 113.

thing; as if it were no more than baptism; or, at most, a change from outward wickedness to outward goodness; from a vicious to (what is called) a virtuous life. I believe it to be an inward thing; a change from inward wickedness to inward goodness; an entire change of our inmost nature from the image of the devil (wherein we are born) to the image of God; a change from the love of the creature to the love of the Creator; from earthly and sensual, to heavenly and holy affections;—in a word, a change from the tempers of the spirits of darkness, to those of the angels of God in heaven.

"There is, therefore, a wide, essential, fundamental, irreconcilable difference between us; so that if they speak the truth as it is in Jesus, I am found a false witness before God. But if I teach the way of God in truth, they are blind leaders of the blind."[23]

I should also add that much of the rage and madness directed toward the people called Methodist throughout the kingdom was aroused by the clergy. I remember an incident in the spring of 1743 in Wednesbury. "While I was speaking, a gentleman rode up very drunk; and after many unseemly and bitter words, labored much to ride over some of the people. I was surprised to hear he was a neighboring Clergyman. And this, too is a man zealous for the church! Ah, poor church, if it stood in need of such defenders!"[24]

Unfortunately our problems were not only from without. In October (1739) I returned to Oxford where "I had a little leisure to take a view of the shattered condition of things here. The poor prisoners, both in the castle and in the city prison, had now none that cared for their souls; none to instruct, advise, comfort, and build them up in the knowledge and love of the Lord Jesus. None was left to visit the workhouses, where, also, we used to meet with the most moving objects of compassion. Our little school, where about twenty poor children, at a time, had been

---

[23]Ibid., Vol. I, pp. 224f.

[24]Ibid., p. 420. Cf. p. 254; pp. 486f. for Wesley's difficulties with the clergy.

taught for many years, was on the point of being broke up; there being none now, either to support, or to attend it: And most of those in the town, who were once knit together, and strengthened one another's hands in God, were torn asunder and scattered abroad. 'It is time for thee, Lord, to lay to thy hand.'

"At eleven, a little company of us met to intreat God for 'the remnant that' was 'left.' He immediately gave us a token for good. One who had been long in the gall of bitterness, full of wrath, strife, and envy, particularly against one whom she had once tenderly loved, rose up and showed the change God had wrought in her soul, by falling upon her neck, and with many tears, kissing her. The same spirit we found reviving in others also; so that we left them not without hope, that the seed which had been sown even here, 'shall take root downward, and bear fruit upward.'"[25]

I must mention that toward the end of that same month, in riding to Bradford, I read over Mr. Law's book on the new birth. I could only judge it to be "philosophical, speculative, precarious; Behmenish, void, and vain! 'O what a fall is there.'"[26]

The evening of that same day, "I was exceedingly pressed to go back to a young woman in Kingswood. (The fact I nakedly relate, and leave every man to his own judgment of it.) I went. She was nineteen or twenty years old; but, it seems, could not write or read. I found her on the bed, two or three persons holding her. It was a terrible sight. Anguish, horror, and despair, above all description, appeared in her pale face. The thousand distortions of her whole body showed how the dogs of hell were gnawing her heart. The shrieks intermixed were scarce to be endured. But her stony eyes could not weep. She screamed out as soon as words could find their way, 'I am damned, damned; lost for ever. Six days ago you might have helped me. But it is past. I am the devil's now. I have given myself to him. His I am. Him I must serve. With him I must go to

[25]Ibid., p. 228; Cf. *Works*, Vol. II, p. 141.
[26]Ibid., Vol. I, p. 234.

hell. I will be his. I will serve him. I will go with him to hell. I cannot be saved. I will not be saved. I must, I will be damned.' She then began praying to the devil. We began, *Arm of the Lord, awake, awake!* She immediately sunk down as asleep; but, as soon as we left off, broke out again, with inexpressible vehemence: 'Stony hearts, break! I am a warning to you. Break, break, poor stony hearts! Will you not break? What can be done more for stony hearts? I am damned, that you may be saved. Now break, now break, poor stony hearts! You need not be damned, though I must.' She then fixed her eyes on the corner of the ceiling, and said, 'There he is; ay, there he is. Come, good devil, come. Take me away. You said you would dash my brains out; come, do it quickly. I am yours. I will be yours. Come just now. Take me away.' We interrupted her by calling again upon God: On which she sunk down as before: And another young woman began to roar out as loud as she had done. My brother now came in, it being about nine o'clock. We continued in prayer till past eleven; when God in a moment spoke peace into the soul, first of the first tormented, and then of the other. And they both joined in singing praise to Him who had 'stilled the enemy and the avenger.' "[27]

The following story has to do with the "stillness controversy." On November 1, 1739, I returned to London to find Philip Molther, a Moravian missionary educated at the University of Jena, who had just returned from Pennsylvania, and my old friend, August Spangenberg, preaching a kind of Quietism called "stillness" to the Society at Fetter Lane. In a remarkably short period of time many of the members were convinced that they did not have true faith and they determined to remain "still," that is (as they explained themselves), to abstain "from the means of grace, as they are called; the Lord's Supper in particular; and that the Ordinances are not means of grace, there being no other means than Christ."[28] I, however,

---

[27]Ibid., pp. 234f. The girl mentioned here was Sally Jones and this is one of many accounts demonstrating what Wesley believed to be "demon possession."

[28]Ibid., p. 247.

was not impressed. In fact, I was greatly distressed. I wrote in my *Journal:* "Satan gained the advantage over us more and more every day. My soul is sick of this sublime divinity. Let *me* think and speak as a little child! Let *my* religion be plain, artless, simple!"[29]

The controversy dragged on until the summer of 1740. Those holding to stillness insisted that my brother and I placed too much emphasis upon the Ordinances, whereas we insisted that those holding to stillness were antinomian.[30] The Moravian fear of works-righteousness made faith possible only by not using (what we term) the means of grace. They determined not to go to church; they stopped communicating, fasting, using so much private prayer, reading the Scripture, doing temporal good and doing spiritual good.[31] A break was impending. On Wednesday evening, July 16, 1740, in hopes of *reductio ad absurdum* (revealing to them the absurdity of their own argument), I took to the Society meeting at Fetter Lane a copy of *The Mystic Divinity of Dionysius* which recently had been put into my hands.[32] I read an extract to the effect that the means of grace are evil to those not born of God. For the unbeliever "to read the Scriptures, or to pray, or to communicate, or to do any outward work, is deadly poison. First let him be born of God. Till then let him not do any of these things. For if he does he will destroy himself."[33] Fully expecting the Society members to see

---

[29]Ibid., p. 248, 256.

[30]It is significant that some years later Wesley denounced Zinzendorf and the Moravians for Universalism, Antinomianism, and Quietism (Ibid., pp. 323ff.). Zinzendorf, in turn, prophesied that the Methodists would "run their heads against the wall," to which Wesley replied: "We will not, if we can help it" (Ibid., p. 517).

[31]Ibid., Vol. II, pp. 27f.

[32]This pseudonymous tract of mystical theology attributed to Dionysius the Areopagite first appeared during the fourth or fifth century. It is essentially a Neo-Platonic mystical exposition of *via negationis*. It was just this *via negationis* (a process of "unknowing" in which the soul leaves behind the perceptions of the senses as well as the reasoning of the intellect in its approach to God, the ineffable Being that transcends affirmation and negation alike) that epitomized all that Wesley had come to detest in mysticism. Thus, this work was taken by John to reveal the utter absurdity of the Moravian stillness once carried to its logical conclusion.

[33]*Works*, Vol. I, p. 281.

immediately the absurdity of such a position, I was amazed (as one can imagine) when Mr. Bell exclaimed, "It is right, it is all right. It is truth. To this we must all come, or we can never come to Christ."[34] Following a brief debate, I was asked to preach there no more. Although I was forced to do battle with Moravian stillness for at least six more years, the final split between the Methodists and the Moravians came on the following Sunday. Again, after reading yet another paper, and without saying anything more, I withdrew, as did eighteen or nineteen of the Society.[35] From that point on we moved to the Foundery which was to serve as our first Methodist preaching house in London.

In the midst of all this, my brother Samuel died at Tiverton.[36] So, many things went through my mind almost at once. I was thankful to God that by the end of August, 1740, I believed that the controversy had subsided. I wrote in my *Journal:* "Disputes being now at an end and all things quiet and calm, on Monday, September 1, I left London. . . ."[37]

It is important to relate yet another chapter in that controversy before I move on quickly to describe the exact organization of the Societies. But first I must take a moment to give you an account of our school at Kingswood. I already mentioned the scene at Kingswood prior to the Revival. By summer, 1739, the miners had been tamed by a gospel of love and peace. "That their children too might know the things which make for their peace, it was proposed to build a house in Kingswood; and after many foreseen and unforeseen difficulties, in June the foundation was laid. The ground made choice of was in the middle of the wood, between the London and Bath roads, not far from that called Two-mile-Hill, about three measured miles from Bristol."[38]

---

[34]Ibid.
[35]Ibid., p. 282.
[36]Samuel, Jr., died November 5, 1739.
[37]Ibid., p. 286.
[38]Ibid., p. 252.

Here a large room was begun for the school, having four small rooms at either end as living quarters for the school-masters and (as it pleased God), some of the poorer children. Two persons were immediately appointed to teach. So, as soon as the house was fit to receive them, the shell of which was nearly finished by the end of the year; our classes were begun.

Thus the Revival began to move into almost every aspect of society. Then, in January, 1741, I was surprised to find that my brother Charles, having been persuaded by Böhler, Gambold, and Hall to be *still* until full faith was his, ceased preaching for more than three weeks. "Was there ever so pleasing a scheme? But where is it written? Not in any of those books which I account the Oracles of God. I allow, if there is a better way to God than the Scripture way, this is it. But the prejudice of education so hangs upon me, that I cannot think there is. I must therefore still wait in the Bible-way, from which this differs as light from darkness."[39] Then, on February 21, 1741, "my brother returned from Oxford, and preached on the true way of waiting for God: Thereby dispelling at once the fears of some, and the vain hopes of others; who had confidently affirmed that Mr. Charles Wesley was *still* already, and would come to London no more."[40]

Lest we lose perspective, I must say that this period (although overshadowed by the Moravian controversy) was actually characterized by a *dual* theme. When I was not fighting stillness, I was exhorting backsliders on to perfection. Backsliding continued to be my chief problem among the Societies, far outweighing the periodic theological disputes. Perfection began to loom as the only effective weapon. I will return to this important theme later on, but for now let me set the proper stage.

I am still convinced that the only lasting arena for perfection is the Society. I have already mentioned the Societies

[39]Ibid., p. 297. We should not be led to believe that Wesley was not himself tempted by "stillness." On April 6, 1741, he writes that his "heart burns within" him; he marvels how he refrained "from joining these men" (*Works*, Vol. I, p. 306).

[40]Ibid., p. 298.

and bands. The Society (a very innocent name, and very common in London for any number of people associating themselves together) consisted of the larger or overall membership of those properly gathered (desiring only to flee from the wrath to come, and to be saved from their sins) frequently consisting of several hundred as those at Bristol, London, and later Newcastle.[41] The general rules of our Societies (though extended considerably through the bands and classes across the years) are quite simply: (1) To

[41]Wesley's thoughts on the development of the Methodist Societies (which were distinct from the "religious" or the "Moravian" societies) are recorded on several occasions. In the *Ecclesiastical History,* for example, he cites three distinct periods of development: the Holy Club (November, 1729); the Georgia society (April, 1736); and the London Society (May 1, 1738). On December 12, 1760, Wesley wrote to the editor of the *London Magazine* that "about thirty years since, I met with a book . . . called *The Country Parson's Advice to his Parishioners.*" This book had been published anonymously in 1680 apparently reporting on the activities of the religious societies formed in 1678 under the influence of Dr. Anthony Horneck (who provided the "rules") and Mr. Smithies (J. S. Simon's *John Wesley and the Religious Societies* provides an excellent account of the development here). There he read: "if good men of the church will unite together . . . disposing themselves into friendly societies. . . ." Wesley, following the example of Dr. Horneck, then adds that "a few gentlemen, then at Oxford, approved of and followed the advice." An interesting interconnection then arises with the statement from Schmidt that Horneck was influenced by the Flemish mystic Anna Maria van Schurmann (as was Wesley) and that his societies had affinities with those of more modern Roman Catholic origin such as the Jesuits or the free societies of the French Count de Renty (Schmidt, *John Wesley,* pp. 318-320). We know from Wesley's *Diary* that about this same time (November, 1729) he began to read and use de Renty's *Life.* In addition, Samuel Wesley, one of the warmest supporters of the religious societies, in "a letter concerning the religious societies" (published in 1699) used de Renty in their defense stating that the religious societies were in "no sense novelties since de Renty had formed such societies as early as 1640" (Bett, W.H.S., Vol. 18, pp. 43-45). De Renty most likely had been discussed in the Epworth rectory and it seems almost certain that Wesley would have read his father's open letter.

It is no coincidence that de Renty also reappears at the second stage in the formation of the Methodist societies (April, 1736). As Wesley writes in his *Diary* for May 20, 1736: "*began* de Renty," Schmidt argues that there could be no immediate dependence on de Renty since this was four to six weeks *after* he had subdivided the Georgia congregation (Schmidt, *John Wesley,* p. 191). Even if we did not already know that Wesley had been acquainted with de Renty for quite some time this argument could be easily overcome: Wesley's use of the word "began" clearly did not necessarily mean for the "first" time, as if he had never

do no harm; (2) To do all the good we can; and (3) To attend upon all the ordinances of God.[42]

As for the bands, it was soon apparent that many within the larger Society wanted some means of closer union. "In compliance with their desire, I divided them into smaller companies; putting the married or single men, and married or single women, together. The chief rules of these bands (that is, little companies; so that old English word signifies) run thus:—

"In order to 'confess our faults one to another,' and pray one for another that we may be healed, we intend, (1) To meet once a week, at the least. (2)To come punctually at the hour appointed. (3) To begin with singing or prayer. (4) To speak each of us in order, freely and plainly, the true state of our soul, with the faults we have committed in thought, word, or deed, and the temptations we have felt since our last meeting. (5) To desire some person among us (thence called a Leader) to speak his own state first, and then to ask the rest, in order, as many and as searching questions as may be, concerning their state, sins, and

---

read it before. There are many examples where the word "began" is used for the same work on successive occasions. Wesley, for example, used the phrase "began the *Light of the World*" (Madame Bourignon's treatise) on February 28 and again on April 4, 1736 (de Renty is also mentioned in a letter dated October 3, 1731). Schmidt, in spite of his misinterpretation of "began," however, goes on to say that in de Renty "he found confirmation of his own action in forming small groups of pious folk. It was an age when Romanic mysticism, Pietism, and the religion of 'free spirits' *(spiritualismus)* were in the air. . . . (Schmidt, *John Wesley*, p. 191n.)

Piette writes that although the societies were Anglican, the rules for the most part were mystical (Piette, pp. 370f.). He goes on to conclude that perhaps this was one of the mystics' greatest contributions to Methodism since these rules were so vitally important for future solidarity. Schmidt states that it is possible that Wesley encouraged the members of his societies to enter into a formal covenant with God, like that which he had come to know in Romanic mysticism from the example of Count de Renty (Schmidt, *John Wesley*, p. 191, cf. *Original*, p. 227). Bett concludes that "we may fairly claim this French marquis of the seventeenth century as the real founder of the class meeting in Methodism" (Bett, Proc. W.H.S., Vol. 18, 0. 45).

[42]*Works*, Vol. VIII, pp. 270f.

temptations."[43] Thus, the bands were the first subdivision for the larger society. In our rules first established for Fetter Lane, the instruction was that the Society so meeting would be divided into several bands, or little companies, none of them consisting of fewer than five, or more than ten persons. It should be added that although the general Society members did not need to profess a confession of faith, the band members were (so we believed) believers. Furthermore, unlike the Society (where the leaders took responsibility), accountability among the band members was left, by and large, to the individual.

Then, in 1742, we realized the need of yet another kind of subdivision. First of all, there was the problem of those who were in the larger Society, not yet confessing faith in Christ, since they were ineligible for the band. Then, there was the problem of locale. Would it not be wise to gather those in a given area into classes regardless of their confession of faith with strong leadership accountability to direct their walk in the Lord? In February we had divided the whole Society in Bristol into little companies or classes—about twelve in each class. One person in each class was appointed to receive the contribution of the rest and bring it to the stewards each week so we could pay off the public debt. Then, two months later in London, I selected "several earnest and sensible men to meet me, to whom I showed the great difficulty I had long found of knowing the people who desired to be under my care. After much discourse, they all agreed, there could be no better way to come to a sure, thorough knowledge of each person, than to divide them into classes, like those at Bristol, under the inspection of those in whom I could most confide. This was the origin of our classes at London, for which I can never sufficiently praise God; the unspeakable usefulness of the institution having been ever since more and more manifest."[44] Our people would not be half-awakened. They would not be left to themselves to fall asleep again. I de-

---

[43]Ibid., 258. Cf. pp. 272f. and p. 307.
[44]Ibid., Vol. I, p. 364.

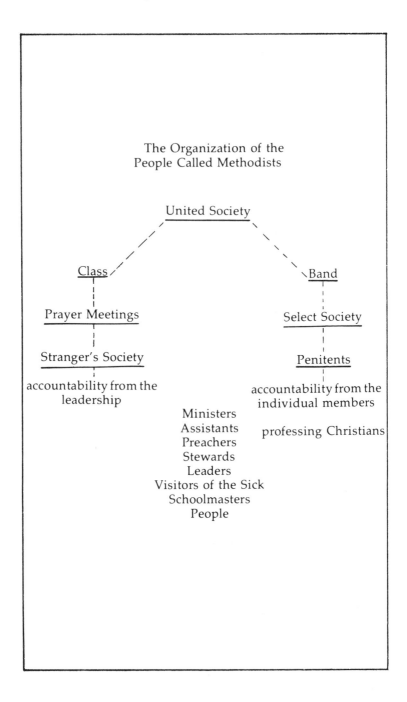

The Organization of the
People Called Methodists

United Society

Class

Band

Prayer Meetings

Select Society

Stranger's Society

Penitents

accountability from the
leadership

accountability from the
individual members

Ministers
Assistants   professing Christians
Preachers
Stewards
Leaders
Visitors of the Sick
Schoolmasters
People

termined, by the grace of God, not to strike one stroke in any place where I cannot follow the blow.[45]

The select societies and penitants complete the subdivision of the Society. The select societies consisted of those who "walk in the light" and originally met with me every Monday morning. "My design was, not only to direct them how to press after perfection; to exercise their every grace, and improve every talent they had received; and to incite them to love one another more, and to watch more carefully over each other; but also to have a select company, to whom I might unbosom myself on all occasions, without reserve; and whom I could propose to all their brethren as a pattern of love, of wholeness, and of good works." Lastly, the penitents consisted of those backsliders who were now determined to renew their first love.

As I have already explained, the key at all levels was strong discipline tempered with gentleness. I constantly "read over the names of the United Society; and marked those who were of a doubtful character, that full inquiry might be made concerning them. At the meeting of that society, I read over the names of these, and desired to speak with each of them the next day, as soon as they had opportunity. Many of them afterwards gave sufficient proof, that they were seeking Christ in sincerity. The rest I determined to keep on trial, till the doubts concerning them were removed."[46] Coupled with this discipline I endeavored to encourage all who were weary and faint in their minds. Most of them, I found, had not been used with sufficient tenderness. "Who is there that sufficiently

---

[45]The following paragraph from "A Plain Account of the People Called Methodist" demonstrates the personal care Wesley took with each member of the classes: "To each of those of whose seriousness and good conversation I found no reason to doubt, I gave a testimony under my own hand, by writing their name on a ticket prepared for that purpose; every ticket implying as strong a recommendation of the person to whom it was given as if I had wrote at length, 'I believe the bearer hereof to be one who fears God and works righteousness.'" This, of course, was the origin of the class ticket.

[46]*Works*, Vol. I, p. 306. Cf. *Works*, Vol. I, pp. 348; 350; 413; 415f; and Vol. II, pp. 10; 118 for an additional word on the importance of "discipline."

weighs the advice of Kempis, *Noli duriter agere cum tentato?* ('Deal not harshly with one that is tempted')."[47] Perhaps the greatest test for the strength of the Society was persecution. Without such close support Satan's advocates no doubt would have won the day. Though some of the mob rioting has already been described, let me give an account or two to put these early Revival days into perspective.

The fierceness of the mobs which plagued us for many years has already been demonstrated. Although much of the trouble occurred outside the larger cities, London itself was not immune. Early in the Revival "as I returned home one evening, I had no sooner stepped out of the coach, than the mob, who were gathered in great numbers about my door, quite closed me in. I rejoiced and blessed God, knowing this was the time I had long been looking for; and immediately spake to those that were next to me, of 'righteousness, and judgment to come.' At first not many heard, the noise roundabout us being exceeding great. But the silence spread farther and farther, till I had a quiet, attentive congregation: And when I left them, they all showed much love, and dismissed me with many blessings."[48]

Again, before moving on to the routine established during these early years, let me describe the practical outworkings (so dear to my heart) of the doctrine, "salvation by faith alone." I am fully convinced "that none shall finally be saved, who have not, as they had opportunity, done all good works; and, That if a justified person does not do good, as he has opportunity, he will lose the grace he has received; and if he 'repent' not, 'and do the former works,' will perish eternally."[49] Early in the Revival we noted in the United Society "that many of our brethren and sisters

---

[47]Ibid., Vol. II, p. 132.

[48]Ibid., Vol. I, p. 284; cf. pp. 353f.; 363; 422; 433; 436ff.; 451f.; 473; 486; 499; 504; Vol. II, pp. 44; 110; 143; 153f. All of the above references demonstrate mob rioting.

[49]Ibid., Vol. I, p. 321. It is interesting that just a few days before the present quotation, Wesley criticizes Martin Luther for blasphemously speaking of good works and of the law of God (Ibid., pp. 315f.; cf. Vol. II, p. 142).

had not needful food; many were destitute of convenient clothing; many were out of business, and that without their own fault; and many sick and ready to perish: That I had done what in me lay to feed the hungry, to clothe the naked, to employ the poor, and to visit the sick; but was not, alone, sufficient for these things; and therefore desired all whose hearts were as my heart, 1. To bring what clothes each could spare, to be distributed among those that wanted most, and 2. To give weekly a penny, or what they could afford, for the relief of the poor and sick. My design, I told them, was to employ, for the present, all the women who were out of business, and desired it, in knitting. To these we first gave the common price for what work they did; and then added, according as they needed. Twelve persons were appointed to inspect these, and to visit and provide things needful for the sick. Each of these was to visit all the sick within their district, every other day: And to meet on Tuesday evening, to give an account of what they had done, and consult what could be done farther."[50]

Bless God, there were only a few occasions in which I found it necessary to separate from the believers some who did not show their faith by their works. Many of our societies singularly distinguish themselves by such works. For example, I must tell you about Tetney. "I have not seen such another in England. In the class-paper (which gives an account of the contribution for the poor) I observed one gave eight-pence, often ten-pence, a week; another thirteen, fifteen, or eighteen pence; another, sometimes one, sometimes two shillings. I asked Micah Elmoor, the Leader, (an Israelite indeed, who now rests from his labour,) 'How is this? Are you the richest society in all England?' He answered, 'I suppose not: But all of us who are single persons have agreed together, to give both ourselves and *all we have* to God: And we do it gladly; whereby we are able, from time to time, to entertain all the

---

[50]Ibid., p. 309.

strangers that come to Tetney; who often have no food to eat, nor any friend to give them a lodging."[51]

For the first three years of the Revival our work had two centers—London and Bristol. Then, in May, 1742, I preached for the first time in Newcastle-upon-Tyne which provided us with a mother society for the northern counties. It was about this time that I set the routine which has remained with me these forty-three years. Most years I spent the winter in and around London traveling on to Bristol in early spring before my annual trip north during the late spring and summer months. Some years later I added an annual trip to the western counties (including Cornwall) in late summer before returning to London. Usually I would announce the time and place of my preaching either at a parish church (though frequently unavailable) or more usually one of our preaching houses, the market cross, or other convenient spots such as a barn or field.[52] I should also mention that I took advantage of these trips to travel with friends, clergy, and our own preachers (though they sometimes regretted it as they were subject to the same abuse), demonstrating not only the content and style of preaching, but also explaining the design, nature, and use of the Christian societies. After preaching, we desired those who determined to serve God to meet us separately from the great congregation for more private instruction.

Then, on July 30, 1742, my mother died in London. Let me describe her death even as I told it to Charles in a letter the following day: "Dear Charles,—Yesterday, about three in the afternoon, as soon as Intercession was ended, I went up to my mother. I found her pulse almost gone, and her fingers dead; so that it was easy to see her spirit was on the wing for eternity. After using the Commendatory prayer, I sat down on her bed-side, and, with three or four of our

---

[51]Ibid., Vol. II, pp. 45f.; cf. Ibid., p. 81. It should be mentioned that one of the first things Wesley did upon entering a town was to visit the sick.

[52]On June 6, 1742, Wesley, being denied the use of the church at Epworth, preached from atop his father's tomb (Ibid., Vol. I, p. 377; cf. p. 408).

sisters, sang a requiem to her parting soul. She continued in just the same way as my father was, struggling and gasping for life, tho' (as I could judge by several signs) perfectly sensible, till near four o'clock. I was then going to drink a dish of tea, being faint and weary; when one called me again to the bed-side. It was past (or just) four o'clock. She opened her eyes wide, and fixed them upward for a moment. Then the lids dropped, and the soul was set at liberty, without one struggle or groan or sigh."[53]

Before moving on to the next phase of the Revival, let me mention our first Conference which took place at the Foundery in London on Monday, June 25, 1744 (and the five days following). Briefly, we carefully considered the doctrine of sanctification including points of discipline, relating chiefly to organization, ministers, assistants (special attention was given to this office), stewards, and leaders.[54] We concluded by discussing the question of union with the Moravians and Mr. Whitefield. I should mention that three years earlier Mr. Whitefield had informed me that "he and I preached two different gospels, and therefore, he not only would not join with, or give me the right hand of fellowship, but was resolved publicly to preach against me and my brother, wheresoever he preached at all."[55] My response? I could only reply: "My brother, my son Whitefield." If he was determined to fight I was determined that he should have that field all to himself. I should add that there were three points in the debate: 1. Unconditional election, 2. Irresistible grace, and 3. Final perseverance. Some have been quick to point out that many in our societies held these doctrines. I only add: "I never ask them whether they hold them or no. Only let them not trouble others by disputing about them."[56] As

---

[53]*Journal*, Vol. III, p. 30n. The date for Susanna's death given in the *Journal* and again on her tombstone in Bunhill Fields is July 23. In this letter and in the *Arminian Magazine*, 1781, p. 312, however, Wesley gives the date as July 30.

[54]It is in the minutes for this conference that "The Twelve Rules of a Helper" first appear.

[55]*Works*, Vol. I, p. 305.

[56]Ibid., p. 274.

for Mr. Whitefield and myself, as God would have it; we were soon once again in each other's arms.[57] Six months later he wrote to me asking for pardon and seeking reconciliation.[58]

As our first decade neared an end I felt confident. So confident, in fact, that about this time I considered, " 'What would I do now, if I was sure I had but two days to live?' All outward things are settled to my wish; the houses at Bristol, Kingswood, and Newcastle are safe; the deed whereby they are conveyed to the Trustees took place on the fifth instant (March 5, 1747); my Will is made; what have I more to do, but to commend my soul to my merciful and faithful Creator?"[59] My old enemy seemed only a shadow quickly fading in the light of God's holy Son.

---

[57]Cf. p. 370. Wesley and Whitefield are together on May 12, 1742, with the Archbishop of Canterbury.

[58]George Whitefield's *Letters* p. 331, Banner of Faith ed., 1976.

[59]*Works*, Vol. II, p. 49.

19

Marriage and the Middle Years [1]

*When I began to make the Scriptures my study, . . . I began to
see that Christians are called to love God with all their heart and
to serve him with all their strength; which is precisely what I
apprehend to be meant by the scriptural term perfection.*

John Wesley

I was in love again! A few years into the Revival I had
met and developed a deep (but noble) affection for Grace
Murray of Newcastle, then living in London. She was the
young widow of a master mariner lost at sea. While he was
alive she had (under the preaching of Mr. Whitefield and
myself) been converted and received into the London Society. At first her husband thought her beside herself and
would have had her committed to the West Garden
madhouse, had not her gentle and affectionate spirit overcome his bitter opposition. I personally made her one of
the band leaders at the Foundery. After her husband's
death, she returned to Newcastle where she lived with her
mother and became one of the first-class leaders. Then, at
the opening of the Orphan House in 1745, she was appointed its housekeeper. The Orphan House also served
as a convenient lodging in Newcastle for our itinerant
preachers.

Grace proved so useful that by the summer of 1748 I
included her among my closest traveling companions, as-
signing her the task of organizing the female classes and
bands. Then the romance progressed so rapidly that by
July, 1749, we were engaged to be married. All that remained before the wedding was (according to the

---

[1]The "middle years" here refer to the period between 1748 and 1763.

Methodist Rules): (1) to satisfy John Bennett (one of my most trusted and successful preachers who had shown more than a little interest in Mrs. Murray, but without a promise); (2) to procure my brother's consent (who I had married to Sarah Gwynne some months earlier)²; and (3) to inform all the societies in England (as my brother had done) by sending an account of the reasons on which I proceeded to every Helper, desiring their prayers.³ This I was most anxious to do as Grace would not be put off indefinitely.

On Monday, July 24, 1749, Grace Murray and I, along with the rest of our company, returned to Bristol, having just completed my third journey into Ireland. The following day we rode to Kingswood where I examined closely the Society and school, putting out those who habitually neglected the Rules. It must have been then that some of the women, apparently jealous of the close relationship between Grace and myself, sought (and not without some success) to cast doubt in her mind concerning my attachment (though they were idle tales which would have easily fallen to the ground in the light of day) to another. Rather than face me directly, she allowed the wound to fester. Satan had planted his seed; the fruit of which caused Grace to renew her correspondence with Mr. Bennett.

The first week of August was one of frustration. Our Conference met at the New Room (having been enlarged and strengthened the previous year) but little was accomplished; Mr. Whitefield and Mr. Harris "flying off" on the finer points of Calvinism.⁴ Because everything was in such disarray, I did not have the presence of mind to notice Grace's coolness toward me. On August 12 we returned to London. While in London we talked, but with very

---

²Charles Wesley was married to Sarah Gwynne in Garth on April 8, 1749.

³We must remember that Wesley insisted upon following the rules to the letter in order to remove any hint of scandal among the societies where attack was expected from every quarter.

⁴The information here actually comes from Charles' *Journal*; John is silent during this period (W.H.S., vol. V, p. 108). Harris is Howell Harris, the staunch Welsh Calvinist.

little satisfaction. We grew apart. On August 23 we left London, arriving in Epworth three days later, where Grace again met John Bennett. I interviewed him myself. I could readily see that Grace would force my hand. On September 6, having reached Newcastle, I asked her plainly: "Which will you choose?" Her reply: "I am determined by conscience, as well as inclination, to live and die with you." Thinking the matter settled, we both wrote to Mr. Bennett the next day; the essence of which was: "That Grace was more and more convinced that both he and she had sinned against God in entering on any engagement at all without my knowledge and consent."[5] My letter to Mr. Bennett was misdirected, but a copy was sent to my brother in Bristol, who quickly journeyed to Leeds where he was informed by two (who should have known better), however innocently, that Grace was engaged to Bennett and that I was resolved to marry a woman who was already promised to another.[6]

In the meantime (after visiting the northern societies), I had left Grace at Hindley Hill, since one of our preachers urged me to come to Whitehaven immediately. I arrived in Whitehaven on September 22. Charles (having left Leeds) found me in Whitehaven and confronted me with protests against the proposed marriage, arguing that "all our preachers would leave us, all our societies disperse." I could not persuade him that he had the matter backwards. He left Whitehaven on September 28, journeyed to Hindley Hill, where he found Grace, and took her back to Newcastle. I arrived at Hindley Hill (having lost my way) two hours later. "I need add no more, than that if I had had more regard for her I loved than for the work of God I

[5]*Journal*, Vol. III, p. 421n. Apparently while in Epworth Grace (unsure of her relationship with Wesley) and John Bennett became engaged though she was already engaged to Wesley.

[6]Charles wrote to Grace at this point: "The case thus appears to me. You promised John Bennett to marry him—since which, you engaged yourself to another. . . . And who is that other? one of such importance that his doing so dishonest an action would destroy both himself, and me, and the whole work of God" (Ibid., p. 439).

should now have gone straight on to Newcastle, and not back to Whitehaven. I knew this was giving up all; but I knew God called, and therefore on Friday the 29th I set out again for Whitehaven."[7] On October 3, my brother succeeded in persuading two bewildered, half-reluctant persons to marry. Sometime later he discovered his great mistake. Instead of preventing me from marrying one betrothed to another, he had coerced poor John Bennett (who was perhaps the innocent party) into marrying the one promised to me. Charles had led Mrs. Murray to believe that I, who had loved her steadfastly for ten years, "had actually expressed the wish that, for the sake of the work of God, she would marry another. It was indeed, not a 'comedy,' but a 'tragedy of errors.'"[8]

Fortunately, an even greater tragedy (if you can believe it) was averted. Stated simply, there was no lasting breach between Charles and myself, which must, at that critical period, have either torn the Methodist society in two, or, more probably, scattered it to the winds. Bless God, the tenderness and tact of Mr. Whitefield quieted the storm. Lest you think me insensitive, an extract from my own account written at the time describes the mood.[9]

"OCT. 1, Sun.—I was in great heaviness, my heart was sinking in me like a stone. Only so long as I was preaching I felt ease. When I had done, the weight returned. I went to church sorrowful and very heavy, though I knew not any particular cause. And God found me there. Not only the lessons, both morning and afternoon, containing the account of the three children in the fiery furnace, of Daniel in the lions' den, and of our Lord's walking on the water and calming the storm, seemed all designed for me; but even the psalms which were sung all the day. I found likewise much refreshment in the sacrament. When I came home, I took up a Common Prayer-Book, and opened upon these words: 'Deliver me not over unto the will of mine adver-

---

[7]Ibid., pp. 432f.

[8]Ibid., p. 440n.

[9]I might add that the extraordinary charity and self-control of Wesley himself (as demonstrated by the account to follow), played an important role as well.

saries; for there are false witnesses risen up against me, and such as speak wrong. I should utterly have fainted; but that I believe verily to see the goodness of the Lord in the land of the living. O tarry thou the Lord's leisure; be strong, and He shall comfort thy heart; and put thou thy trust in the Lord' (Ps. xxvii. 14, &c).

"In the evening my heaviness returned, but with much of the spirit of prayer. It seemed to me that I ought not to linger here, and yet I knew not whither to go; till Mr. P[erronet] asked, 'Will you go to Leeds on Tuesday?' Immediately my mind was easy. I had sent notice of being there on Wednesday evening, but it was gone out of my thoughts. I determined to go; only I was concerned to leave Whitehaven without a preacher.

"We then poured out our hearts before God; and I was led, I know not how, to ask that, if He saw good, He would show me the end of these things, in dreams or visions of the night. I dreamed I saw a man bring out G[race] M[urray], who told her she was condemned to die, and that all things were now in readiness for the execution of that sentence. She spoke not one word, nor showed any reluctance, but walked up with him to the place. The sentence was executed, without her stirring either hand or foot. I looked at her, till I saw her face turn black. Then I could not bear it, but went away. But I returned quickly, and desired she might be cut down. She was then laid upon a bed. I sat by mourning over her. She came to herself and began to speak, and I awaked.

"*Mon.* the 2nd I dedicated to God, in fasting and solemn prayer. We had free access to the throne of grace, and I found my will more resigned. In the evening Joseph Cownley came, and brought me a letter from Mr. Whitefield, pressing me much to meet my brother and him at Leeds on Wednesday evening. My brother had likewise charged Joseph Cownley, 'if I would not come, to come thither himself.'

"*Tues.* 3.—We rode to Old Hutton, and about nine the next night reached Leeds. Here I found not my brother, but Mr. Whitefield. I lay down by him on the bed. He told me,

'My brother would not come till J[ohn] B[ennett] and G[race] M[urray] were married.' I was troubled. He perceived it. He wept and prayed over me, but I could not shed a tear. He said all that was in his power to comfort me, but it was in vain. He told me, 'It was his judgement that she was my wife, and that he had said so to J[ohn] B[ennett]: that he would fain have persuaded them to wait, and not to marry till they had seen me; but that my brother's impetuosity prevailed and bore down all before it.'

"I felt no murmuring thought, but deep distress. I accepted the just punishment of my manifold unfaithfulness and unfruitfulness, and therefore could not complain. But I felt the loss both to me and the people, which I did not expect could ever be repaired. I tried to sleep, but I tried in vain; for sleep was fled from my eyes. I was burning fever, and, more and more thoughts still crowding into my mind, I perceived if this continued long it would affect my senses. But God took that matter into His hand, giving me, on a sudden, sound and quiet sleep.

"*Thurs.* 5.—About eight one came in from Newcastle, and told us, 'They were married on Tuesday,' My brother came an hour after. I felt no anger, yet I did not desire to see him. But Mr. Whitefield constrained me. After a few words had passed, he accosted me with, 'I renounce all intercourse with you, but what I would have with an heathen man or a publican.' I felt little emotion. It was only adding a drop of water to a drowning man, yet I calmly accepted his renunciation, and acquiesced therein. Poor Mr. Whitefield and John Nelson burst into tears. They prayed, cried, and entreated, till the storm passed away. We could not speak, but only fell on each other's neck.

"J[ohn] B[ennett] then came in. Neither of us could speak, but we kissed each other and wept. Soon after I talked with my brother alone. He seemed utterly amazed. He clearly saw I was not what he thought, and now blamed only her; which confirmed me in believing my presage was true, and I should see her face no more."[10]

[10]This account is from a hand-written draft now in the British Museum. It is quoted in the *Journal*, Vol. III, pp. 433ff.

I can only now say: "The Lord gave, and the Lord hath taken away: Blessed be the name of the Lord!" Who can fathom the ways of God, or so it would seem if you will but hear the rest of my story of love and marriage. Less than a year-and-a-half later I was once again clearly convinced that I ought to marry. On Monday, February 18, 1751 (my journey north being delayed a second time due to a stubborn ankle sprain making it impossible to walk), I took Molly Vazeille, the widow of a London merchant, as my wife. [11] We had planned to wed upon my return (giving me an opportunity to fulfill the Rules to the letter); but the delay made it such that I was fearful of putting her off inordinately. [12] Furthermore, my brother Charles was again resisting at every turn; so, I believed it best to settle the matter (even without fulfilling the necessary Rule) that some healing might occur during my absence. [13] Happily, while I was away, he called upon my wife, kissed her and assured her that he was perfectly reconciled to her and to me. [14]

During the early fifties I began making trips into Ireland and Scotland. Thinking the Scots unteachable, I actually

---

[11]The date for the wedding could have been February 19. *The Gentlemen's Magazine* and *The London Magazine* list the two dates (February 18 and 19) respectively. The wedding is not mentioned in the *Journal*. Molly Vazeille was the wealthy widow of a London merchant. She was perhaps introduced to Wesley by Mr. Blackwell (a close friend to both) soon after the Grace Murray episode.

[12]Wesley made a defense before the London Society describing both his intent and purpose, but due to the circumstances (described above) it was not until the night before the wedding.

[13]Wesley did not allow Charles even to know the name of his intended. Charles did not attend the wedding. It is interesting that if Wesley had disregarded the rules earlier he would have married Grace Murray and if he had followed them here (no doubt remembering the episode with Grace, not to mention Sophy) he would not have married Molly Vazeille. Wesley makes surprisingly few references to her in the *Journal*. See, for example, Vol. II, pp. 224, 240, 251, 257, 281, 329, 418, 426.

[14]In fairness it should be mentioned that Charles' fears were not altogether unfounded. His own marriage had proven difficult. Furthermore, the Revival depended upon Wesley's leadership at this point. The character and absolute loyalty to his own principles and methods was all important. He had to be one with himself if the people he led were to follow in unbroken ranks.

made four trips into Ireland (beginning in August, 1747) before entering Scotland in April, 1751. From that time on the trips were made more or less alternately until the present time.

About this time the rest of my yearly routine was more firmly established. Along with the northern journey I added an annual trip into Cornwall, usually in late summer. Throughout the year I frequently preached three times a day with little or no exhaustion.[15] Oddly enough, the more I used my strength the more I had. Even today "I am often much tired the first time I preach in a day; a little the second time; but after the third or fourth, I rarely feel either weakness or weariness."[16]

The work of the Revival has always been interesting and full of surprises. "I find it useful to be in such a state of suspense, wherein I know not what will be the next hour, but lean absolutely on His disposal, who knoweth and ruleth all things well."[17] There were always trials, some large, some small. The mobs, the disputes, always kept us humble. We were continually thanking God for yet another opportunity to grow in grace. I remember one journey almost laughingly: "I had borrowed a young, strong mare, when I set out from Manchester. But she fell lame before I got to Grimsby. I procured another, but was dismounted again between Newcastle and Berwick. At my return to Manchester, I took my own: But she had lamed herself in the pasture. I thought, nevertheless, to ride her four or five miles today; but she was gone out of the ground, and we could hear nothing of her. However, I comforted myself, that I had another at Manchester, which I had lately bought. But when I came thither, I

---

[15]Cf. *Works*, Vol. III, p. 21. where we read that Wesley preached thirty times in eleven days.

[16]Ibid., Vol. II, p. 256. Just a month after his marriage Wesley writes with incredible naivete: "I cannot understand, how a Methodist Preacher can answer it to God, to preach one sermon, or travel one day less, in a married, than in a single state. In this respect surely, 'it remaineth, that they who have wives be as though they had none'" (Ibid., p. 224).

[17]Ibid., p. 268.

found one had borrowed her too, and rode her away to Chester."[18]

At this point, let me put the Revival itself back into larger perspective. By the middle years (or so they may be termed) I was keenly aware of what God was doing among us. In June, 1755, I wrote in my *Journal:* "From a deep sense of the amazing work which God has of late years wrought in England, I preached in the evening on those words, (Psalm cxlvii.20,) 'He hath not dealt so with any nation;' no, not even with Scotland or New-England. In both these God has indeed made bare his arm; yet not in so astonishing a manner as among us. This must appear to all who impartially consider, 1. The numbers of persons on whom God has wrought: 2. The swiftness of his work in many, both convinced and truly converted in a few days: 3. The depth of it in most of these, changing the heart, as well as the whole conversation: 4. The clearness of it, enabling them boldly to say, 'Thou hast loved me; thou hast given thyself for me:' 5. The continuance of it. God has wrought in Scotland and New-England, at several times, for some weeks or months together; but among us, he has wrought for near eighteen years together, without any observable intermission. Above all, let it be remarked, that a considerable number of the regular Clergy were engaged in that great work in Scotland; and in New-England, above an hundred, perhaps as eminent as any in the whole province, not only for piety, but also for abilities, both natural and acquired; whereas in England there were only two or three inconsiderable Clergymen, with a few young, raw, unlettered men; and these opposed by well nigh all the Clergy, as well as laity, in the nation. He that remarks this must needs own, both that this is a work of God, and that he hath not wrought so in any other nation."[19]

It must also be mentioned that one of the most significant reasons for the continuance of our Revival (apart from our manner of preaching and the organization of

---

[18]Ibid., p. 265.
[19]Ibid., p. 335. Cf. an interesting statement on the following page where Wesley gives what he believed to be the reasons for the slowdown of the Revival in Scotland and New-England (Ibid., p. 336).

Societies) was the book and tract distribution.[20] We not only preached the whole gospel (including both justification and sanctification), but plenty of literature ("all true, all agreeable to the oracles of God: As is all practical, unmixt with controversy of any kind; and all intelligible to plain men.")[21] was made available to all our societies, classes, and bands. Although the pressure of time forced me to publish many things either written or abridged while on horseback, the material was sound of doctrine and experience.[22]

I was utterly amazed that some misinformed people would accuse us of profitee. ing.[23] When I settled my temporal business about this t me I commented: "It is now about eighteen years since I began writing and printing

[20]Between 1749 and 1756 *The Christian Library* (a series of extracts from the works of well-known divines composing a fifty-volume collection of works of "Practical Divinity") was published. Cf. Ibid., p. 278.

[21]Wesley, *Christian Library*, "Preface," pp. ivf.

[22]Some might profit from a word concerning Wesley's method of abridgement. Wesley was a master at the art of abridgement, selecting from the material available that which related to his own personal concern and interest and also that which would be of general use to Methodism as a whole. Usually taking the latest English edition, he extracted only the heart, freely modified to suit his own ends, yet still retaining the original meaning. He achieved this by eliminating much of the illustrative, controversial, or irrelevant (to his ends) material, seeking brevity, clarity, and readability through paraphrasing, modernization (e.g., "phanatic" becomes "enthusiast"), and rearrangement. He omitted foreign phrases, and theological and philosophical arguments. He made few additions (except for the preface and summary sections) but his omissions and footnotes (where there are no footnotes he edits more carefully) pinpoint his conflicting opinions. Richard Green states that Wesley carefully weeded out what he thought unscriptural. Monk rightly points out that "Wesley's deletions, changes, and embellishments indicate his theological affinities and differences" (Robert Monk, *John Wesley, His Puritan Heritage*, p. 54).

[23]Cf. *Works*, Vol. II, p. 64. A letter dated July 14, 1747, speaks for itself: "Rev. Sir, I was exceedingly surprised when I was informed yesterday of your affirming publicly in the church, in the face of a whole congregation, 'Now Wesley was sent down for an hundred pounds; and it must be raised directly. Nay, it is true.' O Sir, is this possible? Can it be, that you should be so totally void (I will not say of conscience, of religion, but) of good-nature, as to credit such a tale? and of good manners and common sense, as *thus* to repeat it?

"I must beg that you would either justify or retract this; (for it is a point of no small concern;) and that I may know what you propose to do, before I set out for London." Wesley never received a reply.

books; and how much in that time have I gained by printing? Why, on summing up my accounts, I found that on March 1, 1756, (the day I left London last,) I had gained by printing and preaching together, a *debt* of 1,235 pounds."[24] Although we handed out tracts (most of them written by myself) by the thousands, they were always given away without donation.[25] I personally lost more than 200 pounds on *The Christian Library* alone.[26] Eventually, "a proposal was made for devolving all temporal business, books and all, entirely on the Stewards; so that I might have no care upon me (in London at least) but that of the souls committed to my charge."[27] Even in more prosperous years I never spent more than thirty pounds a year on myself. Any surplus was given to the poor or toward the expenses of the Revival.[28] To this day I have worn neatly mended shirts, never a wig, and frequently cut my own hair to save the price of a barber.

One last word must be said about our distribution of literature.[29] Much of the writing (however unhappily) had to do with the defense of our cause. I remember thinking on numerous occasions: "How much rather would I write practically than controversially! But even this talent I dare not bury in the earth."[30] Most of this work was tiresome. Occasionally I was drawn into the conflict with those who wrote weak, bitter, scurrilous invectives against the people called Methodist. I rarely meddled with such people the second time however. Their writing was "too

[24]*Works*, Vol. II, p. 385. Cf. Vol. III, p. 503, italics mine.

[25]Cf. Ibid., Vol. II, pp. 3, 60, 413. Wesley wrote numerous tracts; including those to a "Swearer," a "Drunkard," and a "Smuggler."

[26]Cf. Ibid., p. 278. Wesley writes concerning *The Christian Library:* "Perhaps the next generation may know the value of it."

[27]Ibid., p. 279. This did little good. Wesley's book account was handled rather clumsily throughout.

[28]Ibid., Vol. IV, p. 243. On another occasion Wesley writes to the tax assessor in London that he had but two silver spoons; one in London and one in Bristol and that he would never have more while men around him still wanted bread.

[29]Wesley not only wrote and published devotionally, he wrote in the secular fields as well, including histories, admittedly oriented toward the Methodist view (Ibid., Vol. II, p. 209); and grammars (Ibid., pp. 175, 223).

[30]Ibid., Vol. II, p. 433.

dirty for me to touch."[31] I would only add: "O that I might dispute with no man! But if I must dispute, let it be with men of sense."[32] The mobs still raged throughout the middle years of our ministry, though this seemed only to unite the strong and weed out the careless. Satan, however, had a more effective tool. Again, the one problem that has plagued us from the beginning is backsliding. Even among our strongest societies consisting of members full of zeal and good desires, experience has taught me to ask: "How long will this continue!"[33] In most, though God has helped them thus far, "only till the fowls of the air come and devour the seed. Many of the rest, when persecution or reproach begins, will immediately be offended; and in the small remainder, some will fall off, either through other desires, or the cares of the world, or the deceitfulness of riches."[34] It was sometimes difficult to be realistic without shortening the arm of God, because of our pessimism. All too frequently "I found many of the first were become last, being returned 'as a dog to the vomit.'"[35] I remember an unfortunate account from Ireland. A certain gentleman "was at the point of death, by a violent rupture: While they were praying for him in the society, he was at once restored to perfect health. He continued in health for several years, and in the knowledge and the love of God: But no sooner did he return to folly, than his disorder returned; and in some months it put an end to his life. He died as stupid as an ox."[36] Another painful memory hangs in my mind. A young man from Rufforth, "remarkably serious and well-behaved, and rejoicing in his first love, who set out but a few minutes before me, was thrown by his horse, and (as it is termed) broke his neck. Just at the instant, a person going by, who

---

[31]Ibid., p. 442. Cf. Ibid., p. 445 where Wesley describes a humorous, if not pathetic, account of a play entitled "Methodism Displayed."

[32]Ibid., Vol. III, p. 81.

[33]Ibid., Vol. II, p. 141.

[34]Ibid., pp. 141f. Backsliding was especially prevalent among the rich (cf. Ibid., pp. 409, 486, 518, 523).

[35]Ibid., p. 184.

[36]Ibid., p. 406.

understood the case, took hold of him, and pulled it into its place. O mystery of Providence! Why did not this man die, when he was full of humble, holy love? Why did he live, to 'turn from the holy commandment' which was then written in his heart?"[37]

It is as true as Jesus is the Christ; the only way to keep Methodists alive is to keep them moving. Since Frederica there has been but one prevention for such violence played upon the souls of well-meaning Christians—going on to perfection. This is an obvious solution, for those who press forward persevere. But alas, though God made such practical divinity necessary, the devil made it controversial. We must, however, "resist the devil," or he will not "flee from us!" So, controversy or not, we preach perfection; a plain account of which (though necessarily brief) I give to you now.[38]

In 1756 I wrote to a friend: "When I began to make the Scriptures my study (about seven-and-twenty years ago), I began to see that Christians are called to *love God with all* their *heart* and to *serve Him with all* their *strength;* which is precisely what I apprehended to be meant by the scriptural term perfection."[39] As for some specifics, I simply and plainly add that perfection, or perfect love (which excludes

---

[37]Ibid., p. 289.

[38]Keep in mind that though Wesley's views on perfection represent his most consistent line of thought reaching back to his religious awakening in 1725 (and for that reason this is the doctrine least affected by Aldersgate; Wesley rarely, if ever, refers to the experience at Aldersgate when explaining the origin and development of this Christian ideal); his opinions do change somewhat (see Analysis, Part IV). The view stated here, except where otherwise defined, represents his more mature doctrine of perfection articulated between the years 1756 and 1763. As Wesley's care of souls extended, he saw more and more the necessity of both justification and sanctification as works of grace. His *Journal* regularly reports the different experiences from this point on (cf. *Works*, Vol. III, pp. 120ff.).

[39]*Letters*, Vol. III, p. 157. In order to establish continuity across the years, Wesley frequently referred to the sermon, "Circumcision of the Heart," first preached before the University in 1733 (cf. *Plain Account of Christian Perfection, Works*, Vol. XI, pp. 367), though it was undoubtedly edited somewhat during the period now under consideration. For a good review of Wesley's thoughts on perfection cf. *Works*, Vol. VIII, p. 429; Vol. X, p. 450; *Letters*, Vol. IV, p. 212; pp. 157f.; *Works*, Vol. XII, p. 397; and Vol. XI, pp. 394f.

sin except by reason of ignorance or mistake) is accomplished by faith alone and is consequently instantaneous (though preceded and followed by a gradual work); and, it should be expected now, at any instant.[40] Lest, however, some should run their heads into a noose, let me caution: It is not absolute (that is angelic or adamic);[41] and it is not merely a moral or ethical aspiration, a set theological creed. It is a doctrine related to practice, a dynamic concept validated by actual experience. The experiences that I have recorded (and there have been hundreds to testify) could be summarized thus: "Constant communion with God the Father and the Son fills their hearts with humble love";[42] that is to say: "They feel no inward sin; and to the best of their knowledge commit no outward sin: They see and love God every moment, and pray, rejoice, give thanks evermore: They have constantly as clear a witness from God of sanctification as they have of justification."[43] Let me illustrate with a particular.

---

[40]Wesley writes on December 5, 1762: "To take away one ground of contention from many well-meaning people, in preaching on, 'The kingdom of heaven is like a grain of mustard-seed,' I endeavoured to show at large, in what sense sanctification is gradual, and in what sense it is instantaneous: And (for the present, at least) many were delivered from vain reasonings and disputings" (*Works*, Vol. III, p. 123. Cf. Ibid., p. 67). The diagram on the following page is designed to assist you in focusing especially upon the acts of grace which are instantaneous and those which are gradual.

[41]Cf. Ibid., p. 126. There was a break among some Methodists as to whether or not perfection was absolute. Maxfield, for example (cf. Ibid., p. 136), made it such that it was unreachable.

[42]Ibid., Vol. II, p. 528. Wesley comments: "Now this is what I always did, and do now, mean by perfection."

[43]Ibid., p. 530. Cf. Ibid., Vol. III, p. 75, for a similar account.

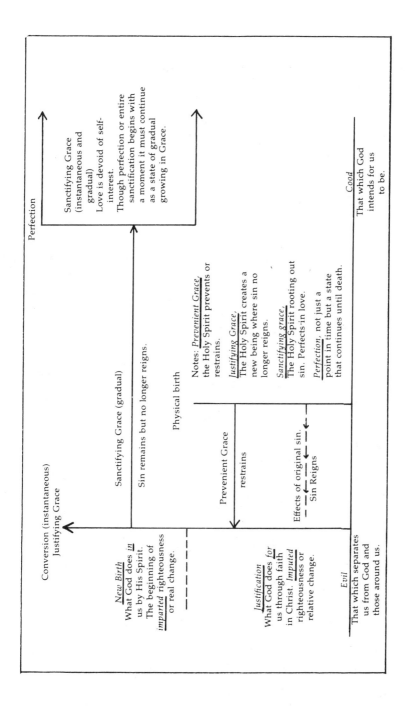

Perfection

Conversion (instantaneous)
Justifying Grace

Sanctifying Grace (instantaneous and gradual)
Love is devoid of self-interest.
Though perfection or entire sanctification begins with a moment it must continue as a state of gradual growing in Grace.

Sanctifying Grace (gradual)

Sin remains but no longer reigns.

Physical birth

Notes: *Prevenient Grace,* the Holy Spirit prevents or restrains.

Justifying Grace, The Holy Spirit creates a new being where sin no longer reigns.

Sanctifying grace, The Holy Spirit rooting out sin. Perfects in love.

Perfection, not just a point in time but a state that continues until death.

Prevenient Grace

restrains

Effects of original sin.
Sin Reigns

New Birth
What God does *in* us by His Spirit. The beginning of *imparted* righteousness or real change.

Justification
What God does *for* us through faith in Christ. *Imputed* righteousness or relative change.

Evil
That which separates us from God and those around us.

Good
That which God intends for us to be.

Judith Beresford "was always an innocent, sober young woman, having the form of godliness, till she was convinced of sin, and soon after justified. She was a pattern both of piety and industry. Notwithstanding her fortune and her sickliness, she was never unemployed; when she had no other work, working for the poor. And the whole tenor of her conversation was such, that it is still a common saying, 'If Miss Beresford is not gone to heaven, nobody ever will.'

"She had a vehement love to the word of God, and spared no pains in order to hear it. Frequently she would not go to bed all night, lest she should miss the morning preaching. She lost no opportunity of meeting with her brethren, to whom her heart was closely united: Nor was she afraid or ashamed to own the poorest of them, wherever she met them, and whatever company she was in. The very sight of them occasioned a joy in her soul, which she neither could nor desired to hide.

"When her weakness confined her to her room, she rejoiced with joy unspeakable: More especially when she was delivered from all her doubts concerning Christian perfection. Never was any one more athirst for this, for the whole mind that was in Christ. And she earnestly exhorted all her brethren, vehemently to press after it.

"The more her bodily strength decayed, the more she was strengthened in spirit. She called upon all that were with her, 'Help me to rejoice; help me to praise God.' Having no fear, but a jealousy over herself, lest she should exceed in her desire to be with Christ.

"As soon as I came to Ashbourn, she sent for me, and broke out, 'I am just at my journey's end. What a mercy, that I who have done so little for God, should be so soon taken up to him! O, I am full of the love of God! I dare not exercise my faith fully upon God: The glory of the Lord is so great, that I cannot bear it: I am overwhelmed: My natural life is almost gone, with the brightness of his presence. Sometimes I am even forced to cry out, *Lord, stay thy hand till I come into glory.'* I asked, 'Have you lately felt any remains of sin in you?' She said, 'I felt pride some weeks ago.' And it seems this was the last time. She added, 'I have now no will; the will of God is mine. I can bring my dearest friends before the Lord; and while I am praying for them, the glory of the Lord so overpowers me that I am lost, and adore in silence the God of heaven.' She cried out, 'Tell all from me, that perfection is attainable; and exhort all to press after it. What a blessing is it, that I have no weary hours; though I am confined to my bed night and day, and can take scarce any thing but water to refresh me, yet I am like a giant refreshed with wine.'

"Afterward she broke out, 'If I had lived in what the world calls pleasure, what a miserable creature should I have been now! What should I be if I had no God on my side? When the fire has made me bright, then I shall go to my God.' She prayed largely for all states of mankind: But particularly for the prosperity of the church; and for the society at Ashbourn, that God would continue and increase his work among them.

"When she altered for death, she called for her mother and brothers, to each of whom she gave an earnest exhortation. Then she said, 'Now I have no more to do here; I am ready to die. Send to Mr. W[esley], and tell him I am sorry I did not sooner believe the doctrine of perfect holiness. Blessed be God I now know it to be the truth!' After greatly rejoicing in God, for two days more, she said one morning, 'I dreamed last night I heard a voice, *Christ will come to-day for his bride.* It is for me. He will come for me to-day.' And a few hours after, without one struggle, or sigh, or groan, she sweetly fell asleep.''[44] Let me at this point anticipate a few of your questions with some notes from the *Plain Account:*

---

[44]Ibid., Vol. II, pp. 400-403. Following a funeral service in the New Room, Bristol (October 28, 1762) Wesley notes: "Many years ago my brother frequently said: 'Your day of Pentecost is not fully come; but I doubt not it will: And you will then hear of persons sanctified, as frequently as you do now of persons justified.' Any unprejudiced reader may observe, that it was now fully come. And accordingly we did hear of persons sanctified, in London, and most other parts of England, and in Dublin, and many other parts of Ireland, as frequently as of persons justified; although instances of the latter were far more frequent than

Question: "Can those who are perfect grow in grace?"

Answer: "Undoubtedly they can; and that not only while they are in the body, but to all eternity."

Question: "Can they fall from it?"

Answer: "I am well assured they can; matter of fact puts this beyond dispute. Formerly we thought one saved from sin could not fall; now we know the contrary. We are surrounded with instances of those who lately experienced all that I mean by perfection. They had both the fruit of the Spirit, and the witness; but they have now lost both. Neither does any one stand by virtue of anything that is implied in the nature of the state. There is no such height or strength of holiness as it is impossible to fall from. If there be any that cannot fall, this wholly depends on the promise of God."

Question: "Can those who fall from this state recover it?"

Answer: "Why not? We have many instances of this also. Nay, it is an exceeding common thing for persons to lose it more than once, before they are established therein."[45]

Question: "What if one should die in a state justified but not sanctified?"

Answer: "I believe they would be saved, because I am persuaded none that has faith can die before they are made ripe for glory. This is the doctrine which I continually teach, which has nothing to do with justification by works. Nor can it discourage any who have faith, neither weaken their peace, nor damp their joy in the Lord. True believers are not distressed hereby, either in life or in death; unless in some rare instant, wherein the temptation of the devil is joined with a melancholy temper."[46]

---

they had been for twenty years before. That many of these did not retain the gift of God, is no proof that it was not given them. That many do retain it to this day, is matter of praise and thanksgiving. And many of them are gone to Him whom they loved, praising him with their latest breath; just in the spirit of Ann Steed, the first witness in Bristol of the great salvation; who, being worn out with sickness and racking pain, after she had commended to God all that were around her, lifted up her eyes, cried aloud, 'Glory! Hallelujah! and died" (Ibid., Vol. III, p. 116).

[45]Ibid., Vol. XI, pp. 426f.
[46]*Letters*, Vol. IV, pp. 10, 13.

Is it any surprise that the more I converse with true believers, the more I am convinced that they sustain a "great loss for want of hearing the doctrine of Christian Perfection clearly and strongly enforced. I see, wherever this is not done, the believers grow dead and cold. Nor can this be prevented, but by keeping up in them an hourly expectation of being perfected in love. I say an hourly expectation; for to expect it at death, or sometime hence, is much the same as not expecting it at all."[47]

As I read over my letters for the years 1756-1763 they are filled with advice related to the pursuit of perfection; that is, to guard them who are saved from sin, and from every occasion of stumbling. I urged those under my care to quit trifling companions;[48] to praise God continually;[49] to reject all comfort which does not flow from the spirit of adoption;[50] to maintain all simplicity, watching unto prayer and yielding not to indolence or spiritual laziness;[51] to control wandering thoughts, bringing all of them into the captive obedience of Christ;[52] and to set aside some time daily for reading and other private exercises.[53]

Toward the close of the middle years I was ill much of the time and even near death on several occasions.[54] In the fall of 1752, for example, I found myself indisposed with an illness that lasted for a full year. One morning I arose extremely sick but believed it would go away quickly. The following day, though I was considerably worse, I could not think of sparing myself; so, "I determined, if it were possible, to keep my word, and accordingly set out soon after four for Canterbury. At Welling, I was obliged to stop;

---

[47]*Works*, Vol. III, p. 113.

[48]*Letters*, Vol. III, p. 206. Cf. *Works*, Vol. II, p. 241. Wesley writes: "A young gentlewoman, who was with us where we dined, hastened away to prepare for the ball. But before she was half dressed, she was struck, and came down in a flood of tears. Nevertheless, she broke through, and in a few hours danced away all her convictions."

[49]*Letters*, Vol. III, p. 208.

[50]Ibid., p. 212.

[51]Ibid., p. 215; cf. pp. 218f.

[52]Ibid., p. 243.

[53]Ibid., p. 240; Vol. IV, p. 103; cf. "Conference Minutes," 1762.

[54]Cf. *Works*, Vol. II, p. 41 where Wesley is rumored dead due to a throw from his horse. He escaped miraculously with only a few bruises which failed to slacken his pace "one hour in the day."

after resting an hour, I was much better; but soon after I took horse, my sickness returned, and accompanied me to Brompton, near Chatham. In the evening I preached to a serious congregation, and again at five in the morning. We came to Canterbury about one, when I was presently seized with the cold fit of an ague. About twelve I fell fast asleep, and waked well at seven in the morning."[55] Within a month the fever, my cough, and the pain in my left breast was so troublesome that my strength almost failed me. Thinking that my end was near I composed the words for my tombstone:

Here lieth the Body
of
JOHN WESLEY
A brand plucked out of the burning:
Who died of a consumption in the fifty-first year of his age,
not leaving, after his debts are paid,
ten pounds behind him:
praying,
God be merciful to me, an unprofitable servant![56]

Early in January, being no better, I took a lodging near the Hot Well (near Bristol) in order to drink the water.[57] I remained there until March 4, but did not resume preaching (after an intermission of four months) until March 26.

---

[55]Ibid., p. 307.

[56]Ibid., p. 309. It is interesting that while Wesley writes: "I ventured to meet the society; and for near an hour my voice and strength were restored, so that I felt neither pain nor weakness" (Ibid.); Charles Wesley writes for the same period: "All last Tuesday they expected his [John's] death every hour" (Charles Wesley's *Journal*, November 29, 1753).

[57]Wesley's routine continued even in the midst of his consumption. For January 7, 1754, he wrote: "I went on now in a regular method, rising at my hour, and writing *(The Notes on the New Testament)* from five to nine at night; except the time of riding, half an hour for each meal, and the hour between five and six in the evening" *(Works,* Vol. II, p. 310).

Although the weakness stayed with me (in varying degrees) for several years, I tried not to indulge my vile body. I continued my regular ministry only seeking to avoid contention, being more sensitive than usual to the opinions of others.[58] In November, 1756, I purchased an electrical apparatus that had proved useful to me personally during the past few years. It usually brought immediate help for a number of disorders.[59] As I studied more carefully the cure of diseases I began asking myself: "Why then do not all Physicians consider how far bodily disorders are caused or influenced by the mind; and in those cases, which are utterly out of their sphere, call in the assistance of a Minister; as Ministers, when they find the mind disordered by the body, call in the assistance of a Physician?"[60]

My illness taught me several valuable lessons, but one in particular. My old enemy had lost his hold. I determined to turn his own tactic against him. The fear of death not only leads to doubt, but also to a serious consideration (however brief) about the things of God. I was in Newlyn, for example, when I was informed that a strong, healthy man was found dead in his bed the morning before. Many were startled: "So I endeavoured to deepen the impression, by preaching on those words, 'There is no work, nor device, nor knowledge, nor wisdom in the grave, whither thou goest.'"[61] Such a method must be used only sparingly, however. This sort of fear soon wears off. Once in Ireland I observed crowds hurrying to witness the execution of a poor deserter. "I believe some of them retained serious impressions for near four-and-twenty hours! But it was not so with the soldiers: Although they walked one by one, close to the bleeding, mangled carcase, most of them were as merry within six hours, as if they had only seen a puppet-show."[62]

[58]Cf. Ibid., p. 288 and *Journal*, Vol. IV, p. 103n.

[59]*Works*, Vol. II, p. 388; cf. Ibid., p. 517, where he revises and perfects the "Treatise on Electricity," and Vol. III, p. 240, 311; Vol. IV, p. 3.

[60]Ibid., Vol. II, p. 479.

[61]Ibid., p. 342.

[62]Ibid., Vol. III, p. 96.

Thus, the Revival continued without decline through the middle years. In London, during the early 60s, "I found the work of God swiftly increasing here. The congregations, in every place, were larger than they had been for several years. Many were from day by day convinced of sin. Many found peace with God. Many backsliders were healed, yea, filled with joy unspeakable. And many believers entered into such a rest, as it had not before entered into their hearts to conceive."[63]

Furthermore, our basic principles were continually being reinforced. "I was more convinced than ever, that the preaching like an Apostle, without joining together those that are awakened, and training them up in the ways of God, is only begetting children for the murderer. How much preaching has there been for these twenty years all over Pembrokeshire! But no regular societies, no discipline, no order or connexion; the consequence is, that nine in ten of the once-awakened are now faster asleep than ever."[64]

Our discipline did not quench the Spirit, however. Spiritual gifts were still prevalent in spite of some dry, formal, orthodox men, who ridiculed whatever gifts they did not have themselves, and decried real, scriptural Christianity as either madness or imposture.[65] This is not to say that our people did not need a word of caution. They were to avoid running to either extreme. Earlier "the danger *was*, to regard extraordinary circumstances too much, such as outcries, convulsions, visions, trances; as if these were essential to the inward work, so that it could not go on without them. Perhaps the danger *is* to regard them too little, to condemn them altogether; to imagine they had nothing of God in them, and were an hinderance to his work."[66]

---

[63]Ibid., pp. 72f.

[64]Ibid., p. 144.

[65]Ibid., Vol. II, p. 204.

[66]Ibid., p. 519. Following this quotation Wesley notes several rules regarding such extraordinary circumstances: "1. God suddenly and strongly convinced many that they were lost sinners; the natural consequence whereof were sudden outcries and strong bodily convulsions: 2. To strengthen and encourage them that believed, and to make his work

At this point, though it pains me, I must relate the account regarding the consequence of my marriage. I have put it off long enough. If we ever properly loved each other (and I doubt that we did), it lasted but a few months. My wife was insanely jealous, refusing to accept the tone and advice of my correspondence (especially with young women) in the spirit in which it was written.[67] I could not perform any of my duties in my usual manner.[68] We lived together only occasionally for twenty years. In 1771 she decided to live with her married daughter in Newcastle, proposing "never to return." I could only comment: *"Non eam reliqui: Non dimisi: Non revocabo."*[69]

From that point on (though her daughter persuaded her to return to me) we lived and traveled together only sparingly. Though she shared our homes both in London and Bristol, for the most part, even while we were together we were apart. Then, years after our separation, she died.[70] I was not informed until four days later. There have been times when I wished that we never had met. I am certain that she must have felt the same way; but surely God will somehow even glorify Himself by this unfortunate match.

more apparent, he favoured several of them with divine dreams, others with trances and visions: 3. In some of these instances, after a time, nature mixed with grace: 4. Satan likewise mimicked this work of God, in order to discredit the whole work: And yet it is not wise to give up this part, any more than to give up the whole. At first it was, doubtless, wholly from God. It is partly so at this day; and he will enable us to discern how far, in every case, the work is pure, and where it mixes or degenerates." (Cf. Ibid., Vo. III, p. 131.) Here Wesley resists such abuse. It should also be noted that at this point Wesley is fascinated by strange stories often recorded in the *Journal* as visions or even apparitions (Ibid., Vol. II, p. 369).

[67]Wesley was counselor to several men and women. I personally have no question whatever regarding the integrity of John Wesley. If some will not believe me then believe Alexander Knox. In an appendix to Southey's *Life* there appears an objective (Knox, a Calvinist, takes issue with Wesley at several points where a theological issue was to be raised) account regarding the moral character of Mr. John Wesley.

[68]Remember, Wesley expected to do just this. He expected married life to change nothing (but his fellowship at Oxford, which he resigned immediately. Cf. *Works*, Vol. II, pp. 231f.). See note 16 of this chapter.

[69]This Latin phrase is translated: "I did not desert her: I did not send her away: I will never recall her."

Utlimately, the work of revival is still God's work. He continues to bless us abundantly, far more than we could ever have imagined. I have few regrets, except perhaps regarding my poor wife. She was so miserably married to a man perhaps already married, *to a cause*.

[70]Molly died on October 8, 1781.

20

A Flame Over England Burned

Many persons in London, in Bristol, in York, and in various parts, both of England and Ireland have experienced so deep and universal a change, as it had not before entered into their hearts to conceive. After a deep conviction of inbred sin, of their total fall from God, they have been so filled with faith and love, (and generally in a moment,) that sin vanished, and they found from that time, no pride, anger, desire, or unbelief. They could rejoice evermore, pray without ceasing, and in everything give thanks. John Wesley

For the past quarter of a century I have continued a work which I firmly believe belongs wholly to God.[1] God, in Revival, never takes sides; He takes over. A striking example of this can be seen in the uncommon work among the young.[2] I remember one incident in particular. I came to Stockton-Upon-Tees where "I was enclosed by a body of children; one of whom, and another, sunk down upon their knees, until they were all kneeling: So I kneeled down myself, and began praying for them. Abundance of people ran back into the House. The fire kindled, and ran from heart to heart, till few, if any, were unaffected. Is not this a new thing in the earth? God begins his work in children. Thus it has been also in Cornwall, Manchester, and Epworth. Thus the flame spreads to those of riper years; till at length they all know him, and praise him from the least unto the greatest."[3] So, the effects of the Revival rose and

---

[1]The period now under consideration includes the years between 1763 and 1788.
[2]Primarily between the ages of 6 and 14.
[3]*Works*, Vol. IV, p. 279.

fell (but never beneath a previous low).[4] We gained both breadth and depth with each new year.

It is significant that we held fast to our original principles. For example, though we built more and more preaching houses to shelter our growing societies, we never quit field preaching.[5] What can shake Satan's cause more? The want of field preaching has been one reason for deadness in several places. "I do not find any great increase of the work of God without it."[6] Though it is still a cross to me, I know my commission and see no other way of "preaching the Gospel to every creature."[7] I go abroad quickly where there is no house or church available, when the crowds are too large to be contained in them, or whenever I find the work decreasing. Some poor sinners will be reached by no other way. As for its continuing usefulness, just last year I preached to as many as 30,000. What more effectual way of overturning Satan's kingdom in a single blow.[8]

In December, 1763, I began to prepare my *Works* for publication. The actual printing (however carelessly)[9] was not to begin for nearly eight years, but as I reviewed the mass of material I began to see some things in a somewhat different light. *The years between 1763 and 1767 mark a somewhat hazy boundary for a rather significant theological readjustment.* By far the most crucial change (an extension of the shift regarding assurance between 1745 and 1747) concerned justification by faith. Though it was more a

[4]The Revival swells seem to be cyclical. Cf. Ibid., Vol. III, p. 418 and Ibid., p. 442, for accounts of rise and fall respectively. Wesley (Vol. IV, p. 18) cites reasons for this periodic decay. Vol. III, p. 199, provides an excellent sketch of this rise and fall within a single society.

[5]There were at this time eighty-four chapels in England, one in Wales, two in Scotland, and thirteen in Ireland. Some of these were built as octagons. Wesley notes (*Works*, Vol. III, p. 71): "I preached at Rotherham, in the shell of the new House, which is an octagon. Pity our houses, where the ground will admit of it, should be built in any other form." Wesley believed that the octagonal design made it easier for all to hear.

[6]Ibid., p. 184; cf. p. 190.

[7]Ibid., p. 479. It is interesting that the day before his 81st birthday he preached in the open air at Epworth.

[8]Ibid., Vol. IV, p. 398.

[9]Cf. Ibid., Vol. III, p. 157; p. 453. William Pine of Bristol first printed the *Works* with reckless abandon, frequently omitting one word or sentence, sometimes many pages.

question of emphasis and perspective than reversal, let me tell you plainly as I remember it now.

I think it was about April, 1763, that I was struck by the destructive forces of disunity among those seeking to proclaim the gospel. I began to see that union among those already "united to one common Head and employed by Him in one common work" could be of tremendous advantage. All too frequently, however, charity was not exhibited in our support one for another. For the first time in many years I felt the horror of despondency beginning to return. Some years later I confided to Charles: "I often cry out, *ditae ne redde priori!* (Give me back my former life!)[10] Let me be again an Oxford Methodist! I am often in doubt whether it would not be best for me to resume all my Oxford rules, great and small. I did then walk closely with God and redeemed the time. But what have I been doing these thirty years?"[11]

In a letter "To Various Clergymen" I expressed the need for flexibility and toleration (vital ingredients for Christian unity). I did not argue for union of opinions, expressions, or outward order, but for union in "love as brethren."[12] That is: "this union . . . is it not the duty of everyone of us to do? Would it not be far better for ourselves? a means of promoting both our holiness and happiness?"[13] I concluded by proposing this union for "them that believe, *that show their faith by their works.*"[14] The response was only polite. My depression grew. Then in December, 1765, I took a sudden fall with my horse. "I was exceeding sick, but was presently relieved by a little hartshorn and water. After resting a few minutes, I took a coach; but when I was cold, found myself much worse; being bruised on my right arm, my breast, my knee, leg, and ankle, which swelled exceedingly."[15]

---

[10]Horace's *Epistles,* Vol. I, vii, 95.
[11]*Letters,* Vol. VI, p. 6; cf. Ibid., Vol. V, pp. 15ff.
[12]Ibid., Vol. IV, pp. 236ff.
[13]Ibid., Wesley writes to John Fletcher (Ibid., Vol. V, p. 4) that "unity and holiness are the two things I want most among Methodists."
[14]Ibid., Vol. IV, italics mine.
[15]*Works,* Vol. III, p. 240. A few years later a subscription was taken among his friends for a carriage to prevent his riding. Cf. Ibid., p. 454.

I recovered slowly. I think the fall weakened the springs of my whole machine. Coupled with the lingering melancholy and the wranglings among ourselves, I began to react. I recall when Mr. Hervey accused me of being *half* a papist. I replied: "What if he had *proved it* too? What if he had proved I was a *whole* Papist? (though he might as easily have proved me a Mahometan). Is not a Papist a child of God? Is Thomas à Kempis, Mr. de Renty, Gregory Lopez gone to hell? Believe it who can. Yet still of such (though Papists) the same is my brother and sister and mother."[16] I began to see that I had been inconsistent with myself. Let me illustrate. Though I had used the lives of mystics like de Renty and Lopez to demonstrate perfection,[17] the year previous, in answer to Mr. Hartley's ingenious "Defense of the Mystic Writers," I had condemned them in a lump.[18] In the heat of a moment I judged "the Mystic writers (rather than mystic theology) to be one great Antichrist."[19] I retract this. It is far too strong. It reveals nothing of the gentleman, nor the scholar, nor the Christian.[20]

---

[16]*Letters,* Vol. IV, p. 293.

[17]Cf. *Works,* Vol. IV, p. 327. On September 22, 1764, for example, Wesley writes to Lady Maxwell: "I want you to be all a Christian;—such a Christian as the Marquis de Renty or Gregory Lopez was." Again in a letter written one week later Wesley applauds the example of Lopez. In fact, by 1767, several of the Roman Catholic mystics (de Renty and Lopez in particular) had become "household words" in many Methodist homes.

[18]Ibid., Vol. III, p. 160. As we have previously established, Wesley reacted against the kind of mysticism (primarily German) that was dark and speculative. Here, however, he writes that *all* the mystics he had seen held justification by works.

[19]Ibid., Vol. X, p. 395.

[20]Ibid. It is not surprising that Wesley's theological shift in emphasis should at the same time affect his attitude toward mysticism. Since 1738 Wesley had consistently affirmed the mystical end of religion while denying their means. There is an obvious paradox in this position in view of the fact that the mystics (especially those mentioned above) apparently manifested ends that their means (according to Wesley's theology between 1738 and 1764) could not possibly produce. During the period of readjustment, however, Wesley no doubt was confronted with this inconsistency. He realized that he would either have to deny the validity of their end (perfection or pure love) or recognize the effectiveness of their means (which, according to his more narrow point of view, meant "works-righteousness"). This was Wesley's dilemma,

Mr. Fletcher (more than any) helped to bring me back to the correct position. He confronted me with a view of mysticism which was not only scriptural but also thoroughly evangelical. I was caught by my own argument. I could not condemn the mystics one moment and praise them the next. Then on December 1, 1767: "Being alone in the coach, I was considering several points of importance. And thus much appeared clear as the day: —

"That a man may be saved who cannot express himself properly concerning Imputed Righteousness. Therefore to do this is not necessary to salvation:

"That a man may be saved, who has not clear conceptions of it (Yea, that never heard the phrase.) Therefore, clear conceptions of it are not necessary to salvation: Yea, it is not necessary to salvation to use the phrase at all:

"That a pious Churchman who has not clear conceptions even of Justification by Faith may be saved. Therefore, clear conceptions even of this are not necessary to salvation:

"That a Mystic, who denies Justification by Faith, (Mr. Law, for instance,) may be saved. But if so, what becomes of *articular santis vel cadentis ecclesiae?* [21] If so, is it not high time for us

Projicere ampullas et sesquipedalia verba; [22]

and to return to the plain words, 'He that feareth God, and worketh righteousness, is accepted with him?'"[23]

The point is that I was now willing to recognize the presence of justifying faith in someone (like the mystics) who chose to express themselves differently. Justification by faith came to mean simply "trusting in the righteousness or merits of Christ," and if the mystics trust in the merits of Christ, even though they deny justification by faith theoretically, they are accepted by God.[24] In my ser-

---

and it is interesting to note how his theology at this time expands to accommodate these mystics.

[21]The grand doctrine by which a church stands or falls.

[22]This phrase is from Horace, *De Arte*, p. 97 and is translated literally: "Reject bombast and words half a yard long."

[23]*Works*, Vol. III, p. 308.

[24]Ibid., Vol. X, p. 391; cf. p. 433.

mon "The Lord our Righteousness" I stated that "if the difference be more in *opinion* than real *experience*, and more in *expression* than in *opinion*, how can it be, that even the children of God should so vehemently contend with each other on the point?"[25]

To put it still another way, I was now convinced that one did not have to *understand* justification by faith to be acceptable to God; you simply had to *have* it.[26] Furthermore, you could know that you were justified either by assurance (a common privilege) or by the ability to perform deeds worthy of repentance (the certain fruit). For me, the holy life was to become a far more telling sign of acceptance with God than full assurance.

This should *not* lead one to believe that I no longer preached the doctrine of justification as I have understood it these past fifty years.[27] Indeed I do![28] It is the *first* principle and can never be enforced too much.[29] So, though I did not relinquish for a moment the fundamental doctrine; I did caution more carefully against the extreme.[30] Again, let me tell you plainly.

I am determined that Methodists will not make mockery of this or any other evangelical doctrine. The doctrine of justification and salvation by faith has been grievously abused by many of our brethren. I will not have it! Frankly, there are times when "I find more profit in sermons on either good tempers or good works than in what are vul-

---

[25]*Sermons*, Vol. II, p. 426; cf. p. 437.

[26]In July, 1765, after reading the Journal of a Quaker, William Edmundson, Wesley comments: "If the original equalled the picture, (which I see no reason to doubt,) what an amiable man was this! His opinions I leave; but what a spirit was here! What faith, love, gentleness, long-suffering! Could mistake send such a man as this to hell? Not so. I am so far from believing this, that I scruple not to say, 'Let my soul be with the soul of William Edmundson!'"

[27]*Works*, Vol. IV, p. 407.

[28]The following references demonstrate the consistency of his preaching on "justification by faith" long after 1767: *Works*, Vol. IV, pp. 80, 85, 89, 91, 366, etc.

[29]Ibid., Vol. IV, p. 399; cf. p. 403.

[30]Ibid., p. 89. Wesley explains the "wrong and the right sense of it." At several points he was openly shaken by those who were vulgarly called "Gospel preachers."

garly called Gospel sermons. That term is now become a mere cant word. I wish none of our Society would use it. It has no determinate meaning. Let but a pert, self-sufficient animal, that has neither sense or grace, bawl out something about Christ and his blood or justification by faith, and his hearers cry out, 'What a fine Gospel sermon!' Surely the Methodists have not so learnt Christ. *We know no gospel without salvation from sin.*"[31] Let me state this still another way.

We dare not stop with justification. I saw clearly, *when preaching to those already justified,* the necessity of enforcing perfection from those grand old verses such as "Work out your own salvation with fear and trembling. For it is God which worketh in you both to will and to do of his good pleasure."[32] Fear not, however: "even the Calvinists were satisfied for the present; and readily acknowledged that we did not ascribe our salvation to our own works, but to the grace of God."[33]

To those already awakened (convinced of sin but not yet having acceptance with God) I preach "Justification by faith," just as I have done for these fifty years.[34]

To those unawakened, justification by faith is like preaching in Greek; it is above their heads. They are far better suited to the terrors of the Lord be it death or judgment of hell ("where their worm dieth not, and the fire is not quenched").[35]

Our most important preaching, however, still focuses on perfection as the particular doctrine committed to our trust. I remember writing some years ago (as I looked back on some late occurrences): God has begun a great work

---

[31]*Letters,* Vol. VI, pp. 326f. (Italics mine.) How is this for a shot at "cheap grace"? And you thought Bonhoeffer said it first. Wesley writes (*Works,* Vol. IV, p. 95): "The next evening I preached on Hebrews 12:14: 'Without holiness no man shall see the Lord.' I was enabled to make a close application, chiefly to those that expected to be saved by faith. I hope none of them will hereafter dream of going to heaven by any faith which does not produce holiness."

[32]Phil. 2:12-13.

[33]*Works,* Vol. IV, p. 196.

[34]Ibid., p. 95.

[35]Ibid., Vol. III, p. 159, 227, 362, 418.

which has continued ever since without any considerable intermission. "During the whole time, many have been convinced of sin, many justified, and many backsliders healed. But the peculiar work of this season has been, what St. Paul calls 'the perfecting of the saints.' Many persons in London, in Bristol, in York, and in various parts, both of England and Ireland, have experienced so deep and universal a change, as it had not before entered into their hearts to conceive. After a deep conviction of inbred sin, of their total fall from God, they have been so filled with faith and love, (and generally in a moment,) that sin vanished, and they found from that time, no pride, anger, desire, or unbelief. They could rejoice evermore, pray without ceasing, and in every thing give thanks. Now, whether we call this the destruction or suspension of sin, it is a glorious work of God: Such a work as, considering both the depth and extent of it, we never saw in these kingdoms before."[36] Indeed, "how shall we escape, if we neglect so great a salvation?" If we do not "go on to perfection," how shall we escape lukewarmness (fair blossoms but no fruit), and hell fire (it is impossible that any should retain what they receive without improving it).[37]

To safeguard the experiences of those who are witnesses of perfection we began the Select Societies.[38] This has been of considerable service in sustaining those who, "being born *into* pure love, now grow *in* pure love. That they *may* fall therefrom I know; but that they *must*, I utterly deny."[39] The United Societies continued to play a vital role in the success of the Revival as well. I have a copy of a letter written in 1764 which is as relevant today as it was then: "There was one thing, when I was with you, that gave me pain: You are not in the society. But why not? Are there not

---

[36]Ibid., p. 156; cf. p. 369.

[37]Ibid., Vol. IV, p. 9; cf. Vol. III, p. 204; Vol. IV, p. 83.

[38]It should be mentioned that "prayer meetings" (Ibid., Vol. IV, p. 375) and "trial bands" (Vol. III, p. 506) begin to appear in the *Journals* about this time. The students of Methodist history might do well to consider these more closely.

[39]Ibid., Vol. III, p. 388; cf. pp. 400, 402, 492; Vol. IV, pp. 24, 84, 283, 328, for references to the Select Societies.

sufficient arguments for it to move any reasonable man? Do you not hereby make an open confession of Christ, of what you really believe to be his work, and of those whom you judge to be, in a proper sense, his people and his messengers? By this means do not you encourage his people, and strengthen the hands of his messengers? And is not this the way to enter into the spirit, and share the blessing, of a Christian community? Hereby, likewise, you may have the benefit of the advices and exhortations at the meeting of the society; and also of provoking one another, at the private meetings, to love and to good works."[40]

The continuing influence of the Societies can be traced to the introduction of the *class*. The class, however, is no stronger than its leader. Let me say a word about this. It is the business of the leader "To see each person in his class once a week; to inquire how their souls prosper; to advise, reprove, comfort, or exhort them: To receive what they are willing to give toward the expenses of the society: And, to meet the Assistant and the Stewards once a week."[41] A leader must remain in his place, however. "In the Methodist discipline, the wheels regularly stand thus: The Assistant, the Preachers, the Stewards, the Leaders, the People."[42] If one wheel of the machine gets out of place, what disorder must ensue! A gradual decay of the work of God in Dublin, for example, can be attributed to the Leaders "who are the lowest wheel but one, but were got quite out of their place. They were got at the top of all, above the Stewards, the Preachers, yea, and above the Assistant himself."[43] Let no one encroach on another, but let everyone move together in harmony and love; upholding the unity of the Spirit in the bond of peace.

This reminds me. I must tell you briefly of the healing of the first breach among the Methodists. The effects of my theological readjustment and the strong desire for union

[40]*Works*, Vol. III, p. 188. In 1767 the membership for the major societies stood at: London, 2,250; Newcastle, 1,837; Bristol (one of the largest towns in the kingdom, and the oldest of Methodist stations, ranked eighth), 1,064.

[41]Ibid., p. 426.

[42]Ibid., p. 428.

[43]Ibid.

among the brethren bore precious fruit in my connection with Mr. Whitefield. In 1766 the plague of bigotry hid its head; love and harmony reigned again. Just before Mr. Whitefield left for America, we had one more agreeable conversation where there was peace and joy.[44] On September 29, 1770 (one year later) he preached in New England for the last time. The next morning "he was not, for God had taken him." In November, I returned to London and had the melancholy news of his death "confirmed by his executors, who desired me to preach his funeral sermon on Sunday, the 18th. In order to write this, I returned to Lewisham on Monday; and on Sunday following, went to the chapel in Tottenham Court-Road. An immense multitude was gathered together from all corners of the town. I was at first afraid that the great part of the congregation would not be able to hear; but it pleased God so to strengthen my voice, that even those at the door heard distinctly. It was an awful season: All were still as night: Most appeared to be deeply affected; and an impression was made on many, which one would hope will not speedily be effaced. O that all may hear the voice of Him with whom are the issues of life and death; and who so loudly by this unexpected stroke, calls all his children to love one another!"[45]

In March, 1776, the Foundery no longer serving us adequately, we considered the plans for a new chapel which we opened on the City Road two and a half years after.[46] The year following we closed the Foundery.[47] What God wrought there in forty years!

During recent years the mobs have slowly begun to subside. I think there are several reasons for this. It is not that we have become "respectable" (God forbid!). Fear comes mainly from ignorance, and as we are able to make our case known, the people themselves come to our defense. I recall an experience in Newcastle some years later:

---

[44]On September 5, 1769, Whitefield embarked for South Carolina.
[45]*Works*, Vol. III, p. 421.
[46]Ibid., Vol. IV, p. 68; cf. references pp. 82, 90, 95, 96, 140.
[47]Ibid., p. 160.

Though it was cold I was obliged to preach outdoors. "One buffoon labored much to interrupt. But as he was bawling, with his mouth wide open, some arch boys gave him such a mouthful of dirt as quite satisfied him."[48] Perhaps the real turning point came toward the end of the middle years when we refused to be daunted. We knew our rights. In Feversham, for example, "I was quickly informed that the mob and the Magistrates had agreed together to drive Methodism, so called, out of the town. After preaching, I told them what we had been constrained to do by the Magistrate at Rolvenden; who perhaps would have been richer, by some hundred pounds, had he never meddled with the Methodists; concluding, 'Since we have both God and the law on our side, if we can have peace by fair means, we had much rather; we should be exceeding glad; but if not, we *will* have peace.'"[49] For the past ten to twelve years things have been relatively quiet.

Since people are perhaps best taught by example, our brethren have won the hearts of many by imitating Christ, doing good to all men, and hating covetousness, which is idolatry. We teach those in our societies that if they must suffer, to suffer for righteousness' sake holding forth the words from 1 Peter: "[To] sanctify the Lord God in their hearts: and be ready always to give an answer to every man that asketh you a reason of the hope that is in you with meekness and fear: Having a good conscience; that, whereas they speak evil of you, as of evildoers, they may be ashamed that falsely accuse your good conversation in Christ."[50] Surely, "the Methodists that do not fulfil all righteousness will have the hottest place in the lake of fire!"[51] The apostle Paul was commissioned not only to "go unto the heathen," but also to "remember the poor."[52] That you might know that we are not undone by our neglect, I add here (to awaken those that sleep) an extract

---

[48]Ibid., p. 41.
[49]Ibid., Vol. III, p. 239; cf. pp. 262, 277, 486, 491.
[50]1 Peter 3:15,16.
[51]*Works*, Vol. III, p. 305.
[52]Galatians 2:9-10.

from a letter not untypical of the people called Methodist: "Since the Lord has not only been gracious to my soul, but has entrusted me with a share of this world's good, I am under an equal obligation to be faithful, in this as in the other gifts of God. Now especially, when help is so much wanted, I ought to be the more careful. Suffer me, Sir, to speak freely of myself: I have about forty-seven pounds a year. As to my disbursements, for apparel, I buy the most lasting and, in general, the plainest I can. I buy no furniture but what is necessary and cheap. I make my own fire, and get my own breakfast and supper. I pay six-pence to one of our friends for my dinner. I drink herb-tea, and thereby save at least a shilling a week. I seldom drink tea in an afternoon, but sup at six, on bread and cheese, with milk and water; so I save at least eight-pence by dropping tea in the afternoon. I fasted much till my health was greatly impaired. Then I used abstinence on Wednesdays, Fridays, and other fast-days, till I was obliged to leave this off too; but not till I was quite indifferent as to what I eat. So I determined, if I cannot retrench a meal, I can retrench the expense of a meal twice a week, as on other fast-days; using potatoes, milk, or some other cheap thing. Thus I have four-pence per dinner twice a week, which, with the one shilling and eight-pence, makes two shillings and four-pence per week, without retrenching one necessary meal. Now this two shillings and four-pence would buy as much meat as, made into broth, would nearly suffice for a small family. To be short, the expense for myself,—meat, drink, clothes, and washing—is not twenty-eight pounds per annum; so that I have near twenty pounds to return to God in the poor. Now, if every Christian family, while in health, would thus far deny themselves, would twice a week dine on the cheapest food, drink in general herb-tea, faithfully calculate the money saved thereby, and give it to the poor over and above their usual donations, we should then hear no complaining in our streets, but the poor would eat and be satisfied. He that gathered much would have nothing over, and he that gathered little would have no lack. O how happy should we all be, if this was the case with us! I mentioned this some time ago in a meeting at London, when a brother said, 'These are but little things.' As I went home, I thought of his words: 'Little things!' Is the want of fire, in frost and snow, a little thing? Or the want of food, in a distressed, helpless family? Gracious God! 'Feed me with food convenient for me! Give me not poverty; lest I steal, and take the name of my God in vain!' "Dear Sir, I know what you feel for the poor, and I also sympathize with you. Here is a hard season coming on, and everything very dear; thousands of poor souls, yea, Christians, dread the approaching calamities. O that God would stir up the hearts of all that believe themselves his children, to evidence it by showing mercy to the poor, as God has shown them mercy. Surely the real children of God will do it of themselves; for it is the natural fruit of a branch in Christ. I would not desire them to lose one meal in a week, but to use as cheap food, clothes, &c., as possible. And I think the poor themselves ought to be questioned, with regard to drinking tea and beer. For I cannot think it right for them to indulge themselves in those things which I refrain from, to help them. My earnest prayers shall accompany yours, that God would give us all, in this our day, to know the things which belong unto our peace, and to acknowledge the blessings which are freely given to us of God!"[53]

This work served a dual purpose. We not only fulfilled the Scripture injunction, but also avoided a grand danger: As Christians "are industrious and frugal, they must needs increase in goods. This appears already: In London, Bristol, and most other trading towns, those who are in business have increased in substance seven-fold, some of them twenty, yea, an hundred-fold. What need, then, have these of the strongest warnings, lest they be entangled therein, and perish!"[54]

One should not be led to believe that our passion for

[53] *Works,* Vol. III, pp. 306f.; cf. pp. 205, 241, 300, 304f.; Vol. IV, pp. 261, 265, 358, 374, and many other similar accounts concerning Wesley's unashamed commitment to social justice.

[54] Ibid., Vol. III, p. 147; cf. p. 187; Vol. IV, pp. 350, 389 and 340 (those in the Bristol society were particularly vulnerable).

social justice related only to the poor, the sick, and the imprisoned. We fought Satan at every level including the regulation of the houses of industry, instituting a humane society, and speaking out against slavery (that horrible practice of buying or stealing poor Africans, and selling them in America).[55]

Speaking of America, I must relate to you the case of our Brethren there. At our Conference for 1769 (our 26th) I mentioned to our Brethren that our first Methodist preaching house had been built in New York and the Society there was in great want of money, but much more of preachers. "Two of our preachers, Richard Boardman and Joseph Pillmoor [Pilmore], willingly offered themselves for the service; by whom we determined to send them fifty pounds, as a token of our brotherly love."[56] Within half a year a great work had been accomplished. Multitudes, both in New York and Philadelphia, flocked to hear, and behaved with deep sincerity; the Society in each place had grown to more than a hundred members.[57]

American Methodism continued to prosper (by the providence of God), though for fifteen years it was virtually deprived of someone who could administer the sacraments of baptism and the Lord's Supper, especially after the establishment of states, which were independent of the English government and of all ecclesiastical authority. So pressing was the need, that on September 1, 1784, I took a step which I had long weighed in my mind. After appointing Thomas Coke to join Mr. Francis Asbury (already in America) as joint superintendent over our brethren in America, I ordained Richard Whatcoat and Thomas Vasey to act as elders in the American Methodist Church about to be constituted.[58]

---

[55]Cf. Ibid., Vol. IV, p. 481, for mention of the "Stranger's Society." Wesley adds: "I do not know that ever I heard or read of such an institution till within a few years ago. So this also is one of the fruits of Methodism."

[56]Ibid., Vol. III, p. 374.

[57]Ibid., p. 385.

[58]It should be mentioned that there is somewhat of a sequence here. Cf. Ibid., Vol. III, p. 337, where Methodist preachers (for their own

The following year the same decision was thought necessary for Scotland. Three well-tried preachers, John Pawson, John Hannby, and Joseph Taylor were set apart for the work in Scotland. For some years I had been convinced that this was my right, rather, my burdensome responsibility, to act thus.[59] I trust God will continue to bless their ministrations and show that *He* has sent them. Many have concluded that these acts constituted separation from the church. Shortly after, "finding a report that had been spread abroad, that I was just going to leave the Church; to satisfy those that were grieved concerning it, I openly declared in the evening that I had now no more thought of separating from the Church than I had forty years ago."[60] Just last year, after meeting the whole Society in London, I told them (since most of the leading men of the society were for separating from the church): "'If you are resolved, you may have your service in church-hours (that is, in conflict with the Church of England); but, remember, from that time you will see my face no more.' This struck deep; and from that hour I have heard no more of separating from the Church."[61] Let me speak more to the point: "The original design of the Methodists, viz., not to be a distinct party, but to stir up all parties, Christians or Heathens, to worship God in spirit and in truth; but the Church of England in particular; to which they belonged

protection) were forced to register as Dissenters. When Wesley's preachers sought licenses the clerk of justice would not register them but as protestant Dissenters to which Wesley replied: "'We are of the Church; we are not Dissenters: But if you will call us so, we cannot help it.' They did *call* them so in their certificates, but this did not *make* them so. They still *called themselves* members of the Church of England; and they believed themselves so to be." Furthermore, at this point, Wesley chose not to appeal to the English bishops (even if they would have consented) for the purpose of ordination "as [so he writes] our American brethren are now totally disentangled, both from the state and from the England hierarchy, we dare not entangle them again, either with the one or the other. They are now at full liberty simply to follow the Scriptures and the primitive church. And we judge it best that they should stand fast in that liberty wherewith God has so strangely made them free." *Journal*, Vol. VII, p. 17n. The American Methodist Church was established at the 1784 "Christmas Conference" in Baltimore.

[59]*Works*, Vol. II, p. 6.
[60]Ibid., Vol. IV, p. 320.
[61]Ibid., p. 357.

from the beginning. With this view, I have uniformly gone on for fifty years, never varying from the doctrine of the Church at all; nor from her discipline, of choice, but of necessity: So, in a course of years, necessity was laid upon me, (as I have proved elsewhere,) 1. To preach in the open air. 2. To pray extempore. 3. To form societies. 4. To accept the assistance of Lay Preachers: And, in a few other instances, to use such means as occurred, to prevent or remove evils that we either felt or feared."[62]

Dear friends, time is pressing, and we must lay this story aside. Let me bring you up to date quickly. During the past fifteen years my health has held remarkably well.[63] I still find the time to visit, even house to house (without which the people will hardly increase, either in number or grace).[64] I recall less than two years ago preaching three times and traveling seventy-six miles in a single day, but I was still no more tired than when I rose in the morning.[65] Bless God for a cause big enough to keep an old man alive.

So, the Revival continues. But, you might well ask, how shall we keep up the flame that over England burns? The answer is simple. "Not by sitting still; but by stirring up the gift of God that is in them; by uninterrupted watchfulness; by warning every one and exhorting every one; by besieging the throne with all the powers of prayer; and, after all, some will, and some will not, improve the grace which they have received. Therefore there must be a falling away. We are not to be discouraged at this; but to do all that in us lies to-day, leaving the morrow to God."[66]

Finally, who can tell how history will judge us. I pray to God that you will look upon us with sympathy and understanding. In the meantime, this old frame teeters on the brink of a long journey. Soon I shall drop into that un-

---

[62]Ibid., p. 450 (cf. p. 451). Although this quotation (April, 1789) is taken from a portion of the *Journal* following the present setting in Macclesfield, these thoughts already would have been clearly in focus. Cf. Vol. III, pp. 260, 337, 353.

[63]Cf. Ibid., Vol. III, p. 402. Wesley felt strong enough to make trips into Holland in 1783 and 1786.

[64]Ibid., p. 473; cf. p. 480.

[65]Ibid., Vol. IV, p. 334.

[66]Ibid., p. 305.

changeable eternity. My old enemy (the fear of death) is now my friend. He seems so much kinder now. I would go with him without hesitation. When the time is come, I ask not even a prayer to hold me back.[67] As for you, press on toward the mark of your high calling. Keep praying, keep reading, keep growing, keep learning, but most of all, keep believing, that I am . . .

.   Your real friend,

John Wesley

[67]See Ibid., Vol. III, p. 225, where Wesley speaks of the necessity of releasing the dying.

The Analysis, Part IV

The righteousness of Christ is doubtless necessary for any soul that enters into glory: But so is personal holiness too, for every child of man . . . the former is necessary to entitle us to heaven; the latter to qualify us for it.   John Wesley

With the biographical data behind us (except for the final three years to be described briefly in the epilogue) we now turn to the analysis of Wesley's theological development during the fifty years of the Revival. The task here is so important, however, I first want to reset the tone for the analysis chapters as a whole. Even after ten years of intensive study (including both the man and his movement) I cannot claim to be totally objective. I am knowledgeable enough to know that at this point in time (after two hundred years of history to follow) fresh, creative insight that is both reliable and inclusive comes only after a *lifetime* of research (I am tempted to say: "Where Wesley is concerned do not trust anyone under sixty"), scratching, and digging into page upon page of primary and secondary sources. Junior scholars have a difficult time with objectivity. They (or should I say "we") are obsessed with being relevant. We tend to mix fact with so much feeling that the character we portray looks more like a man of the twentieth century than a man of his own time. Admittedly, the Wesley of London, Bristol, and Newcastle would act differently in New York, Los Angeles, or Chicago, but Mr. Wesley does not have to be updated to be relevant. It is the *spirit* of the man that communicates, not just his method.

Let me put it another way. If history speaks it must first be told as history. Telling it like it *is,* means first telling it like it *was.* We must then trust the Holy Spirit (who interprets "spiritual truths to those who possess the Spirit") to "enforce" the contemporary word. People are different, not just their spheres of influence. The intent and purpose of the analysis chapters has not been so much to apply any given truth to the present scene (careful readers must and will do that for themselves); it has been to capture the contagious heart of a man totally committed to God. Herein lies the inspiration for each new age.

So, you ask: What has this book to offer? I would say simply: a straightforward interpretation of Wesley as I understand his life and ministry within the context of the eighteenth-century Evangelical Revival. I have made every effort to write from a perspective that is hopefully not only unique, but also informative and interesting enough both to challenge and inspire. I have made an honest attempt to be true to Wesley's spirit. At no point am I aware of yielding to the urge to "clean up" after greatness. Wesley was a man of destiny, but never more than a man. In the biographical chapters the words attributed to Wesley are not (so to speak) my own. They are *his* words as I see him speaking to you, the reader.

Furthermore, I have resisted the temptation to omit the issues that might prove troublesome or even confusing for some as to his teaching on any given doctrine. Again, the analyses attempt to go beyond the events already described in the biographical chapters. Hopefully here, even more of the man and his theology will emerge (and I trust without undue judgment). In short, the effects of his ministry are allowed to stand (or fall) on their own merit alone.

In chapters 17-20 we saw that Wesley began the Revival preaching his "new faith"—justification by faith alone as the "*full* assurance of things hoped for, the evidence of things not seen." What we did not see (because I am not convinced that Wesley would have been aware of it himself) was that, ironically, the Revival years mark the making of a theologian in reverse. Reaction against, more than knowledge from, contributed to the theology of the Revival. Demonstrating this is the primary task of this last analysis chapter. In the interest of time, let me focus primarily upon Wesley's frequently misunderstood reaction to mysticism (though any of the variant influences could be used to the same effect). Let us begin by repeating a hypothesis that relates to justification by faith in reaction to the various stages of mysticism mentioned earlier: of the five mystical stages (1. awakening, 2. purgation, 3. illumination, 4. the dark night of the soul, and 5. union with God) Wesley continued after Aldersgate to practice and encourage the "tools" known to the first three stages.[1] He also admired and commended the many other practical outworkings of these stages manifested in the lives of the mystics whose utter devotion to God was a continual inspiration to him. Similarly, he continued to uphold the mystical concept of perfection (Christian mysticism's fifth stage) as the end of religion. Yet, Wesley detested the vain irrational philosophy which sought to link the noble beginnings of religion (stages 1 to 3) to the ultimate end of religion (stage 5) by the dark night of the soul (the mystical fourth stage involving a lifeless theory of "in orco"), and it was precisely at this point that he substituted the Aldersgate experience of justification by faith in Christ.

Again, Wesley, weary of years without knowing, unable to negotiate the "dark night," wanted to *feel* accepted and opted for faith in the evangelical sense in order to proclaim salvation by faith alone, a doctrine which he continued to preach throughout the Revival, but not without some shift in emphasis along the way. So, having established the beginning, our task now is to describe the "shift" as his theology matured across the years.

The chapters, "The Wider Parish," "Marriage and the Middle Years," and "A Flame Over England Burned," could as easily have been entitled (from a theological perspective), "Salvation by Grace through Assurance: 1738-1747"; "Salvation by Grace through Faith: 1748-1762"; and "Salvation by Grace through Faith as Confirmed by Works: 1763-1788."

It is interesting that at every point of change for fifty years, Wesley is reacting against the extreme. The Moravian split countered the tendency to antinomianism. The shift on assurance guarded against his own view to salvation that had over-

---

[1] E.g., humility, poverty of spirit, and the other instruments of purgation were vital to Methodism. Humility was the first step to faith and the new birth, "a participation in the divine nature." Cf. *Sermons*, Vol. I, p. 321.

reacted against thirteen years of personal fear and doubt. Be-tween 1763-1767 the changes were registered with regard to a view of justification by faith that had apparently excluded those who had faith (demonstrated by their works which only faith could produce), but who lacked the proper understanding (which Wesley no longer deemed necessary).

In order to capture the mind and the heart of the man we should now discuss these changes as they occurred. In chapter 18 we saw the first significant change as it related to the "stillness controversy." Nehemiah Curnock's summary of Wesley's *Journal,* part IV, states that "Methodism was finally cut adrift from the beautiful, dreamy, but wholly impracticable mysticism of German quietism as interpreted by Molther and Bohler and misinterpreted by Bray and Taylor and Simpson."[2] Although Ronald Knox's statement that Molther's stillness re-vealed Moravianism as the seven spirits worse than the first is obviously an exaggeration, Wesley now saw the Moravians in a different light.[3] He objects first to their quietistic mysticism. Ronald Knox claims that the Moravians were going through a phase of incredible childishness.[4] Like the French mystic, Madame Guyon, and her "state of infancy," the Moravians wished to have no brains; they wished to be like "children in arms." In the *Journal* for June 15, 1742, Wesley states, after reading Guyon's *A Short Method of Prayer* and *Les Torrents Spirituels,* that the Moravian riddle is answered; they take their words exactly from "this poor Quietist."[5] Yet Wesley's break with the Moravians involved more than their mysticism. His friend, Alexander Knox, has an interesting theory along these lines. Knox's particular bias emphasizes Wesley's zeal for moral virtue which, admittedly, was uncompromising and intense. According to Alexander Knox, Wesley broke with the

---

[2]*Journal,* Vol. II, p. 500n. Also the hymn entitled, "The Means of Grace," attached to this part of the *Journal* is a statement on the virtue and limitation of Moravian stillness.

[3]It is interesting to note that Wesley's mind was continually changing and eventually he clears the Moravians of much of the responsibility for the split in the society and lays most of the blame at the feet of the English brethren, *Journal,* Vol. II, p. 497; Vol. III, p. 259.

[4]Knox, *Enthusiasm,* p. 414.

[5]*Journal,* Vol. III, p. 18.

mysticism of the Moravians only as they drifted toward moral laxity. He embraced the Moravians as long as they continued to combine their evangelical doctrine of faith with a strong mystical ethic (the Moravian synthesis), but when their quietistic antinomianism began to undermine the latter, he broke. Since there is good reason to believe that Alexander Knox spoke with Wesley personally about mysticism, the following comment (given in full because of its importance) carries added weight: "I can venture to say from my knowledge of Mr. Wesley that if mysticism alone had been chargeable on the Moravians, his objections would have been much more easily obviated. He certainly considered the supposed self-annihilation of mysticism to be in opposition to the tenor of Holy Scripture, which uniformly addresses itself to man's natural thirst for happiness; but still he thought that whatever pernicious consequences were to be feared from the mystical illusion, mysticism itself might co-exist with the deepest piety. In those Moravians, however, he saw it strangely associated with principles leading directly to laxity of practice; and on this account he seems to have animadverted on mysticism *with more severity than was his usual custom.*"[6] He goes on to say that "had he not regarded mystics generally with liberal indulgence, he would hardly have abridged Law's later works and Madarne Guyon's life of herself for circulation among his people."[7]

Although Wesley's war on stillness lashed out with force at the mystical love for darkness and the subconscious which brooded over a sea of silence and isolation, this antagonism should not be exaggerated. Wesley himself continued to maintain a *sane* emphasis upon tranquil tarrying and spiritual quiet as registered, for example, in Charles' hymn: "Bid my quiet spirit hear." Although the "true mystic spirit" would have been almost unintelligible in a Methodist class meeting, Wesley sifted the gold of mystical purification by detachment and countered its extreme quietism with an emphasis on "the social factor" which taught that the spiritual experience is not

[6]Southey, *Life of Wesley*, Vol. II, p. 325 (italics mine).
[7]Ibid., Wesley's opinion of this "poor Quietist" changed enough for him to publish an extract of her life in 1776.

an end in itself, but a means of gathering "a richer harvest of souls."[8] Wesley, therefore, plowed with the Moravian "heifer" and finding their religion to be a melancholy thing, he transformed it (with an emphasis upon the Holy Spirit) into a thing of joy.

The second significant change has to do with Wesley's views on assurance. Since Wesley was himself painfully aware of the necessity for reemphasis along these lines, a few words here will allow us to put this into perspective and then move on quickly to the more important readjustment to follow. Again, Wesley's mind was continually changing in the light of a person's ability to live out his faith. Remember Wesley's correspondence with "John Smith" (a pseudonym, probably for Thomas Secker). John Smith criticized Wesley for what he called "perceptible inspiration," or his doctrine of assurance. Wesley, as has been noted, between 1738 and 1747, virtually taught salvation by assurance: "Every believer hath a direct perceptible testimony" (December 30, 1745). Following this correspondence with John Smith, however (as expressed in the letter to Charles, July 31, 1747), assurance is now only the *common privilege,* as justification by faith does *not necessarily* imply a sense of pardon.[9] It is good to remember that this slight change in 1747 is only a preamble to a much greater change relative to justification by faith nearly twenty years later.

We have already observed that the classical reform doctrine of justification by faith is missing in Wesley's pre-1738 sermons. During and after 1764-1767, however, his sermons exhibit still another change in direction relative to this doctrine.[10] Albert Outler writes that *sola fide* and *sola Scriptura*

---

[8]Workman, *The Place of Methodism in the Catholic Church,* p. 85.

[9]There is a good possibility that "John Smith" was responsible for changing Wesley's mind on assurance. The reference to assurance as an *ordinary privilege* (to my knowledge) first appears in a letter dated March 25, 1747 (*Letters,* Vol. II, p. 91) to John Smith in answer to his charge against "perceptible inspiration" (cf. *Ibid.,* pp. 97ff.).

[10]A comparative study of the pre-1738 and post-1764 sermons on justification would be revealing. Wesley's understanding of "faith" has three phases taking the form of a dialectic: thesis (pre-1738)—faith initiated by inward and outward works; antithesis (1738-1764)—faith initiated solely by God's grace; synthesis (post-1764)—faith initiated by grace and confirmed by works.

means "primarily," especially after 1767. "Faith is the primary reality in Christian experience but not its totality."[11] Wesley states that faith "is only a handmaid to love."[12] Orcibal argues that although Wesley preached justification by faith at first he later recognized with increasing awareness the absolute necessity of the fruits of faith to be manifested by this doctrine.[13] After 1764 Wesley certainly taught that faith not properly nourished by its fruits might well prove illusory. Alexander Knox uses strong words (I believe far too strong, nearly missing the point altogether) to describe this change. Commenting on the respective doctrines of Luther and Calvin, Knox states that "Mr. Wesley came at length to see that the view of *justification* maintained by the one was as unessential as that of *predestination,* contended for by the other, was inadmissable."[14] He goes on to say that Wesley adopted a "practical Christianity" consisting *solely* of "powerful principles and purified affections."[15] He argues that Wesley, after his return to the "plain word" probably never once repeated the well-known homily of salvation which defines faith as a "sure trust and confidence in God, that by the merits of Christ his sins are forgiven, and he reconciled to the favor of God."[16] As we observed in chapter 20, *this is in error,* but although Knox allows his moralistic bias to overstate his case, there is sufficient evidence to support the fact that Wesley undergoes a fairly drastic reappraisal of the doctrine of justification relative to faith and works.

There can be little doubt that Wesley's notion of justification altered to the place where simply to fear God and work righteousness revealed an acceptance by God and a degree of faith.[17] Remember the earlier sermon on "The Almost

---

[11]Outler, *John Wesley,* p. 28.

[12]*Sermons,* Vol. II, pp. 420-441; cf. Outler, *John Wesley,* p. 226.

[13]Orcibal, Jean, "The Theological Originality of John Wesley and Continental Spirituality," *A History of the Methodist Church in Great Britain,* trans. by R.J.A. Sharp. Vol. I eds. Rupert Davies, Gordon Rupp. London, Epworth Press, 1965, pp. 95ff.

[14]Southey, *Life of Wesley,* Vol. II, pp. 339ff.

[15]Ibid.

[16]Ibid., p. 347. This is obviously an exaggeration in light of sermons like #56, 60, 63, and 72 (*Works,* Vol. VII, especially pp. 195f., 236, 260, 332).

[17]A. Knox (Southey, *Life of Wesley,* Vol. II, p. 348) states that Wesley's people expressed no dissatisfaction with his "liberalized principles" because they probably did not fully understand them.

Christian" as compared with the later sermons dealing with the question of the faith of a *servant* and the faith of a *child*.[18] Whereas the "almost Christian" was clearly not accepted by God (Wesley states "good it were for him had he never been born"), the post-1764 concept of the faith of a servant (comparable to that of the almost Christian)—that is one whose faith (however infant) enables him to fear God and work righteousness—is accepted by God and "'the wrath of God' no longer 'abideth on him.'"[19] This point can be further substantiated by Wesley's handwritten marginal notes in his own copy of the *Works,* published in 1771. Opposite the words for February 1, 1738: "not converted," he writes: "I am not sure of this." For the same day opposite the statement: "I am a child of wrath," he writes: "I believe not." He then adds: "I had even then the faith of a *servant,* though not that of a *son.*"

The classic quotation recorded in the last chapter (taken from the *Journal* for December 1, 1767) regarding the faith of those "that feareth God, and worketh righteousness, is accepted with him" was picked up by those who opposed Wesley and contrasted with his earlier view where justification by faith alone is portrayed as absolutely essential to salvation. The point is, however, not so much that Wesley has changed his view of justification by faith as that he is willing to recognize its presence in those who choose to express themselves differently. Again, "justification by faith came to mean simply 'trusting in the righteousness or merits of Christ.'" If one was trusting in the merits of Christ, even though he denied justification by faith theoretically, he was accepted by God.[20]

---

[18]Cf. *Sermons,* Vol. I, pp. 53ff. with *Works,* Vol. VII, pp. 199ff.; 236ff.; cf. also *Sermons,* Vol. I, p. 179 and n; Vol. II, p. 359; and Southey, *Life of Wesley,* Vol. II, pp. 354-360.

[19]*Sermons,* Vol. I, pp. 64f., cf. *Works,* Vol. VII, p. 199.

[20]*Works,* Vol. X, p. 391; cf. p. 433; cf. Green, *Wesley and Law,* p. 175n. Southey states that "there are sufficient indications that in the latter part of his life Wesley reposed in a feeling of catholic charity, to which his heart always inclined him" (Southey, *Life of Wesley,* Vol. I, p. 100). Southey then adds that Wesley, in his later years, printed, and in so doing sanctioned (this is highly debatable), an observation of one of his correspondents: "Perhaps, what the best heathens called reason, Solomon wisdom, Saint Paul grace in general, and Saint John righteousness or love, Luther faith, and Fénelon virtue, may be only different expressions for one and the self-same blessing. The light of Christ shown shining in different degrees under different dispensations. Why then so many words and so little charity exercised among

Wesley, therefore, at long last concluded that many whom he previously thought lost had faith because they manifested the fruits which only faith (by any name) could produce. Although Alexander Knox wrongly implies that Wesley surrendered the doctrine of justification by faith or imputed righteousness, the fact remains that Wesley was now more concerned with the fruits of faith (that *imputed* might become *imparted* righteousness), than with the glib, indeterminate use of phrases which, out of context, lean toward antinomianism. In his sermon, "The Wedding Garment," Wesley strongly objected to the sentiment that the imputed righteousness of Christ implies no subsequent righteousness of *our own*.[21] He stated that "the righteousness of Christ is doubtless necessary for any soul that enters into glory: But so is personal holiness too, for every child of man . . . the former is necessary to *entitle* us to heaven; the latter to *qualify* us for it."[22] Wesley still insisted upon faith, but not as all in all. In a later sermon, "On Faith," Wesley singled out Fénelon who, although a member of the church of Rome, still retained the "faith that *worketh by love*."[23] Wesley continued in that same sermon: "Walk in all the good works whereunto ye are created in Christ Jesus. And then, 'leaving the principles of the doctrine of Christ, and not laying again the foundation of repentance from dead works, and of faith toward God,' go on to perfection."[24]

It is appropriate that this final chapter should close with a word regarding Wesley's views on perfection. Although Wesley argues for (and exhibits) a basic continuity of thought in his understanding of perfection, Albert Outler is right to point out that his more mature doctrine is "strikingly different in substance and form" from his earlier concept.[25] Outler suggests that Wesley was influenced by three distinct mystical traditions: the *voluntaristic* represented by men like à Kempis, Law, and Castaniza (Scupoli); the *Quietistic* represented by mystics like Molinos, Guyon, de Sales; and the mysticism of *early*

Christians about the particular term of a blessing experienced more or less by all righteous men!" (Ibid.).

[21]Cf. *Letters,* Vol. V, p. 5.
[22]*Works,* Vol. VII, p. 314.
[23]Ibid., p. 201 (italics mine).
[24]Ibid., p. 202.
[25]Outler, *John Wesley,* p. 9n, #25 and 26; pp. 251-252; 275.

and eastern spirituality represented by men like Macarious and Ephraem Syrus.[26] Outler goes on to imply that Wesley's earlier doctrine of perfection focused on the first two traditions and the more mature doctrine on the latter. Our study, however, proves this to be a misleading oversimplification. A comparison of Wesley's extracts with the originals he abridged (on the basis of what he retained and omitted) demonstrates that he both accepted and rejected portions from all of these "traditions" in his more mature doctrine. For example, Outler defines voluntaristic mysticism as "a mysticism of the will that issues in a strenuous program of self-denigration aimed at total resignation."[27] This may be true but it is wrong to imply that this characteristic does not appear in the other traditions as well or in Wesley's more mature understanding of perfection. Resignation was an important factor in the schemes of all the mystics whom Wesley abridged and Wesley himself argued in 1777 that "total resignation to the will of God, without any mixture of self-will" was basic to the character of Christian perfection.[28]

Similarly, Outler's statement may be true that "if Wesley's writings on perfection are to be read with understanding, his affirmative notion of 'holiness' *in the world* must be taken seriously"; but it is wrong to imply that this characteristic of "active holiness in *this* life" appears only in Macarius and Ephraem Syrus and not in the other mystical traditions or in Wesley's earlier doctrine.[29] Admittedly, Wesley expressed the necessity of sanctification before death in much stronger terms during later years.[30] His *Journal* for September 15, 1762, stated

---

[26]Ibid., pp. 251f.

[27]Ibid., p. 252.

[28]*Works*, Vol. XI, p. 422, cf. p. 436. Typical of Wesley's resignation is the advice (common among the mystics) that the death of loved ones should set us free "to a more full and absolute dedication of your soul and body to Him" (*Letters*, Vol. III, p. 141); cf. *Journal*, Vol. IV, p. 311; Wesley asks a girl thought to be dying: "Do not you desire life or death?" She replied: "No; I leave all to Him. But if it was His will, I should be glad to die." Wesley frequently cites de Renty's example along these lines.

[29]Outler, *John Wesley*, p. 252; cf. Wesley's pre-1738 sermons where holiness is clearly a goal to be realized in this life.

[30]*Sermons*, Vol. II, p. 202; *Works*, Vol. VII, p. 266. Passages here suggest that this perfection is not absolute.

that one should hourly expect to be perfected in love.[31] On June 27, 1760, Wesley wrote to Miss March exhorting her to read and pray looking for full salvation at any moment.[32] In fact, Wesley believed and taught that God would not take the Christian in death until he was perfected—ripe for glory.[33] The only reason that perfection was usually delayed until the moment just before death was because Christians were not sufficiently encouraged to expect it *now*.[34] Wesley, however, was undoubtedly introduced to this Catholic view of sanctification by the mystics (especially Macarius, de Renty, and Lopez) early in his ministry; and it would be unwarranted to imply that this was not a part of his earlier understanding simply because it was more clearly articulated at a later date. Yet, even if Dr. Outler's dichotomy is misleading, the fact remains that Wesley's more mature doctrine of perfection is different, especially in its relation to the atonement.[35] Let's take a moment to discuss this difference.

Before Aldersgate Wesley would never have been able to speak of perfection in terms of "the full assurance of faith." Wesley's theological and philosophical break with mysticism enabled him to reach a state of perfection only by completely by-passing the mystical means of the dark night of the soul. Wesley insisted that "so long as they believe, and walk after the Spirit, neither God condemns them, nor their own heart."[36] Dunn Wilson, in an effort to fit Wesley into some kind of a mystical scheme, states that Wesley taught his followers to accept a dark night. Nothing could be further from the truth.[37]

---

[31]*Journal,* Vol. IV, p. 529.
[32]*Letters,* Vol. IV, p. 100.
[33]Ibid., p. 13; cf. p. 158. It is interesting to note that although perfection can be achieved in this life, Wesley usually states that "he who claims it has it *not.*" Cf. Ibid., Vol. V, p. 6, for a possible exception to this where Wesley states that it is our duty to declare our sanctification.
[34]*Journal,* Vol. IV, p. 529.
[35]Green, *Wesley and Law,* p. 199, cites Wesley's *Works* (Vol. XI, p. 369) to show that Wesley's mature doctrine of perfection relative to the atonement can be traced to the influence of his trip to Germany following his evangelical conversion.
[36]*Journal,* Vol. I, pp. 167f; cf. *Sermons,* Vol. II, p. 272.
[37]Wilson, unpublished thesis, "The Influence of Mysticism on John Wesley," pp. 278-292. Wilson (p. 292) apparently following the mistaken example of Atkinson Lee (*Methodism in the Modern World,* edited by Lidgett and B. Green, London: 1929, pp. 119-137), seeks to demonstrate a parallel between Wesley's "scheme of salvation" and the mystical stages of awaken-

Wesley admits that "heaviness" might occur as a result of illness or nervous disorder: but this is far removed from the "darkness" which results from the loss of God's favor.[38] Wesley no more taught his followers to expect darkness than to expect backsliding or apostasy.[39] His sermon on "The Wilderness State," like the sermon "Against Backsliding," taught one not to expect darkness, but offers remedy and encouragement in case it should occur. This darkness has its origin not in the arbitrary withdrawal of God's presence (as the mystic believed), but in *sin*. Wesley argued time and again that Christians from the moment of justification *need never lose* the joy and peace consistent with the constant awareness of the presence and love of God.[40] God never withdraws the awareness of His presence arbitrarily. According to Wesley, sin alone occasions what the mystic refers to as darkness.[41] Consequently, perfection for the mystic involved a call or a challenge as he sought to establish a high standard of Christian holiness through the mystical means of spiritual discipline, prayer, and the dark night of the soul (naked "faith"). On the other hand, Wesley's more mature doctrine of perfection involved an ap-

---

ing, illumination, darkness, and purgation (Wilson's order here is indeed strange; cf. Underhill, *The Mystic Way*, p. 54: awakening, purgation, illumination, darkness, and union). Wilson is in trouble from the very start. He begins by associating awakening with Wesley's doctrine of the "new birth." The mystical awakening, however (which could be called an *ethical* new birth, cf. Wilson, p. 354), says little or nothing about justification by faith expounded so uncompromisingly in Wesley's sermon "The New Birth" which describes the experience at Aldersgate (to associate the awakening with the 1725 experience is more feasible). Wilson then complains (as well he might from his so-called mystical scheme) that Wesley's pattern of spiritual growth following the new birth appears obscure and confused. Without attempting to defend Wesley (as this is not our task) this writer concludes that Wilson's hypothesis (in this regard) is not only unconvincing, but also incomprehensible.

[38]Cf. *Letters*, Vol. IV, p. 270; the wilderness state has *human*, not *divine*, origin.

[39]Cf. Ibid., Vol. III, p. 215. Wesley writes: "It is no more necessary that we should ever lose it (the sense of God's love) than it is necessary we should omit duty or commit sin."

[40]*Sermons*, Vol. II, p. 253; here Wesley attacks mysticism for teaching that Christians "are not always to walk in luminous faith." Wesley strongly denies that one should leave "those sensible comforts" (for the mystic an "inferior state") to live by naked faith.

[41]*Sermons*, Vol. II, pp. 249, 272; cf. *Letters*, Vol. III, pp. 214f.; 218.

peal, an offer, a gift of God; and although he attempted earlier to achieve perfection along the mystical lines, he found it to be unattainable by these means. There can be little doubt that although Wesley continued to agree with the mystics that perfection was God's purpose for all men and that it involved total communion with God, the mystical disregard for the historical significance of the Incarnation became the greatest area of incompatibility. It was futile to speak of man's love for God without first speaking of God's love for man; after all, "we love him because he first loved us."[42]

Furthermore, the nature of the Aldersgate experience convinced Wesley that sanctification (like justification) was granted in an instant. Although Wesley recognized the need for gradual growth before and after sanctification, his insistence on an experience wrought in an instant remained a point of contention between Wesley and the mystics.[43] Social holiness also played a much greater role in the later doctrine.[44] After 1738, Wesley lost all patience with the theological and philosophical tenets which encouraged the contemplative, solitary, or passive life, and by virtue of these tenets discouraged (at least in theory) good works.[45] There was no "hermitic ideal" in Wesley's more mature doctrine of perfection. His later doctrine also apparently alters with regard to "absolute" perfection. In a sermon preached in 1736, he speaks of flesh being "changed into an angelical condition."[46] On November 2, 1762, however, he writes Thomas Maxfield that he dislikes

---

[42]Cf. *Sermons,* Vol. II, pp. 77, 80; *Works,* Vol. VIII, p. 24. Wesley's later concept of grace adds depth to the mystical emphasis on man's love of God and to his own pre-1738 understanding of perfection.

[43]Cf. *Works,* Vol. III, p. 329.

[44]Cf. *Sermons,* Vol. I, p. 382. Christianity cannot subsist "without society, without living and conversing with other men."

[45]During the period under consideration, Wesley continually emphasized the theme of works following justifying faith. Faith must precede works; but, where works, as the fruits of faith, appear there must be faith since "they have *faith* who have fruits which nothing but faith can produce," *Letters,* Vol. IV, p. 35; cf. pp. 28f., 173ff. It is interesting to note by way of preview that after 1767 Wesley applies this same rule to the mystics. They must have faith since they manifest its fruits.

[46]*Works,* Vol. VII, p. 515.

his "supposing man may be as perfect as an angel."[47] Lindstrom adds that not only is Wesley's later doctrine not angelic, it is not Adamic.[48] Adam's perfection was objective and absolute *while Wesley's perfection was subjective and relative involving, for the most part, intention and motive.* Wesley frequently asserted that perfection could be achieved as far as willful sin was concerned, but that ignorance would always make one liable to involuntary sin, or as Wesley preferred to say—"mistakes." Only omniscience implies infallibility.[49] At one point in his thesis, Wilson contrasts Wesley's dynamic concept of perpetual growth with what he refers to as the Catholic idea of an absolute state of perfection hinted at by such terms as deification and absorption.[50] None of the mystics whom Wesley abridged, however, seriously contended for such a position (with the possible exception of Molinos). In fact, in some respects the perfection of the Roman Catholic mystic is *less* absolute and *more* dynamic than Wesley's. Although Wesley states that "when ye have attained a measure of perfect love . . . think not of resting there. That is impossible. You cannot stand still; you must either rise or fall"[51]; he still criticizes Lopez and the papists for not holding a high enough view of perfection. Even more surprising is the letter dated July 7, 1761, where after defining perfection as "perfect love: loving God with all the heart; receiving Christ as prophet, priest, and king, to reign alone over all our thoughts, words and actions," he adds that "the Papists neither teach nor believe this."[52] He continues, "they teach there is no perfection here

---

[47]*Letters,* Vol. IV, p. 192; cf. *Works,* Vol. VII, p. 266; *Sermons,* Vol. II, p. 202. The last two references suggest that absolute perfection is beyond the grave. Closely related to this is Wesley's negative view of the body discussed by Wilson ("The Influence of Mysticism of John Wesley." 354ff.); cf. *Sermons,* Vol. II, p. 29, 155; *Works,* Vol. VII, pp. 347f.

[48]Lindstrom, p. 153.

[49]*Works,* Vol. XI, p. 374.

[50]Wilson, *"Influence of Mysticism,"* pp. 317ff. Later on Wilson cites W. T. Stace (*Mysticism and Philosophy,* London, 1961, pp. 222f.), who denies that mystics contend for deification.

[51]*Works,* Vol. XI, p. 426; cf. *Sermons,* Vol. II, p. 202. This growth extends even into eternity. Cf. also *Works,* Vol. II, p. 429. Wesley states that the classes at Kingswood are "steady but not zealous. It is impossible they should stand here long; they must go on or go back."

[52]*Letters,* Vol. IV, pp. 157f.

which is not consistent with venial sins; and among venial sins they commonly reckon simple fornication."[53] Who can say what might have prompted Wesley to make such a charge? At this point one must simply conclude that somewhere between the Catholic concept of absolute perfection talked about by Wilson and the Catholic concept of perfection consistent with venial sin talked about by Wesley lies the healthy doctrine of perfection expounded by mystics like Macarius, de Renty, and Fénelon which influenced Wesley far more than he was frequently willing to admit.[54]

If there are differences in Wesley's early and later concepts of perfection relative to the mystics, there were also many characteristics which remained unchanged.[55] Perfection, especially its moral and ethical implications, is still the one "purpose of religion." Lindstrom emphasizes the fact that "with Wesley as with the mystics everything was directed towards a *change* which would qualify man for glorification. In this general position just as in the teleological alignment of his theology, Wesley, after, as well as before 1738, agrees with practical mysticism."[56] The willingness to sell all to purchase the "pearl of great price" and the largely *ethical* nature of a transformation grounded in "gospel obedience and holiness of life" mark the real points of contact between Wesley and the mystics which extend beyond Aldersgate as an ultimate influence and an invaluable tool for the Evangelical Revival. Eric Baker states that "*ethical* mysticism" was thought by Wesley (and Law) to represent a truth inherent in Christianity preserved in the mainstream of Catholic piety and reinforced by the Homilies of the Church of England.[57] That this basic ethical flavor was present in Wesley's earlier and later doctrine can be demonstrated by his works. Compare, for example, the 1733 sermon "The Circumcision of the Heart" and the 1765 statement on perfection in the letter to John Newton.[58] In both,

---

[53]Ibid.

[54]It should be pointed out that Wesley tended to exclude the Roman Catholic mystics from the criticism normally aimed at "Papists" as such.

[55]Cf. Lindstrom, *Wesley and Sanctification,* pp. 129ff.

[56]Ibid. (italics mine).

[57]Baker, Eric W. *Herald of the Evangelical Revival.* London: Epworth Press, 1948, p. 73.

[58]*Letters,* Vol. IV, p. 299.

perfection is stated in terms of "faith that worketh by the love of God and man, all inward and outward holiness." Lindstrom sees an obvious parallel in the concept of perfection outlined in these works and that of ethical or practical mysticism in the Roman Catholic tradition.[59] On another occasion Wesley states that more and more of God's image is "transfused into your soul; that from disinterested love, all other divine tempers will, as it were naturally, spring."[60] When you love God thus, "then the commandments of God will not be grievous."[61] Wesley assumes that as one's love for God is perfected, so one's delight in doing His will is perfected. These characteristics of holiness along with his ethical, moral, and evangelical views after Aldersgate were not only retained, but insisted upon as a legitimate pattern for Christian perfection. Wesley's emphasis on purity of intention (that man is actuated by a single motive); wholehearted devotion to God requiring an inward obedience of heart and an outward obedience of word and action (a perfect inward and outward conformity with Christ); and the absolute supremacy of love for God and neighbor never wavers and provides a fairly consistent image of perfection throughout a lifetime of teaching.

To conclude on a more comprehensive note it should be stated that there comes a time in most men's lives when they must stop and weigh the cost of greatness. One road often leads to compromise, comfort, and mediocrity, while another leads to self-discipline, self-sacrifice, and greatness. When Wesley was confronted with this choice by Taylor, à Kempis, Law, and others, he never hesitated to take their lead. Although many stand staring as if hypnotized, Wesley charged ahead and never turned back. He was directed and sustained by the example of a lifetime of influences, especially by those whose piety had been won after years of conflict; and whose wholehearted devotion to God had persisted through years of painful, yet rewarding experience. The result was a man equipped to instruct those in unavoidable ignorance, to encourage those in expressible despair, to assist those in inescapable poverty, to

---

[59]Lindstrom, *Wesley and Sanctification,* pp. 129ff.
[60]*Works,* Vol. VIII, pp. 198f.
[61]Ibid., p. 199.

challenge those in alienable sin, and to exhort those who responded to that exalted, but nonetheless, attainable perfection. Wesley was an immensely practical man, but he was also a visionary. Perhaps this, after all is said and done, was his genius. To be sure, all misguided professions of possessing divine illumination which are not warranted and sealed by purity of life are either lies or self-delusions. On the other hand, cold-blooded intellectualism will never force the locks of the kingdom: those who come there must have clean hands and a pure heart, and only those who have the love and longing for God will have a lasting effect upon men.

Bibliography, Part IV[1]

Primary Sources

John Wesley, *A Christian Library.*

———, *Christian Perfection as Believed and Taught by John Wesley,* Thomas S. Kepler, ed., Cleveland (1954).

———, *A Collection of Hymns.*

———, *Notes Upon the New Testament.*

———, *Journal,* Curnock, ed.

———, *Letters,* Telford, ed.

———, *Poetical Works.*

———, *Sermons on Several Occasions.*

———, *Standard Sermons,* Sugden, ed.

———, *Works,*Pine.

———, *Works,* Jackson, ed.

Green, Richard, *Bibliography.*

Union Catalogue of Publications.

Secondary Sources

Abbey, C. J., *The English Church and Its Bishops.*

Arminian Magazine, The. Consisting of Extracts and Original Treatises on Universal Redemption (1788-91).

Baker, Frank, *Charles Wesley.*

———, *A Charge to Keep.* London (1947).

———, *John Wesley and the Church of England.* London (1970).

———, "The Beginnings of the Methodist Covenant Service," LQHR, 180 (1955), 215-20.

———, "Bishop Lavington and the Methodists," W.H.S. Proc., XXXIV (1963/64), 37-42.

———, "John Wesley's Churchmanship," LQHR (July, 1960), 210-5 (October, 1960), 291-8.

———, "John Wesley on Christian Perfection." W.H.S. Proc., XXXIV (1963/64), 53-7.

———, "Study of Wesley's Readings," LQHR.

———, "Wesley's Ordinations," W.H.S. Proc., XXIV (1944), 76-80, 101-3.

---

[1]For details on abbreviated sources see Bibliographies for Parts I, II, and III.

Bett, H., *The Spirit of Methodism*. London (1937).

Cannon William R., *The Theology of Wesley*.

_____, "John Wesley's Doctrine of Sanctification and Perfection," *The Mennonite Quarterly Review*, XXXV (1961), 91-5.

Cell, George C., *Rediscovery of Wesley*.

Coke, Thomas, and Moore, H., *Life*.

Davies, Rupert E., *The Church in Bristol*.

Edwards, M. L., *John Wesley and the Eighteenth Century*. London (1933).

Fletcher, John W., *The Works*. London (1800-04), 9 vols.

Flew, R. N., *The Idea of Perfection in Christian Theology*. London (1934).

A Form of Discipline for the Ministers, Preachers and Members of the Methodist Episcopal Church in America, Considered and Approved at a Conference Held at Baltimore . . . 27th of December, 1784. Elizabethtown, New Jersey (1788).

Jackson, Thomas, *Life of Charles Wesley*.

Knox, Ronald A., *Enthusiasm*.

Lawson, John, *Notes on Wesley's Forty-four Sermons*. London (1946).

Léger, A., *La Jeunesse de Wesley*.

Lindström, Harold, *Wesley and Sanctification*. Stockholm (1946).

Lyles, Albert M., *Methodism Mocked—the Satiric Reaction to Methodism in the Eighteenth Century*. London (1960).

Minutes of Several Conversations Between Thomas Coke, Francis Asbury and Others at a Conference Begun in Baltimore . . . the 27th of December, in the year 1784. Composing a Form of Discipline. Philadelphia (1785).

Moore, Henry, *Life*.

Orcibal, Jean, "L'originaute theologique de John Wesley et les spirituantes au continent." Rev. Hist., CCXXII (1959), 51-80.

Outler, Albert C., *John Wesley*.

_____, "Towards a Re-appraisal of John Wesley as a Theologian," *The Perkins School of Theology Journal*, XIV (1961), 5-14.

Overton, J. H., *John Wesley*.

———, *The Evangelical Revival in the Eighteenth Century.* London (1886).

Piette, Maximin, *John Wesley.*

Rattenbury, J. E., *The Evangelical Doctrines of Charles Wesley's Hymns.* London (1941).

———, *Wesley's Legacy to the World.* London (1928).

Sangster, W. E., "Wesley and Sanctification," LQHR, 171 (1946).

Schmidt, Martin, *John Wesley.* Vol. II, parts 1 and 2.

Simon, John S., *Wesley and the Methodist Societies.*

———, *John Wesley and the Advance of Methodism.* London (1925).

———, *John Wesley, the Master Builder.* London (1927).

———, *John Wesley, the Last Phase.* London (1934).

———, *The Revival of Religion in England in the 18th Century.* London (1907).

———, "Mr. Wesley's Notes Upon the New Testament," W.H.S. Proc., IX (1913/14), 97-105.

———, "Wesley's Ordinations," ibid., 145-54.

Southey, Robert, *Life.* 2 vols.

Telford, John, *Life.*

Todd, John M., *John Wesley and the Catholic Church.* London (1958).

Tuttle, Robert G. Jr., "Influence of the Roman Catholic Mystics on Wesley."

Tyerman, Luke, *Life of John Wesley.*

———, *Life of Whitefield.*

Vulliamy, C. E., *John Wesley.*

Wakefield, Gordon S., *The Spiritual Life in the Methodist Tradition.* London (1966).

Wesley, Charles, *Journal.* Telford, ed.

Wesley Historical Society, *Publications* and *Proceedings.*

Whitefield, George, *The Works.* Gillies, ed.

———, *Journals,* Murray, ed.

Whitehead, John, *Life.*

Williams, Colin, *Wesley's Theology Today.*

Yates, A. S. , *The Doctrine of Assurance.* London (1952).

Epilogue

Can we suppose that this active mind, which animates and moves the dull matter with which it is clogged, will be less active when set free? Surely, no; it will be all activity.

John Wesley

Wesley, between April 4, 1788 (when we left him in Macclesfield) and March 2, 1791 (the date of his death), continued his work among the people called Methodist, sustaining and strengthening the breadth and scope of the Evangelical Revival. He continued to exhort Christians to read and pray. A letter to one of his preachers reads:

What has exceedingly hurt you in time past, nay, and I fear to this day, is want of reading. I scarce ever knew a preacher read so little. And perhaps by neglecting it you have lost the taste for it. Hence your talent in preaching does not increase. It is just the same as it was seven years ago. It is lively, but not deep; there is little variety; there is no compass of thought. Reading only can supply this with meditation and daily prayers. You wrong yourself greatly by omitting this. You can never be a deep preacher without it any more than a thorough Christian. O begin! Fix some part of every day for private exercises. You may acquire the taste which you have not; what is tedious at first will afterwards be pleasant. Whether you like it or no, read and pray daily. It is for your life; there is no other way: else you will be a trifler all your days, and a pretty superficial preacher. Do justice to your own soul; give it time and means to grow. Do not starve yourself any longer. Take up your cross, and be a Christian altogether.

Yours &c.[1]

Furthermore, he continued to teach his preachers to preach sermons designed to convict the unawakened, to convert the sinner, and to convince those justified to pursue perfect

---

[1]*Letters*, Vol. IV, p. 103.

love. He continued to train class leaders to organize societies. In May, 1788, he wrote: "There is no other religious society under heaven which requires nothing of men in order to their admission into it, but a desire to save their souls. Look all around you, you cannot be admitted into the church, or society of the Presbyterians, Anabaptists, Quakers, or any others, unless you hold the same opinions with them, and adhere to the same mode of worship.

"The Methodists alone do not insist on your holding this or that opinion; but they *think and let think.* Neither do they impose any particular mode of worship; but you may continue to worship in your former manner, be it what it may. Now, I do not know any other religious society, either ancient or modern, wherein such liberty of conscience is now allowed, or has been allowed, since the age of the Apostles. Here is our glorying; and a glorying peculiar to us. What society shares it with us?"[2]

During these last three years, believing that "man was not born in shades to lie," Wesley made two trips into Scotland and one to Ireland. He continued to travel throughout England and Wales, once walking the six miles between Kingswood and Bristol exclaiming that he was "ashamed, that a Methodist preacher, in tolerable health, should make any difficulty of this."[3] He continued to visit classes and preach in the open air (to 25,000 in Cornwall) saying: "Let us work now; we shall rest by and by."[4]

Only in the last year did his strength and sight decay, but his mind stayed alert enabling him both to write and to preach until the week before his death. He commented: "Can we suppose that this active mind, which animates and moves the dull matter with which it is clogged, will be less active when set free? Surely, no; it will be all activity. But what will be its employments? Who can tell?"[5]

---

[2]*Works,* Vol. IV, p. 419 (italics mine). It is interesting to note that Wesley himself established the origin of the nonconfessional United Methodist polity.

[3]Ibid., p. 436.

[4]Ibid., Vol. IV, p. 471.

[5]*Journal,* Vol. VIII, p. 132.

Wesley attended his last Methodist Conference (the Conference had previously been assigned the sole right of appointing the preachers after his death) in Bristol, August, 1790. Here one of his preachers, James Rogers, and his wife Hester Ann, were appointed to attend Mr. Wesley personally. Hester Ann, ill herself, soon had to yield to Elisabeth Ritchie who nursed him until the end.[6]

The *Journal* ends abruptly on October 24, 1790 and the *Diary* on February 24, 1791, after a short journey to Leatherhead, less than a week before he died. Both established the continuity of his tireless routine. The activity recorded on the last page of the *Diary*, for example, could easily be substituted for that on a page at any given point during the previous fifty years.

To conclude, permit me a final word of commentary. Wesley was unquestionably a great man; but the Revival (if such comparisons can be made) was greater, far greater. Again, revival is always the work of God; and, as with all God movements, it was bigger than the instrument used to create it. In a way, Wesley himself could not measure up to all its demands upon the believer. For the whole of his life, John Wesley (like Moses) remained a hairs-breadth outside of his movement. John Wesley never received the abiding full assurance of faith, apparently experienced by so many of those he loved and admired. He seemingly had doubts until the very end; but, nonetheless, he persevered. John Wesley never achieved the entire sanctification he preached to others. He wrote: "I have told all the world I am not perfect. . . . I have not attained the character I draw."[7] Nonetheless, he held tenaciously to a doctrine that was the hallmark of Methodism. Finally, John Wesley could not bear witness to the kind of death he boasted about among so many of those perfected in love. He wanted Methodists to die rejoicing, not just in peace. He frequently asked those in the moment of death: "Do you

---

[6]Elisabeth Ritchie's detailed account of Wesley's last days appears in the *Journal*, Vol. VIII, pp. 138ff.

[7]*Works*, Vol. III, p. 273.

see Jesus? Do you see Jesus?" Then, in the moment of his own death, when those around him had every right to ask the same question of him, he had strength only to proclaim: "The best of all is, God is with us." But John Wesley "died well!" A few hours later, he whispered one last word: "Farewell."

Index

287.092 W513t 1978

Tuttle, Robert G.,
    John Wesley

287.092 W513t 1978

Tuttle, Robert G.,
    John Wesley